Caregivers'
Bible

Helping Older Adults with
Behavioral and Emotional Quandaries

William Matteson, Ph.D.

Matteson, William, Ph. D.
Caregivers' bible : helping older adults with
behavioral and emotional quandaries / William Matteson.
p. cm.
Includes bibliographical references and index.
LCCN 2007900033
ISBN-13: 978-0-9655563-0-9
ISBN-10: 0-9655563-0-1

1. Older people--Mental health. 2. Older people--
Psychology.   I. Title.

RC451.4.A5C76 2007   618.97'689
                            QBI07-600015

First Edition, December 1997
Second Edition, January 2004
Third Edition, May 2007
10 9 8 7 6 5 4

Cover design by 1106 Design
Text design by Sheryl Mehary

Matteson Media
16707 Sunset Boulevard
Pacific Palisades, California 90272

Caregivers' Bible

Helping Older Adults with
Behavioral and Emotional Quandaries

William Matteson, Ph.D.

Matteson Media
Pacific Palisades, California

"How far you go in life depend on you being
tender with the young,
compassionate with the aged,
sympathetic with the striving,
and tolerant of the weak and strong.
Because someday in life,
you will have been all of these."

George Washington Carver (1864–1943)

"Age is of no importance
unless you are a cheese."

Billie Burke (1886–1970)

Contents

Section One

Caring for
An Aging America

Chapter One

Ageism

During the year following the end of World War II, fifteen million soldiers suddenly came home. This rush of returning young men and women resulted in an explosive rise in our population, spawning the generation now known as the baby boomers.

Over the next several decades, while the boomers were growing up, advances in sanitation, nutrition, and medicine led to an unforeseen increase in life expectancy, and an unprecedented increase in the number of elder Americans.

The baby boomers and their parents are getting old. In the years ahead, millions of these aging Americans will face an escalating need for health care. But our youth-oriented society has not prepared itself to deal with the demands of this rapidly-growing segment of the population.

Elderly Americans deal with myriad typical problems associated with aging, but also come face-to-face with another less-anticipated problem — the bias and prejudice our society has developed against growing old and being old.

Behavioral Objectives

At the end of this section, participants will be able to:

Understand the meaning and consequences of age bias in the treatment setting.

Describe emotional reactions in working with the elderly.

Take steps to improve the well being of older people in need of care.

Describe the factors contributing to ageism in our culture.

Current Life Expectancy

The average life span is now 75 years, up from 47 years in 1900.

In 2004 lifespan was:
• white women 80
• black women 74.7
• white men 74.3
• black men 67.2

In 1900, 4% of the population was over 65.

In 2030 it will be 20%.

The elderly are the fastest growing segment of the population.

In 2007, 35 million Americans will be over 65.

By 2030 the number will reach 85 million.

During this time the number of older Caucasians will increase by 97%.

African Americans by 265%.

Latino Americans by 530%.

With the maturing of the baby boomer generation, the United States has evolved into a culture of youthfulness. Age is out — youth is in.

The signs are everywhere: the cosmetic surgery business is exploding; book-stores burst with books on how to reverse the aging process; cable television channels' infomercials spew promises of eternal youth and fitness. It's no surprise then that our first years are valued more than our last.

Today's 75-year-old may actually live another 25 years, but few place much value on those years. Instead we are taught by our culture and our media to devalue and denigrate aging and the aged, as evidenced by the number of derogatory terms like, "over-the-hill," "geezer," "old coot," and, "old biddy," replete in our language. This bias is ageism — youth is positive, age is negative. And ageism touches every part of our culture.

To understand the societal effects of ageism, consider the value of giving a 20-year-old a new heart that will extend her life another twenty-five years. Of course there would be no medical or social hesitation. Next, consider the value of performing the same operation on an 85-year-old. Is it worth the expense? Does this aged person deserve a new heart? Many would say, "No, she's too old. Let her die."

Ageism was also at play in the mid-1900's, when the culture of youth began to affect blue-collar workers. These workers were forced, for the first time in our history, into retirement and were replaced by younger people. Experience had become less valuable than youth.

Many factors have contributed society's current emphasis on youthful beauty, power, and self-centeredness. The baby-boomers' generation is the first reared under the relentless influences of mass-media. It is the first generation in history whose primary sources of information were external to their immediate or extended family.

In recent decades, our television programs and movies have romanticized youth and devalued age. An extreme example is the 1976 film *Logan's Run*, in which all citizens were killed when they reached thirty. Our cultural heroes never grow old — after all these years, Superman and Barbie have gained nary a pound or a wrinkle.

Soap-operas of the late forties and early fifties, with titles like, *Right to Happiness* and *Life can be Beautiful* taught baby-boomers and their parents they could expect to have their every need or desire fulfilled. Taking rather than giving was the new mind set.

Television, radio, movies, magazines and comics have had an immeasurably profound impact on post-World War II generations. Rather than absorbing the wisdom of their elders, baby-boomers were barraged by the superficiality of young, powerful, and attractive "celebrities." As technology began to outpace the average person's ability to assimilate it, the experience and knowledge of elders seemingly became less valuable and less useful. These older people came to be seen as liabilities rather than assets. The favorite cries of the 70s youth generation were, "Never trust anyone over thirty," and, "I hope I die before I get old."

These "children of the media" baby-boomers, typically enjoyed extended and privileged childhoods. It was during the boomers' school years that adolescence came to be seen as the latter part of childhood, rather than the early part of adulthood. Kids grew up more slowly, and left home later.

Programs like the GI bill and generous government loans enabled thousands of middle class people to attend college, prolonging their "childhood" and delaying their entry into the work force.

Other changes were under way as well. During the fifties, more people bought homes than in any time in history. A new type of neighborhood — the suburb — emerged, and led to another unprecedented phenomenon — the two-car family. And so emerged the American obsession with conspicuous consumption, replacing achievement as the hallmark of success.

Growing prosperity and the mass media's promotion of the much publicized American Dream as being within reach, created very high — and frequently unrealistic — expectations in an entire generation.

These factors are vitally important today, because they bespeak the lack of preparedness on the part of the baby-boomer generation as they now age, and as they are increasingly faced with caring for aging parents. This is exacerbated by the fact that today's family is highly mobile — the average family moves once every ten years. Friends and relatives are left behind, and the sense of support of family and community has drastically dwindled.

Only a few generations ago the extended family was the American norm, with several generations often living in one house. Age was seen as synonymous with wisdom. Children were taught to revere and respect their elders, and Grandpa was truly grand. People grew, aged, and were cared for and allowed to die at home.

As a society expecting to have its needs met and its problems solved, we have increasingly come to depend on others for solutions. We live in the era of the expert, with the consultant having replaced the cowboy and the trouble-shooter having replaced the six-shooter.

The result is the overwhelming likelihood that baby boomer children of aging parents will out-source the job of caring for parents. They will turn over caregiving responsibilities with very high expectations, as their investment in eternal youth and power has given them an unrealistic view of what medicine can do.

Many of today's adult children, rather than possessing a sense of compassion for and devotion to their parents, react to the deterioration of their once healthy and productive progenitors as an intolerable, narcissistic injury. Watching parents age may remind the "youth-forever" generation of their own mortality, inducing unpleasant thoughts and feelings. For these people, the care of aging parents is considered a burden obviously to be shouldered by others.

Those who cannot cope with the their own mortality, or the loss of their narcissistic, fantasies, cope by blaming outside forces for their fears and frustrations. Being unable to recognize age as a natural and inevitable part of life, they blame the health care industry for failing to "fix" what they fear. This blame is often projected onto the people who are caring for their parents. While they themselves may be shunning their responsibilities, they are often quick to criticize, eager to oversee, and fail to comprehend the scope of the task they have handed over to the caregivers. It is important for caregivers to keep in mind when dealing with such families that it is not their anger, but their fear that speaks so loudly.

The effect of all of these forces, combined with the high expectations of caregivers themselves, has been to create a predisposition in many elderly people to see themselves as bitter and helpless victims of the forces around them.

Caregivers are not immune to the effect of societal ageism and familial buck-passing and blame. Without realizing it, some caregivers infantilize, demean, and talk down to their elderly clients. Exposed each day to the wizened and weathered faces of age, they may become reflexive rather than responsive. Constantly confronted with the very thing they so strongly wish to avoid, some actually come to hate those whom they had so earnestly pledged to help.

Faced with sweeping negative reactions to age, many elderly people may come to devalue themselves, to lose their feelings of power, their sense of worth, and their feelings of lovability — the three basic components of self-esteem. Youthful disdain for the aged may

Consequences of Ageism

Infantlizing

Using baby talk.

Calling residents "honey".

Assuming dementia

Attributing all memory or cognitive impairments to dementia.

Charting "dementia due to ageing".

Failuire to diagnose depression.

People over 70 are seven times less likely to be screened for depression.

Devaluing

Assuming older people are useless.

be internalized by the elderly and exhibited as feelings of being useless, used up, and in the way.

Such negative, self-deprecating perceptions on the part of the elderly often lays the groundwork for depression, withdrawal, and deterioration.

Age bias is a cause of many of the difficulties observed in long-term care facilities. One of the best examples of age bias appears in Nancy Wexler's book, *Mama Can't Remember Anymore.* In the book, Paul E. Ruskin, M.D. explains,

"I was invited to present a lecture to a class of graduate nurses who were studying the "Psychological Aspects of Aging" I started my lecture with the following case presentation:

'The patient is a white female who appears her reported age. She neither speaks nor comprehends the spoken word. Sometimes she babbles incoherently for hours on end. She is disoriented about person, place and time. She does, however, seem to recognize her own name. I have worked with her for the past six months, but she still doesn't recognize me.

She shows complete disregard for her physical appearance and makes no effort whatsoever to assist in her own care. She must be fed, bathed and clothed by others. Because she is toothless, her food must be pureed; because she is incontinent of both urine and stool, she must be changed and bathed often. Her shirt is generally soiled from almost constant drooling. She does not walk. Her sleep pattern is erratic.

Often, she awakens in the middle of the night, and her screaming awakens others. Most of the time she is very friendly and happy. However, several times a day she gets quite agitated without apparent cause. Then she screams loudly until someone comes to comfort her.'

After the case presentation, I asked the nurses how they would feel about taking care of a patient as the one described. They used words such as, frustrated," "hopeless," "depressed," and "annoyed," to describe how they would feel.

When I stated that I enjoyed taking care of her and that I thought they would too, the class looked at me in disbelief. I then passed around a picture of the patient: my six-month-old daughter.

After the laughter had subsided, I asked why it was so much more difficult to care for a ninety year-old patient, than a six-month-old with identical symptoms.

We all agreed that it's physically easier to take care of a helpless baby weighing 15 pounds than a helpless adult weighing 100 pounds, but the answer seemed to go deeper than this.

The infant, we all decided, represents new life, hope, and almost infinite potential. The demented senior citizen, on the other hand, represents the end of life with little potential for growth. We need to change our perspective.

The aged patient is just as lovable as the child. Those who are ending their lives in the vulnerability of old age deserve the same care and attention as those who are beginning their lives in the vulnerability of infancy."

As Ruskin so effectively points out, the solution to these problems is in the realization by both caregivers and the elderly that an older person is still a person; that deference and dignity do not expire when social security begins; that to be old need not be an imposition, but a valuable part of the human experience.

This book is dedicated to total quality caregiving — the notion that, once we recognize and tame our own demons, we can make caring for the aged a rewarding experience for patient and caregiver alike.

Chapter Two

Leaving Home

After the 1906 San Francisco earthquake, psychiatric patients in Napa State Hospital had to be housed in tents because of heavy damage to the building. Physicians and administrators at the hospital were astounded to find immeasurable improvement in their patients' health under these somewhat unusual circumstances. When the building was repaired and the patients were moved back, their behavior deteriorated; they reverted to their more disturbed and bizarre behavior.

Albert Mehrabian
Public Places and Private Spaces (1976)

Behavioral Objectives

At the end of this section readers will be able to:

Describe the losses associated with relocation.

Name the five phases of relocation adjustment.

Define relocation stress syndrome.

Take steps to reduce the trauma of relocation.

Although most families make heroic efforts to care for their ailing elders, many eventually are forced to consider placing them in a professional care facility.

The decision to admit a parent, a spouse, or any family member to a such a facility is a difficult and painful one. It usually is made when all other alternatives have been exhausted, seldom made without guilt, remorse, hurt and anger, and results in a profoundly difficult transition for both new resident and the family.

The family must deal with the loss of the familiar. They must adjust to living without their loved one,

Symptoms of Relocation Stress Syndrome

- loneliness
- depression
- anger
- apprehension
- anxiety
- sleep disturbance
- changes in eating habits
- increased dependency
- insecurity
- lack of trust
- excessive need for reassurance

while grappling with the reality that they are not equipped to give adequate care. They must lick their wounds and learn their limitations, yet provide strong positive support for the loved one, who is now beyond their care.

The person entering the professional care facility must deal with multiple losses: loss of home, privacy, and independence. Friends, treasured objects, lifestyle, and much of what was loved and familiar are gone forever. This overwhelming sense of multiple loss usually is accompanied by anxiety, depression and disorientation. In most cases, the stress of transition is temporary, but in some it persists, leading to a condition known in psychiatric literature as an adjustment disorder.

Leaving home and entering a care facility clearly is traumatic, but relocation from one facility to another also takes a heavy toll on the physical and psychological health of elders. Studies of the effects of transferring residents have found elevated mortality risk between 2 to 3 times greater than those patients who were not transferred.

This phenomenon was officially described and named in 1992 as *Relocation Stress Syndrome*. The United States Administration on Aging calls this problem *Transfer Trauma*, and notes that relocation is associated with depression, increased irritability, serious illness and elevated mortality risk.

The fear and grief that the person — newly placed in a facility or moved from one facility to another — is experiencing are often expressed as anger. Fear is disabling, while anger is empowering. A person suffering the loss of personal power and position may exhibit anger and resistance in an attempt to have an impact on the unfamiliar and frightening world.

Understanding the origin of this behavior allows caregivers to reach beyond the anger and gently touch the person's pain. A kind word and an understanding attitude can make this difficult transition much more bearable.

Preparing for Departure

The stresses of moving to a care facility were carefully examined by Thomas Coffman in 1981. He pointed out that the traumatic stress was not only from the move itself, but the also in the person's perception of the quality of care and the social support they would receive at the facility. In other words, it wasn't just the change, but the emotions that surrounded that change, that were critical.

Coffman also found that carefully planned moves, carried out with adequate warning and in consultation with the person, had far better outcomes.

Relocation went most smoothly when the person was given information far in advance of the move, was allowed visits to the new facility several times, and was given opportunities to become acquainted with the staff before the move. Thus, the person was able to enter an environment that was familiar, with a staff already familiar.

Planning for Arrival

Planning effective care giving and behavioral management, and ensuring resident and staff satisfaction, involves the careful implementation of the following important steps.

1. Obtain a thorough personal history, physical examination, and detailed description of existing problems in advance of the person's arrival. Learn everything you can about the person, and inform the new staff so they know what to expect.

2. Based on information obtained, establish the apparent cause of any existing behavior

Fear is disabling, while anger is empowering. A person suffering the loss of personal power and position may exhibit anger and resistance in an attempt to have an impact on an unfamiliar and frightening world.

problems. Be aware that behavioral problems often are caused by changes in daily routines, relocation, physical or mental illness, environmental stressors, and medication problems. (All of which will be discussed later.)

3. Based on information obtained, establish a preliminary intervention plan. Typically, this person has been brought to a particular facility because he or she has decompensated, is experiencing acute medical or behavioral problems, is gravely disabled, or has become too difficult to care for in his or her previous location. A good number of people arrive at a residential care facility already exhibiting disruptive behavior.

4. Do not put a new person in the proximity of others before completing a medical assessment, behavioral assessment, and observing the person's capacity to interact socially. The presence of a new person often is disruptive to other residents, potentially causing existing residents to exhibit behavioral and emotional problems. New residents may become combative, explosive, and potentially dangerous to others.

5. Establish a structured daily care, social activity, and free time schedule based on the person's history and preferences to ensure each day is enjoyable and predictable. This routine should be shared with all staff members, be posted in the person's room and reinforced with the resident frequently.

6. Schedule sessions of physical activity to match the person's energy cycle.

7. Provide rest periods each day during which the person can listen to music, sit in a recliner, or nap as appropriate. (Note: Naps are appropriate if the person is accustomed to napping, but not to relieve boredom.)

8. Minimize isolation and idle time. Isolation leads to decompensation, and idle time increases self-stimulating behavior. Too much idle time also promotes napping, which will interfere with normal sleep.

9. Monitor the use of visual and hearing aids. Help the resident establish a routine of using these devices, as people who do not use their glasses and hearing aids typically spend significantly less time socializing. Be aware that over half of all adults with hearing impairments do not use their hearing aids. (More information on vision and hearing impairment appears in chapters 12 and 13.)

10. Assign a specific person to be the primary caregiver so rapport can be established. Realize it may take time, to find the best fit, matching personalities, caregiving styles and communication skills.

11. Assign the minimum number of staff necessary to a specific resident, so the staff members become the caregiving team and give the person a feeling of familiarity and safety.

Labeling

New environments are confusing. Already upset and disoriented, people newly entering long-term care facilities frequently will exhibit signs of depression, dementia, or other cognitive problems. Careful organization of the environment, with labeling and other signage, can significantly reduce agitation and disorientation, and make it easier to correct unwanted behaviors that may occur.

People with dementia have great difficulty storing and retrieving new information from their long term memory, so orientation, instructions, and directions are soon forgotten. Many residents can no longer read,

The most common complaints of long term care residents are:

Incompatible roommates

Ignoring food preferences

Theft or loss of personal belongings

Distrupting or ignoring long standing sleep-wake cycles or routines

Staff ignoring call lights

Disrespect and infanilization

Staff doing things for resident that they could do for themselves (a phenomenon called *excess disability*)

because they can no longer see or comprehend written words. Thus, it is extremely important to:

1. Clearly label objects and the location of stored objects. Signs are easier to see if the background is dark and the symbol light, rather than the reverse. Avoid blues and greens because those colors often are difficult for older people to see.

2. Use large, high contrast, pictures when possible, rather than written instructions. Ensure the person is able understand the message of the picture. Ask him or her to tell you what it means.

3. Use pictures or objects that remind residents of where they are, where important locations are, and what they are to do in each location. For example, putting the resident's picture on the door to his or her room will remind him or her of where it is, while putting a picture of a knife and fork on the cafeteria door reminds the resident where to eat.

    For residents with more advanced dementia, use pictures of them that were taken before they began to suffer from the disorder, as many people with dementia do not recognize pictures of themselves taken following the onset of symptoms.

4. Use multiple labels. For example, put a rest room label with a direction arrow in the hall and put another label on the rest room door.

5. Place all labels so they can be seen clearly, whether from a standing position or a wheel-chair.

6. Fasten a brightly colored ribbon to the door knob of the person's room, and put a ribbon of the same color on the person's wrist, enabling the person to find the room by matching the ribbons.

Prepare a Safe Environment

Keep the environment clean and simple, with as few distractions as possible. The residents' short attention spans and difficulty processing information make complex stimuli incomprehensible and disturbing. To avoid this possibility, it is important to

1. Minimize the use of intercoms, televisions, buzzers, bells, and other noises. Many residents become frightened by these noises, while those suffering from psychotic disorders may incorporate such sounds into their delusions

2. Place residents confused by too much stimulation in small groups. Avoid putting them in large, noisy, multi-purpose rooms which may result in many becoming over-stimulated and agitated.

3. Remove unnecessary mirrors, confusing signs, intricate wallpaper and boldly-patterned bedding People with moderate to severe dementia sometimes mistake their image in a mirror for another person, and become agitated. Demented or psychotic people often get caught up in the patterns and details of their environment, which can then become sources of hallucinations.

4. Put residents who are disturbed by noise in quiet rooms. Monitor the rooms yourself to determine the noise level of each. At one facility, staff members volunteered to spend a night in each of the rooms, thus discovering that several rooms were too noisy to sleep in. In addition, one room was situated across from the nurses' station in such a way that the light from the station shined directly on the bed. Putting the staff in the residents' rooms for a night gave them a first-hand appreciation of the light and noise level found in each room, as well as the knowledge with which to make adjustments as appropriate.

Minimize Danger

Because newly-arrived residents are often frail, confused, unfamiliar with the surroundings, and possibly medicated, they are at high risk of falling or hurting themselves. Those with dementia are at even greater risk because, with their impaired judgment and probable poor vision and depth perception, they are unable to recognize potential dangers in their environment. Therefore, it is important to:

1. Maintain similar lighting in the hallway and in the residents' rooms. As older eyes take a longer time to adjust to changes in light intensity, walking from a well lighted hallway into a dimly lit room may result in falls and injuries.

2. Use ample non-glare lighting in halls and resident rooms, and night lights in all rooms.

3. Reduce the glare from shiny floors and other polished surfaces.

4. Remove furniture and other objects with sharp edges. Keep furniture and other equipment in good condition. Loose parts and exposed edges are potential sources of injury.

5. Remove any spoiled food or nonfood substances that could be accidentally swallowed.

6. Carefully monitor smoking, and restrict it to certain areas.

7. Put all unattended beds in a low position.

8. Remove all trash and other clutter frequently.

9. Check that clothing is on properly. In particular, ensure shoes are on correctly and securely tied.

10. Check that all personal items are stored in a safe place, and that all personal items are labeled with the person's name.

Personalize the Environment

Every person has the need for personal space. When residents enter a hospital or care facility, they lose control of personal territory, often having to share rooms, bathrooms, and eating areas with strangers. Arguing and fighting often occur because of disagreements about space previously understood to be personal. To assist in this transition,

1. Ask the family to provide inexpensive personal belongings to decorate and personalize the person's room. Include as many personal items in the person's environment as possible.

2. Inventory all the personal items so both staff and family are aware of what is in the room. Ensure that staff working with the person are familiar with the resident's belongings so there is no confusion about property ownership.

3. Mark all personal belongings with identification, and, where possible and practical, fasten the personal objects to the wall or furniture to ensure their security.

4. Make the room as pleasant and comforting as possible. Avoid odors from cleaning supplies, deodorants, sanitizing sprays, and substances designed to mask other unpleasant odors, which are often overpowering. Provide pleasant and familiar aromas, such as those emanating from cooking, the aroma of freshly-brewed coffee flowers, a newly-mowed lawn, or even outdoor air — fragrances rarely experienced by people in institutions. Common comforting sights of leafy trees, and the sounds of morning songbirds also may be absent from the older person's resident facility environment. Providing opportunities to enjoy these everyday pleasures, whether actually or artificially, greatly enrich the person's quality of life.

Chapter Three

Families

It can be put down as one of the advantages of a hospital that the relatives and friends do not take care of the patients. It is much better for them not to be under the care of anyone who is overconcerned for them.

New York Times Dec 31, 1900

Interactions with family members are important to a successful care plan. The family can be a valuable resource, providing essential historical information about personal preferences, routines, medical and mental health histories, and past successful types of caregiving. In addition, family members also can provide a powerful source of comfort and support for the resident.

At times, however, families present problems. Family members may have become accustomed to being the primary caregivers, and may be over-involved with the patient. While meaning well, they may disagree with caregiving methods or plans, and sometimes actually interfere with treatment. A family member who has taken on the role of caregiver may

Behavioral Objectives

At the end of this section readers will be able to:

Describe the five stages of coping with cognitive decline.

Explain the function of denial and minimizing of a family member's illness.

Use constructive methods to help family members deal with their concerns.

Effectively involve family in the treatment regimen.

strongly identify with that role and be very reluctant to relinquish it.

According to researchers Paul Teusink and Susan Mahler, families of elderly patients with progressive cognitive decline undergo a predictable step-wise process as they attempt to cope with the disorder, and that families coping with debilitating disease exhibit similar reactions to those of families coping with death.

Caregivers need to provide the families with information and education about this coping process to enable them to understand that what they are feeling is normal. With this support, guidance and knowledge, a family can successfully work through feelings and reactions, mourn the loss of the previous family structure, make the necessary decisions for elder care, and re-establish a new family equilibrium.

Denial

In the beginning, family members may notice memory lapses and behavioral differences in their aging loved one, but explain these changes away by saying that they are just the result of "stress," or a normal part of getting old. The family may insist there is nothing wrong with their loved one in spite of growing evidence to the contrary. This familial reaction may be the result of the family's lack of education about aging, but it is also a conscious or unconscious desire to deny what they are seeing.

Denial defends against the pain of loss, and makes any objective assessment, decision-making, or treatment-planning difficult. Increasingly frequent family fights about how to handle the loved one's illness may actually be a way for the family to postpone dealing with what is occurring within their family structure, and, consequently, postponing their grief.

Families exhibiting excessive denial must be helped — through support, education and, at times, outright confrontation — to recognize the extent of the disability of their family member. Although this process may be difficult and emotional, only when denial is overcome will the family be able to make sound decisions and realistic plans for treatment.

Over-involvement

Denial often is followed by family members' intense over-involvement with the patient. As the deterioration of the afflicted loved one becomes more obvious, family members may increasingly take over daily tasks and responsibilities in an effort to compensate for the deficits.

A role reversal begins to occur, as a family member more and more frequently becomes a parent to his or her own parent. This can be one of the most difficult adjustments families face. The family member often must assume the patient's former family role, involving important legal and financial responsibilities. This task can be difficult and stressful, and family fights may break out, and sibling rivalries re-emerge.

Often, an adult child must take on the spousal role even if the parent's spouse is still living. Tasks and responsibilities that were accomplished by one spouse for many decades may be incomprehensible to the non-ailing partner. Some spouses have never written a check or paid a bill, while others have never prepared a meal, and — in combination with the stress of dealing with illness in their spouse — find such tasks overwhelming.

When involvement with an aging parent becomes an obsession, family members may sacrifice their personal lives and become consumed with the care-giving task. Even while recognizing they are in over their heads, they may be reluctant to seek professional help, thinking that to do so is to betray their parent. Some sons or daughters are raised to believe that they must care for their parents regardless of how disruptive it may be to their own lives. They believe that to not do so will result in ostracism and ridicule by their family and community. Adherence to this belief often stretches them to the breaking point. Such people must be helped to understand what is within their power to do and what is beyond their limits, and to act on that knowledge.

Professional caregivers must recognize the difference between a normal reaction and over-involvement within a given family and its particular culture. They must provide the family members with solid evidence of what problems familial over-involvement is causing for the patient, the staff, and the rest of the family, and must help the family realize its over-involvement may actually be a hindrance to achieving successful caregiving.

Anger

Inevitably, an over-involved family member, unable to shoulder the tremendous burden of caring for their loved one, nor tolerate his or her increasingly bizarre or socially inappropriate behavior, reacts in anger. Anger also can erupt in a family member from the feeling of having been abandoned by a still-living but now helpless parent or spouse.

Regardless of its source, this anger is often projected or displaced onto the very people who are trying to help the family deal with their overwhelming sense of helplessness — the caregiving professionals. These professionals must recognize when this is occurring, and, rather than becoming defensive, angry, or alienating in return, must help the family confront and deal with their anger appropriately. Without this guidance, families may fail to realize they are projecting their own painful feelings onto caregivers, and may accuse them of neglecting the patient and causing what is in reality the naturally-occurring deterioration of the progressing illness.

Guilt

As anger lessens, family members' feelings of guilt may become more obvious. They may feel guilt as a result of their anger, or from the need to make medical and financial decisions that may be objected to by the loved one, or even from having unexpressed and personally unacceptable wishes that their suffering family member die.

Guilt may result from family members believing they waited too long before seeking professional help for their loved one, and thus caused avoidable suffering. Another source of guilt may be the re-awakening of old feelings — feelings of lack of attention to their parent or spouse in earlier times, or remembrances of abrasive and cruel comments from years passed. Family members may mix their guilt with a dash of failure: they tried their best to care for their loved one, but the task was more than they could bear.

Unfortunately, this guilt sometimes gets translated into a need to dictate orders to the staff and caregivers. They confuse interference with involvement. One such case involved Jim Stevens and his father.

> Jim Stevens brought his father to the nursing home because caring for his dad was disrupting his job to the degree that he was at risk of being fired.
>
> He told the administrator that he wanted to be notified of any and every problem his father was experiencing. He made it clear that no treatment of any kind was to be administered to his father without his approval.
>
> In reality, Mr. Stevens was very difficult to reach. He seldom returned phone calls, and sometimes could not be reached at all. This resulted in impeding any semblance of quality care.
>
> The administrator invited Mr. Stevens to a meeting and said, "Mr. Stevens, I know you care for your father

a great deal. I know you worry about him. And we are all impressed with your concern and your involvement. It is true that you want the absolute best for your dad, isn't it?"

"Of course," he replied.

"Well the absolute best care we can give requires immediate intervention at times. If we have to wait, your father may suffer unnecessarily. You wouldn't want to stand in the way of helping him, would you?"

"No. Of course not," he said.

"Then I guess we both agree that when we cannot reach you, we should do what we feel is in your father's best interest, right?"

"I suppose so," he said.

"Great," She said, "then I would like you to sign this agreement stating that if we cannot reach you within an hour, we can do what is best for him."

In this interchange several things happened. The administrator validated Mr. Steven's feelings and concerns. She got him to agree that the best care was the most important issue. She got him to agree, in writing, they could proceed with treatment if they could not reach him. The written agreement assured there would be no misunderstanding.

Health care professionals can most effectively deal with family members' guilt by discovering its cause, and taking corrective steps to alleviate it. A major early step may simply be to educate the family about the illness itself, thereby providing reassurance that the family has not harmed the patient. More extensive counseling may be needed to help the family make difficult but necessary decisions, some of which may be objected to by the patient.

Acceptance

Acceptance comes once a family is able to truly understand the disease or disability and its progressive effects on their loved one. They have worked through the bulk of their anger and guilt, and have arrived at the realization their loved one is no longer the person they once knew, and can accept the loss.

In cases of dementia, acceptance can be especially difficult. This disease's insidious onset and long, slow progress give false hopes to family members that things will remain as they are. The patient's relatively normal appearance during the early stages of the illness makes the illness appear less serious than it really is.

A case study of the problems associated with a lack of acceptance is described by Teusink and Mahler:

> Mrs. K, a profoundly demented 76-year-old Jewish widow, was transferred from a long-term-care facility to the Cornell Medical Center for an evaluation of agitated behavior including constant pacing, verbal abusiveness, and at times combativeness.
>
> Although Mrs. K had exhibited symptoms of Alzheimer's disease for approximately one and a half years, she had worked in her family's garment manufacturing business until one year before her transfer to the center.
>
> In the transfer summary, the nursing home complained of difficulty with the patient's 50-year-old son, who was running his mother's business.
>
> During the initial phase of his mother's hospitalization in our facility, Mr. K was unable to accept his mother's progressive deterioration and was insistent that certain signs, such as intact long-term memory, were proof that she was less impaired than he had been told. He believed that his mother's wandering stemmed from her boredom at not having work to do and from the lack of staff initiating engaging her in activity.
>
> Mr. K visited his mother nightly and brought her dress patterns to cut. When she was unable to perform the tasks he expected of her, he displaced his disappointment and anger onto the nursing staff in a hostile, abusive, and accusatory fashion, thus engendering staff defensiveness and resistance to empathizing with his pain. Mr. K was critical of all aspects of his mother's treatment and expected the hospital to find a miracle cure for her illness.
>
> Engaging Mr. K in family therapy was difficult since he saw both the doctor and social worker as his adversaries. He was seen in weekly sessions, where he

was encouraged to talk about his frustration at our inability to make his mother well.

At the same time, we educated him about Alzheimer's disease — its manifestations, course, and treatment.

Mr. K eventually revealed his concerns that the illness was hereditary or contagious, and his feelings of helplessness in caring for his mother. He had attempted to have her live with his family before placing her in a nursing home, but he and the family were unable to control her wandering and disruption of family life.

As Mr. K began to discuss his family history and his feelings about his mother, it became clear that he had a conflict-ridden, ambivalent relationship with her.

Mrs. K had worked long hours in the family's business since Mr. K was a young child and had left his care to an older sibling. Mr. K had felt neglected and abandoned, and had developed angry feelings toward his mother.

Having to put his mother into a nursing home reawakened these repressed feelings of anger and abandonment, and aroused concerns that he was now abandoning her. He was still unable to see his mother as anything other than the strong, capable, working woman he had known in the past, and although he was capable of running the family business, he was experiencing self-doubts. In addition, he was furious at his sibling, who lived out of town and was not involved with his mother's care.

Mr. K's reminiscences about his mother helped him to realize the source of his angry feelings and he became less critical of the staff.

His lessened anger enabled him to understand the symptoms of Alzheimer's disease, to more realistically assess his mother's illness, and to mourn her loss.

When Mrs. K was discharged from our facility, we talked with the social worker in the long-term care facility where Mrs. K would return, so that we could apprise her of Mr. K's conflicts and encourage her to provide him with continued support.

In other cases, family members have become estranged from the patient, and eschew any involvement at all, allowing unresolved feelings of anger, frustration, helplessness, grief, and fear to interfere with healthy family interaction. Family therapy and family support groups can be very useful in these cases.

Unfortunately, there are the rare cases in which family members have not only been neglectful, but abusive as well. In a 1988 survey, researchers Karl Pillemer and David Finklehor discovered that about four percent of elders experienced abuse by family members. In the majority of cases, the abuser was the patient's spouse. They also discovered that only one in fourteen cases were ever reported.

Social support plays an important part in setting the stage for abuse. Elderly people who are isolated from all but their caregivers are four times as likely to suffer abuse than those who have social support. Men are more likely to be abused than women, because elderly men are more likely to live with a caregiver.

Regardless of who they are, how they act, and what they have done, family members must always be treated with respect, deference, and consideration. A professional caregiver working in a caregiving facility must remember that residents and families are considered to be customers, and a caregiver's job is to serve them.

Family Visits

A frequent problem of long term care residents is loneliness. Most residents complain that families don't visit enough, often because they actually don't visit often, but frequently because the resident simply doesn't remember the visits. Photographs, video or audio tape recordings taken during visits is useful in reminding residents they are not alone.

Family visits can be an unfortunate source of trouble when negative interactions with visiting family members irritate and agitate a patient. Encourage the family to keep the climate of the visit positive, as

Video and audio recordings of family visits can be a significant source of comfort for residents.

fighting and friction during a visit can cause behavioral problems in the resident for several days.

Residents may see family visits as opportunities to complain about the facility and the quality of care. Although these complaints may be valid, in some cases, residents complain of poor care either because they cannot remember many of the things that are done for them, or because they get pleasure out of stirring up trouble. For instance,

> Mrs. Whitkin's daughter would visit twice a week. She would arrive at ten o'clock, and spend an hour with her mother. During these visits Mrs. Whitkin would complain incessantly about not being fed, not being cared for, and being generally neglected.
>
> We suggested to her daughter that she come to facility unannounced at different times during the day and stand where her mother could not see her, so that she could observe the things we did for her mother. In this way, she was able to see that we were in fact doing the things that Mrs. Whitkin claimed we did not do. The daughter then realized that much of what we were doing was simply forgotten.

Behavioral Interventions to Help Family Members

1. Spend time with the resident's family. Get to know them, and learn about their expectations, attitudes, and concerns.

2. Acknowledge and validate the family members' feelings and concerns. If they are not forth-coming with these feelings, offer family members information on typical feelings and concerns and ask if they are experiencing any of them. For example, you might say, "It's common for families to feel frightened, depressed, defeated, or guilty about the decision to seek professional help. It would not be unusual for you to be feeling any or all of these things."

3. Family members sometimes express their concern and anxiety as anger. When this happens, it is very important that you not internalize a family member's anger. Rather than taking their anger personally, validate their anger and offer solutions. Be responsive, not reactive. Say, "I can hear that you are very upset. I understand. Let's see what we can do to solve the problem."

4. Tell family members about the resident's current condition. Carefully explain the symptoms and problems that the resident is experiencing. Explaining problems and unusual behaviors helps the family understand and cope with what they are seeing.

5. Explain how the resident's current condition creates specific needs, and show how these needs can best be met.

6. Explain the facility's policies and procedures. It is useful to give a written summary of the policies and procedures to all family members, along with a list of answers to the most frequently asked questions, so that there are no misunderstandings about what the facility can and cannot do. Taking the time to prepare this summary may save hours of explanation later.

7. Involve the family in the care plan whenever possible. Invite the family to care-planning meetings. Even minimal participation greatly increases family compliance, gives them a feeling of power and participation, and allows them to provide valuable information and insight about any problem behaviors.

8. Inform family members of any change in the care plan, and provide the rationale for the change.

9. Inform all staff members of who the family members are, and how they are to be involved in care giving.

10. Explain to the family how the quality of each visit affects the quality of life of their loved one.
11. Encourage the family to join a support group.
12. Put the family in touch with community resources.

Section Two

Factors Affecting
Behavioral Problems

Chapter Four

Memory, Cognition, and Concentration

A great number of emotional and behavioral problems present in elderly people are actually caused by difficulties with mental function. As the aging mind begins to falter, a person may become anxious and fearful. In the beginning stages of dementia, for example, many people experience anxiety. The more they grapple with remembering information that once came effortlessly, the more they fear the worst. Early on, dementia patients may be acutely aware they are losing their memory. It is not uncommon to hear someone say, "Please help me, I'm afraid I'm losing my mind."

As the memory loss and cognitive problems continue, a person may experience depression, making matters even worse as depression further interferes with memory. It is vital that the person be screened for depression, and be treated for it if present. Often treating underlying depression results in a significant improvement in memory problems. (For more about depression see chapter 7.)

Behavioral Objectives

At the end of this section readers will be able to:

Describe the types of memory.

Explain the differences between memory, cognition, and concentration.

Identify the types of memory deficits a person may exhibit.

Help people cope with memory problems.

Types of Memory

Episodic Memory:
A person's memory of past events.

Episodic memory problems are often signs of Alzheimer's disease.

Semantic memory:
A person's knowledge of the world, including language and recognition of objects.

Problems with semantic memory, such as word finding and categorising words are often signs of Semantic dementia.

Many problems resembling memory problems are actually caused by other factors. To understand this, it helps to review how the memory process actually works.

Input Problems

All memories begin with a stimulus, a source of information that is new to the mind. Most memories originate from the stimulation of our senses: sight, sound, taste, touch or smell. Stimulation is the key to good memory function.

It's common for people to become less physically and socially active as they grow older, seeking out less and less sensory stimulation. In caregiving environments, many elderly people do very little each day but sit and watch television. This is seldom discouraged by the staff; it is not disruptive and it occupies the person, but it also deactivates the person.

Unfortunately, this understimulation causes problems. Lonely and forgotten people are seldom spoken to, seldom touched, and rarely encouraged to engage in social activity. Under-stimulation is literally the hobgoblin of healthy minds. An under-stimulated brain will actually begin to atrophy, shrink, and deteriorate, even within weeks.

Chronic under-stimulation can actually lead to hallucinations. The brain needs a certain amount of stimulation to function properly, and if it cannot obtain it from the environment, it will manufacture it by causing hallucinations. Experiments in sensory deprivation show that deprived of external events, the brain will begin to generate stimuli within a few hours.

Residents in long-term care facilities may talk to themselves not because they are mentally ill, but merely because talking is their only source of stimulation. Rocking, wandering, and masturbation also provide stimulation.

Exposing a person to new experiences and novel environments can actually cause neurons to grow new connections. Stimulation helps the brain stay healthy. Therefore, the more active the person, the better-functioning the memory

Keep in mind, however, that too much stimulation can overload an ailing brain. It can make people anxious, irritable, and withdrawn. Too much input may confuse people, and overtax their mental filters.

Receptors

Information coming from the outside world is picked up by millions of specialized cells called receptors. Eyes, ears, noses, mouth and skin all contain receptors, and all humans process information reaching these receptors in the same manner. Most people, however, have preferred modes of processing this information. Visually-oriented people would rather watch something, which people with a preference for sound would rather hear it. This preference for a specific type of information is caused by the action of stimulus filters, which are discussed below.

Many years ago, children with hearing impairments were classified as retarded, considered unteachable, and often were shunned by society. Eventually it was discovered that hearing-impaired children were just as capable of learning and remembering as anyone; they simply had a receptor problem. In the elderly, loss of hearing — a receptor problem — may be mislabeled as dementia.

For any stimulus to be picked up by the nervous system, it must be strong enough to trigger the receptor. Scientists call this minimum intensity the *stimulus threshold*. A mosquito is often able to land on the body, puncture the skin, and leave without our awareness because its delicate touch is below the stimulus threshold of the touch receptors in the skin. We

Working Memory:
A person's ability to solve problems, comprehend the environment, and focus on specific tasks or thoughts. This type of memroy includes attention and concentration.

Problems with working memory may be a sign of Frontotempoaral dementia.

Procedural Memory:
A person's skills, including routines, habits, and activites aof daily living.(Also called ADLs and IADLs.)

Problems with procedural memory occur in white matter vascular dememtia.

typically only become aware of the insect's visit because of the itching caused by the bite.

Many memory problems begin with stimulus thresholds. As people age, stimulus thresholds increase. Older people lose sensitivity to touch, taste, smell and sounds. Because people cannot remember what they do not perceive, when receptors fail to transmit information, no memory is stored.

For example, aging causes the sense of touch to falter, as the stimulus threshold increases and the skin loses some of its ability to detect stimuli. Elderly people become less aware of clothing and personal items such as jewelry, and may not notice when an item falls off or becomes lost. When they later discover they have lost a favorite sweater or a piece of jewelry, they have no conscious recollection what happened.

Elderly eyes dim, and ears no longer hear as well as they once did. This decrease in function is usually slow and insidious, and may not be noticed for a considerable time. Many people will deny that they have a hearing or vision problem even when it is apparent to others around them. As hearing begins to fail, they complain that others are not speaking clearly or loudly enough. They misunderstand and misinterpret what they hear. (More information about hearing loss appears in chapter 12.)

Of course, when hearing fails, auditory memory suffers — what cannot be heard cannot be remembered. For this reason, people begin to exhibit what looks like memory problems, when what is actually happening is a loss of the ability to detect or understand sound.

It's important to be aware that many older people also lose much of their ability to smell and taste. This often results in a decrease in the pleasure of eating. When eating decreases, malnutrition may occur, which can have a profound effect on memory and cognition.

Screening a resident for receptor problems is essential in evaluating cognitive deficits and behavior problems. Checking sight, hearing, touch, taste, and smell can often pinpoint and correct problems before they become debilitating and disruptive.

Filtering

Although we encounter millions of bits of information each day, we actually remember only a small portion of them. What we do remember is controlled by the mechanism of filtering out what is unimportant and focusing on a task at hand.

Like any filter, this mechanism eliminates unwanted material. Stimulus filters scan all incoming information, and allow into consciousness only the most important data of the moment. The result of these filters is the ability to focus, which is called attention.

Each person develops a unique set of stimulus filters — an array of natural talents and abilities that make it easy to remember certain types of information. This is true in part because of individual differences in the hard wiring of the brain. Just as people differ in hair color, eye color, and height, each person's brain structure is unique. In the last few years, researchers have actually found physical differences in brain structure that correspond with different abilities and professions

Some people excel in certain types of memory, while others suffer specific deficits and are said to have learning disabilities. Elderly people with learning disabilities, like their younger counterparts, may be unable to process certain types of information, and therefore cannot store it.

This deficit in storage has often been mistaken for a memory problem, but it's actually a processing problem. Because learning disabilities such as attention deficit disorder and dyslexia were not diagnosed a generation ago, they are seldom considered in the elderly, and thus often misdiagnosed as dementia.

Elderly people with learning disabilities, like their younger counterparts, may be unable to process certain types of information, and therefore cannot store it.
This deficit in storage is often mistaken for a memory problem.

The process by which stimulus filters decide what to attend to is called the *orienting response*. Orienting is an automatic, unconscious process, active even when we are sleeping. It is this response that allows a new mother to sleep through the noise of a police siren, only to be awakened a moment later by a slight whimper from her newborn. The orienting response is in play when we converse with someone in a room full of people, automatically focusing on what the other person is saying and subconsciously filtering out all other conversations are filtered out. But if someone across the room calls our name, this same response refocuses our attention, and we turn our heads to see who called us.

Concentration Problems

Concentration is the ability to focus on one from of input, while filtering out other stimuli. As people age, input becomes harder to filter. By the time we hit our forties, our frontal lobes begin to lose cells, causing problems with attention and concentration. Background noises begin to interfere with conversations, and too much stimulation becomes confusing and distracting. Some people react to this phenomenon by withdrawing, as may happen when some residents in long term care facilities prefer to stay in their rooms — the outside world has become too noisy and confusing.

Hearing aids often interfere with filtering. When a person with a hearing aid is in a room full of people it is sometimes impossible to filter out noise, resulting in an incomprehensible roar.

Stress also causes stimulus filters to break down, with nothing in the environment getting filtered out. The resultant stimulus overload affects short-term memory, which can't handle this much input. The person becomes unable to focus and unable to transfer the information into long-term memory. The net result is that the brain stops processing new information. Later on, when the stress is over, people find they can't remember events that happened during the time of stress.

As a stressed person is also preoccupied with concerns about being stressed, this preoccupation interferes with the ability to learn new information and can block the person's ability to recall what the person already knows.

When older people feel stressed, they instinctively try to get away from noise and distraction they can no longer filter — thus the phrase "getting away from it all." It is important to realize that some of the isolating behavior residents engage in is actually an attempt at reducing stress. In these cases, providing the person with quieter surroundings, less stimulation, and an uninterrupted flow of information will improve both the ability to store and to recall that information

As mentioned earlier, it's common for new residents in a care facility to experience a great deal of stress. Everything around them is new and different, and they may exhibit temporary confusion and memory loss. As residents become familiar with the their new facility, these problems tend to go away. (For more on confusion, see chapter 5.)

Working Memory

Once a piece of information has been selected by the orienting response and passed through the stimulus filter for processing, it enters working memory. Working memory holds only a small amount of information — enough for about one phone number — and holds it for a very short period of time — about twenty seconds.

Beginning at age forty, there is also a gradual decline in working memory. This problem occurs because of frontal lobe atrophy, which results in distraction.

You've probably had the experience of looking up a number in a phone book, walking over to the phone, dialing part of the number, and suddenly realizing that you have forgotten the rest of it. What do you do? You look the number up again, and this time say the number over and over to yourself until you reach the phone. If you're successful in dialing the number, you finish your conversation, and hang up. But if you have to call again in a few minutes, you find you have again forgotten the number. These are the limitations of working memory storage.

People suffering from dementia often can carry on a sensible conversation although storage of the conversation — which is done in long term memory — doesn't occur. Because working memory and language function is intact, the person appears normal. However, a moment after a conversation has ended, the person with dementia has absolutely no memory of it. Conversations often go like this:

> I introduce myself to Mrs. Irwin, saying, "Hi, Mrs. Irwin. My name is Dr. Matteson."
> "Hi, Dr. Matteson," she replied, "That's an easy name to remember, isn't it?"
> "Sure is," I said, "Can you tell me how long you've been here?"
> "A few days," she told me. (She had actually been here for six months).
> "Do you know my name?" I asked.
> "I don't believe you told me your name."

Working memory is still intact. But what is lost is the ability to transfer the information from short-term to long-term memory. People can hold onto an idea long enough to respond to it, but a fleeting moment later, it is whisked away and gone forever.

Problems with this type of memory also cause deficits in *cognition:* the ability to problem solve.

Long Term Memory

The final stage in the memory process is the retrieval of the stored information. Most of the time, the inability to remember something is caused by a failure in the storage process just described. The most common cause of not remembering is the simple failure to transfer information from short-term to long-term memory.

One way to help older adults store new information is to repeat it many times in many places, and to review it frequently. Repetition sends a message to the memory system that the information is important and should be stored. Repeating information many times in many circumstances causes an increase in cue density, and increases the person's ability to store and recall new information. Even in people with noticeable memory problems, repetition and spaced practice often result in learning.

Another way to increase learning is through the use of pictures, either drawn by the persons to correspond with the information they wish to learn, or having the information drawn for them. For example, when I want patients to remember my name, I tell them, "My name is Dr. Matteson. Think of Madison Square Garden."

Semantic Memory

As people get older, retrieval of information takes longer. Even in people with normal memory, search and retrieval slows down with age. Word finding also becomes more difficult. The storehouse of information in the brain, located in the temporal lobes, is called *semantic memory.*

In most people, words are stored in the left temporal lobe, which is accessed by using a part of the brain called the hippocampus, the index to the temporal lobe. When a person needs a word or phrase, the hippocampus retrieves it and delivers it to working memory. In healthy adults, the decline in word retrieval begins at about forty years of age, and progresses with increasing age. Studies show that the first category of words that become inaccessible are proper names. This is followed by nouns, adjectives, and then verbs.

When a person says he or she cannot remember something, ask the question in a different way. This causes other pathways to be activated, and increases the chance of recall. If this doesn't work, ask the question again later — what is unavailable at one moment often can be recalled without effort a few moments later.

Remote Memories

Family members of elderly people often comment on the person's remarkable ability to remember events from years ago, but not from last week. *Remote memory* is the storehouse for the events of childhood and youth. Unlike other types of memory, this type is durable and long lasting. Even in the intermediate stages of dementia, remote memory usually stays intact.

People with memory problems remember remote events better than recent ones for several reasons. First, as just stated, remote memory is the last type of memory to be affected by dementia. Second, people often tell the same stories over and over, which keeps the memory fresh in their minds. Third, it's impossible to tell whether these memories are accurate. Because they happened so long ago, there is usually no way to verify them. Even if the stories are recounted with conviction, they may have little resemblance to what actually happened.

Many older people don't remember recent events well because their life is dull, repetitive, and uninteresting. When nothing memorable happens, nothing is remembered.

Procedural Memory

Procedural memory is the storehouse of all habits, skills and routines. A procedural memory (such as playing a musical instrument) may take a long time to learn, but once the memory is acquired, it is done without effort.

The most important quality of procedural memories is that they do not require consciousness. Most of us have had the experience of driving down the street only to suddenly find we don't know where we are. After a few anxious seconds, we scan the environment and reorient ourselves. We were driving on autopilot, relying on our procedural memory.

As people age, short-term memories, long-term memories and semantic memories decline. At the same time, eyes and ears lose their sensitivity. The result of these changes is an increasing reliance on procedural memory, which we call our habits and routines.

As an elderly man, for instance, comes to rely on his habits, we might call him "set in his ways." Because it is more difficult to learn new routines, he avoids change. But when moved from a home he may have lived in for decades, all routines and habits are shattered, and he becomes bewildered. The words we use for this condition are *disorientation*, *confusion,* and *delirium*. Although all three words describe a confused individual, as discussed in the following chapters, they mean different things, and the distinctions are often critical to successful treatment.

Chapter Five

Confusion

Have you ever awakened in a hotel room in the middle of the night and had no idea where you were? Perhaps you didn't remember until you'd groped for your glasses and turned on a light.

Now imagine that you're in a hospital. You have bilateral cataracts, are hard of hearing, and took a sleeping pill a few hours ago. You're awakened by the presence of a shadowy figure. Alarmed and still drowsy from the medication, you strike out at the intruder.

After she leaves, you try to get up to urinate, but what are those bars on the bed? You climb over them and tumble to the floor. As you lie there, you lose control of your bladder. The shadowy figure returns, straps you back in bed, and sticks a tube into your bladder. Then she goes to the nurses' station where she writes in your chart, "Confused, combative, and incontinent."

According to Gayle Anderson, an expert in geriatric assessment who wrote the words above, about half of the people entering a care facility will go through a period of disorientation. But this is only one of many causes of confusion.

Behavioral Objectives

At the end of this section readers will be able to:

Define differences between disorientation, confusion and delirium.

Help people with disorientation.

List the causes of confusion.

Discuss medical causes of confusion.

Causes of Delirium
Infections:
- acute meningitis
- viral
- chronic meningitis
- tuberculosis
- fungal
- neurosyphilis
- brain abscess
- pneumonia
- pyelonephritis
- cholecystitis
- diverticulitis
- endocarditis

Hypo or Hyperthermia
Hypoxia:
(decreased cerebral oxygen)
- acute myocardial infarction
- congestive heart failure
- arrhythmia
- vascular occlusion
- pulmonary embolism
- hypotension
- transient ischemia (TIA)
- ventilatory failure
- chronic lung disease

Anemic hypoxia:
- iron deficiency anemia
- pernicious anemia
- folic acid deficiency
- gradual blood loss

Brain Disorders
- head trauma
- subdural hematoma
- concussion/ contusion
- intracerebral hemorrhage Normal-pressure-hydrocephalus

Disorientation

Disorientation means the lack of awareness of time, place, and person. It is the specific loss of ability to know a person's location, what time it is, what day, month, season, or year it is.

Disorientation can be caused by dementia, confusion, or delirium, but it can also be a function of the person's environment and lifestyle. For example, some hospital wards have no windows, which makes it impossible to tell whether it is day or night. Some facilities have few clocks, calendars, of any other external cues to orient the person.

Keep in mind that many elderly people have lost their sense of time because every day is exactly the same. While structure is important, complete lack of change makes the days pass by uneventfully. Not only does this sameness lead to disorientation, but it impairs memory as well. Children of elderly parents often comment that their parents remember things that happened years ago, but not what happened last week. This is caused in part by the fact that nothing happened last week!

Intervention for Disorientation

1. Ensure the environment has cues for orientation, including clocks, calendars, and signs stating the day, month and year. There also should be signs stating the name and location of the facility.
2. Structure each day differently, so that the week contains a variety of daily activities. Elderly people do not get weekends off, and they do not have regularly-scheduled vacations. Unless there is a clear way for them to tell one day from another, they will lose orientation to time.

Confusion

Confusion is a group of behaviors that include distractability, an impaired attention span, loss of memory for recent events (and later for remote events), impaired judgment, inability to comprehend the environment, and the inability to understand or follow instructions. Unlike delirium, confusion does not always include loss of alertness, and is not always caused by a medical condition.

None of these terms includes all behavior — few people become confused about everything, are constantly delirious, or remain totally disoriented. Instead, these conditions are usually intermittent and patchy in occurrence. It is important to remember this intermittence, because if caregivers make the assumption that the symptoms are the result of old age or senility, and therefore irreversible, they may overlook a potentially dangerous medical condition, or unnecessarily restrict a person's rights.

Irreversible confusional states are found in about 50 percent of the institutionalized elderly and in a large number of elders cared for by families. These types of confusion are caused by brain damage, are progressive, and are collectively known as dementias (More information on dementia appears in chapter 6). Alzheimer's disease or multi-infarct dementia account for 80 percent of the dementias of old age. However, much of what may look like dementia can, in many cases, be reversed.

Reversible Confusion

One of the diagnostic distinctions between permanent and reversible confusion is that the latter type usually has a rapid onset. There is often a sudden loss of cognition, orientation and memory for recent events. During this time, the person may experience

Drugs that cause delirium

Antiparkinsonian Drugs
Amantadine
(Symmetrel)

Carbidopa/levodopa
(Sinemet)

Levodopa (Larodopa)

CNS Depressants
Meperidine
(Demerol)

Codeine

Morphine
Hydromorphone
(Dilaudid)

Tricyclic antidepressants
Amitriptyline
(Elavil)

Doxepin

Imipramine
(Tofranil)

Nortriptyline
(Pamelor)

Drugs that cause delirium

Anticholinergics
Atropine
Benzotropine (Cogentin)

Scopalamine
(Methyexyphenidyl trihexane)

Benzodiazapines
Taken alone:

Diazepam (Valium)

Temazepam (Restoril)

Triazolam (Halcion)

Taken alone or in combination with Tagamet:

Alprazolam (Xanax)

Clorazepate (Gen-Xene)

Tranxene

Flurazepam (Dalmane)

Prarepam (Centrax)

visual hallucinations and the inability to organize thoughts or actions. Even so, the person's orientation and social protocols may be unimpaired.

The person suffering this reversible type of cognitive impairment has trouble following directions or focusing on anything for any meaningful length of time. Later, when no longer confused, the person may be able to remember his or her own previous thoughts and actions as if viewed in a movie.

There are many causes of confusion, most of which are result from a major change in the person's physical or emotional state. Confusion often happens after surgery, an accident, an illness, or because of an acute metabolic imbalance.

Although confusion is usually caused by a medical condition (see margins of these pages for a partial list of such conditions), the confused behavior may actually be the first sign of the problem. The treatment for rapid onset confusional states should begin immediately, including obtaining an accurate assessment, screening, diagnoses, and a close observation of the person's behavior.

Interventions for Confusion

1. Conduct a complete physical examination, including a basic laboratory screening. Check the person's vital signs, test for mental impairment, and compare historical information to recent changes in the person's behavior. Obtain information about the person's personal history and lifestyle, and assess ability to follow directions and maintain attention to surrounding events.
2. If there is no evidence of a metabolic imbalance disease, consider recent life events which could have caused undue stress. Look at factors such as recent losses, change in visits, and changes in the environment.

3. Use frequent statements of orientation These statement help the person restore his contact with reality while the physical and social stressors are being assessed and treated.

Following is an example of an effective intervention:
Mrs. Harris was being admitted to the hospital because of wandering, incontinence, disorientation to time and place, and several chronic medical conditions. She was frightened and disoriented. During the admission process she continued to cry out, "Help me, I can't get out of here, help me, I'm lost!"

The nurse was able to calm her through touch and repeating the statements, "Mrs. Harris, I am Mrs. Posner. Look at my name tag. See it has my name and the name of this hospital on it. I'm your nurse. You are in Alameda Hospital. I will be caring for you. This is your room, here is your bed, and this is where we are going to put your belongings. You are perfectly safe."

This repeated intervention eventually oriented the person to her new surroundings.

The treatment for reversible confusion always consists of treating the cause. For example, the treatment for confusion from dehydration is to relieve the dehydration while maintaining the safety of the person. The treatment for pernicious anemia is to begin immediate vitamin B12 replacement.

Confusion resulting from relocation, sudden environmental changes, sensory overload, and other environmental stressors, improves only when the stress in the environment is identified and reduced. If these factors are not addressed, behavioral intervention will be ineffective.

Delirium

Delirium is also called *acute confusional state* (ACS). However it differs from the type of confusion described above, in that it usually is caused by a

Causes of reversible confusion

Metabolic Imbalances:
- Renal failure
- Dehydration
- Hyponatremia (low salt)
- Hypernatremia (high salt)
- Blood volume depletion
- Acid-base imbalance
- Hypoglycemia
- Hyperglycemia
- Liver failure
- Hypothyroidism
- Hyperthyroidism
- Hypercalcemia
- Hypopituitarism
- Cushing's Syndrome

Physical:
- Fractures
- Recent surgery
- Fecal Impaction
- Urinary retention

Environmental: Relocation
- A sudden change inenvironment
- Sleep Deprivation
- Sensory Deprivation
- Sudden change in temperature
- Sudden Change in food habits
- Adding or stopping a medication
- Catastrophic loss (such as death of spouse)
- Sudden change in daily activity schedule

medical illness, an infection, or drug toxicity, and always involves periods of diminished consciousness. It may also be caused by fever, organ failure leading to toxicity, or any acute infection. While dementia is a problem with memory and cognition, delirium is a problem with attention. A delirious person cannot remember from moment to moment, because he cannot attend to the information long enough for it to register in memory.

Delirium is a sign of danger, and if not treated, can lead to death. The delirious state is usually transient and fluctuates in intensity. In the majority of cases, the person recovers within four weeks. However, in elderly patients, delirium lasting up to six months is not uncommon, especially when arising because of chronic liver disease, a carcinoma, or a subacute bacterial infection. (In the elderly a common cause of delirium is a urinary tract infection.) Delirium is treated by finding and treating its cause.

While dementia is a problem with memory and cognition, delirium is a problem with attention.

Chapter Six

Dementia

I vowed to learn to live with this person who was inhabiting the body of the man I cherished.

Joanne Koenig Coste
Learning to Speak to Alzheimer's

The word *dementia* means literally to lose one's mind. Dementia is a set of brain dysfunctions characterized by multiple deficits in cognitive abilities without loss of alertness (see the previous chapter's discussion of delirium, which involves the loss of alertness.).

In 1900 there were fewer then three million people over the age of 65 in the United States. At the time of this writing, there are about 35 million, and this number is expected to double by the year 2050. It is estimated that one percent of people between the ages of 65 and 74 years old, seven percent of those from 75 to 84 years old, and 25 percent of those over 85 suffer from severe dementia. Currently about two million people in the U.S. suffer from advanced dementia, while another five million suffer mild-to-moderate symptoms.

Behavioral Objectives

At the end of this section readers will be able to:

Describe the general progression from the early through the late stage of Alzheimer's.

Assess the extent of memory and cognitive loss in a person.

Communicate effectively with a person suffering from dementia.

List the behavioral complications of dementia.

Pharmaceutical acetyl-cholinesterase inhibitors:
Donepezil hydrochloride
(Aricept®)

Galantamine hydrobromide
(Razadyne®)

Rivastigmine tartrate
(Exelon®)

Tacrine hydrochloride
(Cognex®)

Natural acetylcholinesterase inhibitors:
Huperzine A

Black tea

Green tea

Dementia is caused by brain damage. The parts of the brain that are most affected are the association areas of the brain, which integrate sensory information, thought, memory, and purposeful behavior. When extensive damage to these regions occurs, the affected person may begin to engage in bizarre behaviors that have no link to the external environment. They also may become verbally and physically agitated and abusive.

Dementia always includes the loss of memory and cognition, and causes the loss of the ability to make sound judgments, and to maintain an ongoing sense of being. Very often, the ability to comprehend and express ideas is also impaired, and there are problems with social interaction, daily living skills, and thinking.

While more than 60 disorders have been identified as causing dementia, Alzheimer's disease, also called Dementia of the Alzheimer's type (often abbreviated in the literature as DAT), is responsible for more over half of all dementia cases. Vascular disease, also called *multi-infarct dementia* or *vascular dementia,* accounts for another 20 percent.

Some people suffer from potentially reversible dementias caused by brain tumors, infections, toxins, nutritional deficiencies, over-medication, metabolic problems, and other neurological disorders.

It is important to distinguish the existence of a mental disorder from the symptoms of dementia, as mental disorders often mimic the symptoms of dementia, but are treatable. In addition, a person suffering from dementia may exhibit worse symptoms as a result of a co-existent mental disorder.

For people suffering from dementia, the move from home to a caregiving facility is particularly difficult. Already confused, they have lost most of what has become familiar — their homes, friends, lifestyles, familiar objects, and much of their independence. With the loss of a familiar environment, their habits and routines are shattered as well.

This multiple loss, combined with the dementia-induced cognitive and memory problems, usually results in residents having extreme difficulty adjusting to their new environment. They don't know where they are or where their personal and familiar belongings have gone, and they become frightened.

The Stages of Alzheimers Dementia

Early Stage

Have you ever walked into a room and realized you had no idea why you were there? Demented people have this experience every day.

In the early stages of dementia, the loss of the ability to think and remember is intermittent and patchy. An afflicted person may forget who a caregiver is on Monday, but have no trouble recognizing the person a day later.

People in the early stage of Alzheimer's disease may begin to show a loss of interest in their environment, their personal hygiene, and their personal affairs. Semantic memory begins to decline. Word finding becomes difficult, usually beginning with the inability to remember names, and then nouns. They may have difficulty attending important social events, such as holidays or birthday parties. Social graces, politeness, and social protocols begin to break down. One of my patients, for example, went home in the middle of his birthday party because he did not remember why he was there, and decided it was time to take a nap.

People in this stage suffer uncertainty and confusion in initiating actions. A thought may occur to the person to do something, but a moment after having begun the action, he has forgotten the intention of the action. A demented person may pick up an object with clear intent, then wander aimlessly around with the object, not remembering what to do with it.

At this early stage of the illness, people may be able to live at home, albeit with supportive care. Although they may appear to be thinking clearly, usually, they will need assistance in such tasks as paying bills and managing money. Frequent and regular assistance is of particular importance if the afflicted person lives alone.

Although most dementias are irreversible and essentially untreatable, at this stage, proper health care — including a regimen of antioxidants such as vitamin E, Vitamin B12 and non-steroidal anti-inflammatory drugs, and anticholinesterase inhibiting drugs — along with the reduction of environmental change and stress, may reduce symptoms, slow the disease process and prolong independence.

A person in early stage dementia, while perhaps still able to drive, may become easily lost and forget the way home. Neighbors and friends can be enlisted to watch for any changes in the person's living habits which may warrant increased vigilance. Relocation, change in residence, or illness will often mark the point at which the person slips into the next stage.

Intermediate Stage

Dementia's progress can be marked by a loss of what health care providers call activities of daily living (ADL). Health care and personal hygiene become neglected. The person shows a diminished ability to care for personal needs or affairs. The person loses the ability to comprehend, remember, or follow simple directions, and, as motor faculties begin to break down, may begin to engage in meaningless behavior.

Obvious memory losses begin to arise, in recall, recognition, and retention, and continuing until most of the simple tasks of life — bathing, brushing teeth, getting dressed — become confusing and incomprehensible. An activity as simple as putting on a shirt may become overwhelming. Personal possessions are lost or inexplicably hoarded and hidden.

Biological clocks begin to falter, and time disorientation occurs to such a degree that the person may not be able to tell if it is day or night. The person may wake at midnight and ask for lunch.

Severe deficits in the ability to think and remember require that business affairs be turned over to a conservator or family member with power of attorney. At this point, families with a good support network may still be able to care for the person. Without it, most families find the caregiving overwhelming and begin to look for a higher level of care

Later Stage

As the disease advances, screaming, aimless wandering, and combative behaviors begin to manifest in the patient. A person in the later stage of Alzheimer's disease can no longer walk from one point to another, and often is disoriented as to time and place. The ability to recognize people becomes impaired, and a caregiver may be mistaken for a family member. Fine motor skills, such as the ability to write and manipulate objects, disappear, and the person now needs help with the most basic activities, such as eating, getting dressed, and toileting.

Speech becomes garbled and incoherent, often requiring the use of non-verbal communication. The patient begins to exhibit a compulsive need to touch, to hoard, and to examine all objects with the mouth.

The patient may display a complete loss of emotion, may have altered dietary habits, ranging from anorexia to binge eating, and may exhibit inappropriate sexual behavior. Interestingly, with all of these problems and aberrant behaviors, a person in this phase still may be able to engage in and enjoy physical activities such as walking and group activities, and likely will continue to enjoy music.

Normal human behavior, however, literally has fallen to pieces and motor faculties are shattered into fragments. The person may get up suddenly, stop, look around, touch the wall, and sit down again, all the while oblivious to such actions.

The later stage dementia patient requires 24-hour care. Removal from the home and placement in a care facility may become essential, regardless of the fact that the lack of familiar surroundings and faces in the new facility typically results in a total loss of orientation. Personal hygiene at this stage is done entirely by a caregiver. Sleep is severely impaired, with agitation and confusion often occurring upon awakening, and before bedtime.

Terminal Stage

In the end stage of this cruel siege, an affected person may lose the ability to walk, stand up, or communicate in any meaningful way, and requires total nursing care. The patient is dependent on support for all physiologic processes, is non-responsive and cannot not recognize family members or familiar objects. Further deterioration is usually halted by death from an infection, renal failure, or pneumonia.

Assisting Families

Losing a loved one to this disease is a painful and devastating process. Family members undergo prolonged anticipatory grief and require frequent support from staff and from each other. Some family members may not be able to tolerate seeing the mindless, ravaged body of a person who no longer recognizes them, and, to protect themselves from the pain, may stop visiting the patient. Strongly supporting family members during this time is vital to preventing abandonment.

Interventions for Working with Dementia Patients

Behavioral complications of dementia include depression, wandering, endless pacing, aggression, agitation, hallucinations, paranoia, disturbed sleep, inappropriate verbalizations, rummaging, pica (eating non-edible items), hyper-sexuality, self-abuse, and repetitive questioning. Many of these behavioral problems are discussed later in this book.

Communicating with a person who is suffering from dementia requires skill and patience. Some important suggestions for communicating include:

1. Never approach people from behind. They will be startled and become upset.

2. Stand directly in front of the person when speaking to them. Touch their arm or shoulder gently to focus their attention.

3. Always treat the person with dignity and respect.

4. Be attentive to tone of voice and facial expressions. People with dementia are very sensitive to nonverbal communication. Even when they have lost the ability to understand what a caregiver is saying, they will react to the delivery.

5. Speak slowly and simply, but remember that the demented person is an adult. Avoid talking to them as if they were children.

6. Assess the person's ability to comprehend verbal commands. Research shows that as dementia progresses, people lose the ability to comprehend complex verbal commands. However, even those with relatively advanced dementia maintain their ability to comprehend single stage commands. Quickly assess the person's comprehension ability by asking them several one-, two, and three-step commands, such as

One-step: Close your eyes.

Pick up the brush.

Two-step: Pick up the brush and give it to me.

Pick up the paper, and put it in the book.

Three-step: Take this piece of paper, fold it in half, and place it inside the drawer.

Pick up the book, put the paper in it, and hand it to me.

If the person can comprehend and respond to three step commands, use them. Using one step commands with these people will not maintain their attention. For those with impaired comprehension, use one-step commands and yes or no questions.

7.   Do not expect a quick response. People with impaired thinking skills take longer to comprehend what was said to them. Give the person time both to comprehend what you've said, and then to respond.

8.   Pay attention to the voice and gestures for clues to words demented people may be having difficulty in finding. They may say one word but mean another. Provide the proper word, and ask them if this is what they meant.

9.   Use gestures and visual clues to clarify what meaning.

10.   If something must be repeated something, do so using the same words.

11.   Discuss only concrete actions and objects, not abstract concepts.

12.   Don't force a person to engage in conversation. If the person has difficulty speaking or comprehending what is said, conversation will make them feel inadequate and they will react by becoming agitated.

13. Avoid asking questions whenever possible. Answering a question requires searching one's memory, forming a thought and translating the thought into speech, which is a difficult process for a person with a malfunctioning brain. Not knowing the answers may embarrass and upset people, and they may become agitated and snap something like, "Stop asking so many stupid questions!" It's important to be aware that people suffering from dementia cannot store memory — no matter how many times you tell them something, they will forget it a moment later. This can be frustrating for caregivers because, although they may get to know residents quite well and spend months helping them, the residents have absolutely no memory of them or what they have done.

14. Use Musical Cues. Since even advanced dementia patients retain memory of music, specific pieces of music can be used to announce activities such as mealtime and bedtime, or to identify bathrooms and eating areas.

Chapter Seven

Depression

In healthy adults, depression beginning late in life is uncommon — less than two percent of healthy elders suffer from late onset depression. Despite the occasional inconveniences that accompany healthy aging, most older adults actually experience an increase in life satisfaction.

On the other hand, depression is rampant in older people who are medically ill — the greater the severity of the illness, the greater the likelihood a person will become depressed.

Thus, depression is widespread among aging disabled, hospitalized, and long-term care patients. Depressive symptoms are found in 40 to 50 percent of nursing home and geropsychiatric hospital residents, and, in a recent study of several nursing homes, major depression was found in twenty-five percent of the cognitively intact residents and ten percent of cognitively impaired residents.

It is vital for all elderly people to be screened for depression. Depression in cognitively intact individuals can mimic the signs of dementia, while depression in

Behavioral Objectives

At the end of this section readers will be able to:

Describe the extend of depression in the elderly.

List the symptoms of depression.

Discriminate between grief, sadness, and depression.

Discuss the medical causes of depression.

Depressive symptoms

Thought
Negative self-evaluations
Negative expectations
Negative interpretation of
    events
Memory loss
Confusion
Impaired attention span
A focus on past mistakes
All or nothing thinking
Unwanted thoughts
Poverty of thought
Hopelessness
Helplessness
The wish to be dead
Suicidal thoughts
The conviction of being a
    burden

Emotion
Ambivalence
No sense of humor
Feeling inadequate
Chronic apathy
Sadness
Guilt
Powerlessness
Emotions are dulled
No motivation

Symbols
Destructive fantasies
Nightmares
Bothersome images
Punishment from God

people with cognitive problems can make their problems worse.

The Diagnostic and Statistical Manual of Mental Disorders (DSM) emphasizes emotional symptoms such as sadness and anhedonia as the quintessential criteria for the diagnosis of depression. In the elderly, however, physical symptoms may be more prevalent. One study of patients with major depression found physical symptoms to be the chief or exclusive complaint for almost 70 percent of those identified. These symptoms include headache, back pain or non-specific musculoskeletal complaints, weight loss, constipation, a bad taste in the mouth, lack of interest in sex, and insomnia. Physical symptoms not usually associated with depression are also common, including gastrointestinal complaints. One study of irritable bowel syndrome showed markedly higher occurrences in depressed patients vs. controls.

When emotional symptoms among the elderly with depression are reported, they are likely to be complaints of agitation, anxiety and panic attacks, irritability, and obsessive concern with bodily functions.

Brain function may explain symptomatic differences between older and younger sufferers of depression. The two halves of the brain communicate through a bundle of nerve fibers called the *corpus callosum*. Some clinicians believe that during the aging process, cell loss occurs in these fibers, impeding the transmission of emotions generated in the right hemisphere into the left hemisphere language centers. Thus, older affected people would be less aware of, and less willing to talk about their depression.

It is also possible that the inability or unwillingness to express emotional distress is cultural, that is, that the older generations (those born before the 1940s) were taught not to speak about emotions.

Both of these factors probably contribute to this lack of verbalization of emotion, with the result that many older people do not verbalize that they are depressed, and may actually deny the possibility when asked.

Depression's Impact on Health

Depression in the elderly can be expensive and lethal. Medical costs are 47 to 51 percent higher in depressed elders compared with non-depressed cohorts, and depressed elders have 50 percent higher risk of heart attack than those free of depression.

Heart disease and stroke are the leading causes of death and disability among older Americans today. Depression is associated with increased mortality in patients with ischemic heart disease.

Although cardiovascular disease is linked to many factors, such as sedentary lifestyles, hostility, cynicism, smoking, and alcohol abuse, the presence of depression is the most potent predictor of mortality.

Studies show that even when controlling for the effects of smoking, depression remains a significant independent predictor of mortality among heart patients and stroke survivors. The relationship between depression and heart disease is also reciprocal, with each condition exacerbating the other.

There is a growing body of evidence indicating that recovery from heart attack and stroke is influenced by depression, with researchers pointing out that the heart is not only a pump delivering blood to all vital organs, but also a sense organ responding to emotional upset.

Disability and loss of stamina following a heart attack is often accompanied by major depression. The emotional impact of this type of traumatic event brings people face-to-face with their own mortality, and often suggests to them that they are much more vulnerable than they once believed. This revelation may be accompanied by bouts of hopelessness, anxiety, and

Depressive symptoms

Behavior
A change in activity level
Aggression
Destructive acts
Crying spells
Suicide attempts
Slowed speech
Substance abuse
Impulsiveness
Violation of personal values
Agitation
Perfectionism

Relationships
Victim stance
Dependency
Highly reactive
Social isolation
Avoidance
Approval seeking
Martyrdom
Passive-aggressive behavior
Boundary problems
Hypercritical
Poor communication skills

Physical
Multiple physical complaints
Sleep problems
Appetite changes
Weight changes
Change in sex-drive

depression, a dangerous response in that it can impede physical rehabilitation and compliance with treatment.

Biological Causes of Depression

Research suggests that depression has a genetic component, and its occurrence runs in families. This predisposition to depression, researchers believe, also is related to chronic pain and cardiovascular disease.

It has long been known that many people with depression exhibit low levels of serotonin. Recently it has been suggested that the link between vascular disease and depression may be because blood platelets and brain neurons share the same serotonin transporter protein, and are moderated by the same gene.

Other research suggests that this link has a genetic component, that is, depression often runs in families. Even in people without heart disease, platelet activation (the process by which platelets stick to one another and tissue, forming a plug or clot) is increased in late-life depression, and is most often found in elderly depressed subjects with a specific gene (called 5HTTLPR l/l). Several studies have linked this gene with mood disorders, suggesting that there may be a common pathway to blood flow problems both in the brain and the heart through which depression increases mortality in the elderly.

However, genetic factors seem less important in late-onset depression. Rather, depressions occurring for the first time an an older person is more likely to be triggered by stress and loss, nutritional deficiencies, medical problems, and adverse reactions to medication.

Nutrients and Depression

Calcium.
Excessive milk drinking, steroid hormone therapy, parathyroid disorders, and hypothyroidism all can

contribute to a condition called hypercalcemia, which may in turn contribute to depression.

Magnesium.

Depression may result from a magnesium deficit caused by chronic alcoholism and alcohol withdrawal. Magnesium sulfate often can reverse the depression.

Potassium.

Although the exact mechanism is not known, excess potassium, as often seen in uremic patients, has been associated with depression. A deficiency of potassium is also associated with depression and is most commonly seen in patients with frequent vomiting or prolonged diarrhea and people receiving diuretics or steroids.

Sodium.

Elderly people with heart problems, particularly those in cardiac failure, often eliminate sodium from their diets. Depression may occur as a result, but can usually be corrected by the addition of a minimal amount of sodium back into the diet.

Vitamin C.

Rarely, chronic vitamin C deficiency has been shown to cause both hypochondriasis (a preoccupation with bodily symptoms) and depression. Vitamin C interacts with many central nervous system receptors.

B12 and Folic Acid.

Low folic acid and B12 levels have been observed in a large proportion of care facility residents suffering from various emotional problems, especially depression.

Although B12 deficiency is common in depression, monitoring levels of B12 in the blood is not always useful as B12 deficiency may not become apparent until long after serum levels have been greatly reduced, and depression has begun.

In studies of elderly people with depression, as many as 30 percent were shown to be deficient in folic acid. In one study, 67 percent of the residents admitted to a geropsychiatric hospital were deficient. Folic acid deficiency also can cause chronic forgetfulness, insomnia, apathy, and other dementia-like symptoms.

Niacin and Biotin.

Both niacin (vitamin B3) deficiency and biotin deficiency can exacerbate depression and memory problems, as well as cause emotional instability. Pantothenic acid (vitamin B5) deficiency can cause restlessness, irritability, and depression. Low levels of these vitamins are very rare.

Thiamin.

Thiamin (vitamin B1) deficiency is very common among alcoholics, and can lead to a condition called Korsakoff's psychosis, which causes profound memory loss, depression, apathy, anxiety and irritability. Thiamin deficiency in the brain results in a condition called metabolic acidosis, which upsets the neurotransmitter balance.

Depression sometimes can be caused by allergies or exposures to environmental toxins. Solvents like those used in paints, furniture making, and boat-building have been reported to cause depression, confusion, and memory loss in people exposed to the fumes.

Medications that Cause Depression

Although depression is most often caused by loss, isolation, or a biochemical imbalance in the brain, it also can be caused by nutritional deficiencies or excesses, prescription, over-the-counter, and illegal drugs, alcohol, caffeine and nicotine, hypoglycemia, and hormonal imbalances. In fact, research suggests that almost any chronic biochemical imbalance can cause depression.

Many medications, used alone or in combinations, may cause depressions. Reducing the dosages, elimination of use, or modifying certain combinations often will correct the problem. A few of the most common culprits include

Antiemetics.

Antiemetic drugs are used to prevent nausea, and may, if used in large doses or over a period of time, cause depression. Discontinuing use of the drug or using a smaller dose usually reverses the symptoms in two weeks.

Sedatives.

Sedative drugs are often used — and misused — by elderly people to promote sleep and reduce anxiety. Chronic use of these drugs often leads to addiction, abuse and an increased risk of depression and suicide. Some states now use computer tracking to prevent people from obtaining these addictive medications from more than one doctor.

Corticosteroids.

Steroid drugs, used for their anti-inflammatory properties, may cause depression, usually when used over a long period of time.

Antihypertensives.

Blood pressure medications also can cause depression and subsequent behavioral problems. In spite of this relationship being quite widely known, many doctors are unaware of the frequency with which people suffer from drug-induced depression, and fail to connect depressive symptoms with the medication they prescribe.

Harvard researcher Dr. Jerry Avorn and his colleagues looked at how often antidepressants were prescribed to people taking beta-blockers such as Inderal, Lopressor, and Corgard. Examining the medical records of 143,253 residents, they found that 23 percent (almost one out of four) of those taking beta-blockers were also taking antidepressants. This study revealed that doctors often give patients additional prescriptions to overcome side effects of another medication without realizing that the problems could actually be solved by eliminating the first medication.

Medical Causes of Depression

Vascular depression.

In the 1800's, German psychiatrist Robert Gaupp coined the phrase "arteriosclerotic depression." Gaupp observed that many elderly depressed people also suffered from hardening of the arteries. Felix Post later also suggested that vascular disease in the brain was a significant factor in the development of depression in late life.

With the advent of computer tomography (CT) and magnetic resonance imaging (MRI), it has become possible to evaluate subtle vascular changes in the brain of elderly depressed patients. Vascular changes are seen as hyper-intense signals in both the white matter and gray matter.

In 1987, Dr. Ranga Krishnan found that over 70 percent of patients with late-onset depression (defined as onset over age 50), had hyper-intense signals on the MRI images. The main locations of the gray matter changes were in the basal ganglia, in the caudate and putamen, the cingulate gyrus, and in the frontal lobes of the brain. These are the areas of the brain responsible for processing both physical and emotional pain.

Risk factors for vascular depression include diabetes, hypertension, and atherosclerosis. Cardiac surgery also increases risk.

Post-Stroke Depression.

Although typically easy to diagnose, strokes with or without physical impairment or disability — often cause depression. Strokes may be major or minor, and minor ones may produce as severe a depression as a major stroke. The most effective treatment for post stroke depression is antidepressant drug therapy.

Toxins.

Depression can also be caused by allergies or exposures to environmental toxins. For example, solvents like those used in paints, furniture making, carpet manufacturing, and boat-building have been reported to cause depression, confusion, and memory loss in people exposed to such fumes.

Although rare, another potential cause is chronic exposure to heavy metals. Because elderly people may have an impaired ability to eliminate toxins from the body, these factors should be ruled out before further intervention.

Thyroid.

Depression is often one of the first signs of thyroid disease. Even subtle decreases in thyroid hormone can induce depression, and, in the elderly, depression may be the only sign of thyroid dysfunction. Depressed residents should be routinely screened for thyroid problems, particularly if they complain of depression and fatigue.

Adrenal Insufficiency.

Dysfunction of the adrenal gland also has been associated with depression, so adrenal function should also be checked.

Tumors.

Temporal lobe tumors are particularly inclined to cause depression, and are frequently masked by the psychological symptoms of headache and paresthesias.

Other contributing factors to depression can be physical problems such as hearing loss, vision problems, foot problems, and even dental problems. I was once called for a consultation on a patient who had been isolating, refusing to leave her room, and refusing to participate in groups or mealtime. Although this woman had a history of depression, during the interview she told me, "I'm not leaving this room until I get my new dentures. I look so ugly without my teeth." In this case, a dental consultation cured the problem.

Depression, Grief, and Sadness

Distinguishing grief from sadness is important when working with an elderly person. Sadness usually is a transitory state, and very often the result of revisiting a painful memory. Temporary bouts of sadness are common for older people; most of them have had many losses, and from time to time they will revisit these memories. At these times, helping to refocus a person on more pleasant thoughts can often ameliorate the feelings of dejection.

While sadness may be a fleeting feeling, grief, the process of mourning a significant loss, is an emotional process that may last for months or years. Most elderly people, especially those in long-term care facilities, have undergone several significant losses — the loss of spouse, of home, of friends, and, perhaps most importantly, the loss of their independence. These losses are monumental and must be grieved.

Grief has specific stages, (discussed later in this chapter) one of which is depression. Unlike clinical depression, however, which may not have a recognizable cause, grief is always the result of a catastrophic loss.

Caregivers should never minimize losses by telling a grieving person, for instance, "Cheer up, it's not so bad." This misguided effort to comfort a person, actually discounts and trivializes the losses being grieved. Also, it is not useful to tell a grieving person, "I understand how you must feel," since, unless caregivers have actually suffered a similar loss, they don't know how the grieving person feels.

Caregivers cannot measure the extent of another person's attachment or loss, and no loss is trivial, as illustrated in this example.

> Mrs. Peterson was brought to the hospital because she was losing weight, was isolating, and was suffering frequent bouts of crying. She had told others that she wanted to die. It was discovered at the intake interview that she had recently lost her parakeet — her closest companion for the last ten years. No one had recognized the enormity of her loss. In fact, the board-and-care administrator had told us, "I wish she would quit crying about that stupid bird." When this loss was validated and acknowledged, she was allowed to work through it, and eventually recovered.

Loss and Grief

Loss clearly has a significant affect on mood, but what is less noted is the fact that loss also disrupts fundamental patterns of living. Consider the case of Mrs. Johnson, who recently lost her husband, after having spent forty years with him. During all this time she developed and stored thousands of patterns of behavior which allowed her and Mr. Johnson to accomplish the tasks of daily living. The patterns range from mundane routines such as going grocery shopping and cleaning the house, to more profound patterns such as solving problems together, coping with the challenges of life, and interchanges of intimacy.

The loss of Mr. Johnson is catastrophic, and requires grieving, but it also means the loss of dozens of patterns of behavior. Loss of patterns means immobilization and isolation — two events that can completely disable Mrs. Johnson. So while grief work is the fundamental task of recovery from loss, learning new patterns is essential for re-entry into the world.

Recently a pilot program designed to address this problem was conducted at the University of Washington School of Medicine in Seattle by Dr. Paul Ciechanowski and associates. Called the PEARLS program (Program to Encourage Active, Rewarding Lives for Seniors), it was a community outreach intervention program that help seniors integrate patterns.

Ciechanowski evaluated the effectiveness of this home-based program in a group of 138 mostly homebound seniors (average age, 73) who had been diagnosed with minor depression or dysthymia. Seventy-two percent of the study's participants were referred by social agencies, and 28 percent were self-referred. Seventy two percent lived alone, 42 percent belonged to an ethnic minority group, and 36 percent received antidepressant medications at baseline.

Over a period of 19 weeks, participants in the program received an average of 6.6 visits from social workers. The substance of the visits was a combination of problem-solving therapies and focused on the patients becoming regularly physically active and increasing their behavior patterns outside of the home. PEARLS recipients who completed this program showed a 50 percent improvement in depression scores or complete remission by the end of 12 months. They also had fewer hospitalizations than the control group. The improvements in the participants not only restored their quality of life, but significantly decreased caregiver burden. While the program clearly resulted in a high degree of success in re establishing participants' connections to the world, a significantly important element of this program was its cost — $630 per patient.

Grief

Grief is a normal response to loss. Sadness and depression as part of the grieving process should not be considered behavioral disorders. When a resident appears to be depressed, a loss history should be taken immediately to obtain an accurate historical survey of the person's recent and remote losses. Losses may include the death of loved ones, but also may be the loss of a job, a pet, a limb, or social standing.

A person is suffering from unresolved grief must have those losses identified, and then the losses must be grieved. One of the most effective ways to help people grieve is to explain the typical stages of grief to them (see below), which normalizes the emotions they are feeling, and allows them to take the time necessary to work through and resolve the grief.

The Stages of Loss

1. Denial. Denial is a reaction to the shock of loss.

   The first reaction is, "No, this can't be true. This can't happen to me." Getting stuck in denial feeds the fantasy that the loss did not happen.

2. Emotionality. Once denial is broken through, an emotional roller coaster begins, running from anger, to guilt, to sadness, and back to anger. Typical thoughts that accompany this stage are, "I'll show you...," "If only I'd...," "You've hurt me," "...I hate you."

   Getting stuck in anger results in the persecution of the lost person, and the angry person spends the rest of their life blaming the lost one for their own misery.

Getting stuck in guilt can result in and endless persecution of one's self. Guilt-ridden people often become convinced that they are evil, and would be better off dead.

3. Bargaining.   Bargaining is magical thinking, or the fantasy that if the grieving person can just do or say the right thing, the loss can be recovered.

    Bargains may be made with one's self, with the lost person, or with God. People stuck in bargaining may become obsessed with the lost one, believing, for example, that someday their mate will return, even though they may have remarried and started a new family.

4. Depression.   The depression stage is character- ized by the loss of the internal presence of the lost person or object, leaving the griever with the feeling of a gaping black hole in the soul, and with the sense that every moment is an eternity. This stage feels as if it will last forever, but it doesn't. However, becoming stuck in depression causes the grieving person to shut down, withdraw from the world, and self-isolate.

5. Acceptance.   Acceptance is the realistic obser- vation that the loss is permanent, and involves re- focusing on what was gained from the experi- ence and memories of the lost one and recon- necting with the world.

The grieving process for a catastrophic loss can last well over a year, and, depending on the severity of the loss, the person's coping skills, and the effective- ness of a social support system, the loss process can last anywhere from three months to three years. During this time the person is at increased risk for suicide, illness, or a serious emotional breakdown. Allowing the person to talk frequently about the loss speeds the healing process.

Depression, Memory and Cognition

Depression is one of the most common under-diagnosed causes of memory problems. Depression, which has a profound effect on the ability to think, reason, and remember, may cause symptoms so severe that it can be difficult to determine whether a person is suffering from depression or dementia. Several diagnostic tests have been developed to sort out the differences between these two memory-destroying disorders appropriately identify the illness at hand.

People suffering depression become focused on internal events, such as memories of tragic losses, or real and imagined transgressions. In addition, they may focus the physical symptoms of depression, such as body aches and pains. This internal preoccupation inhibits attention to the outside world. What is not attended to is not remembered.

Brain activity in the depression-afflicted person slows down, impairing memory and thought-processing. Depressed people often are said to exhibit poverty of thought — the inability to process thought at all — accompanied by feelings of helplessness and hopelessness. The sufferer begins to ignore input from the outside world; they just don't care about anything.

Depression has been linked to decreased levels of chemicals in the brain called neurotransmitters. The neurotransmitters involved include serotonin, melatonin, dopamine, adrenaline, and noradrenaline — substances which also play an important role in memory. Antidepressant drugs are considered to work by raising the levels of these chemicals.

Psychotic Depression

Prior to the 1940's, the term *"psychotic depression"* was quite common. As many as two-thirds of hospitalized depressed patients at that time were diagnosed as psychotically depressed. Today the term has fallen out of favor, and less than ten percent of depressed patients are considered psychotic.

Psychotic depression, however, happens more frequently in the elderly, often mimicking dementia with symptoms such as hallucinations, delusions, and other bizarre behaviors. It's important to remember, though, that depression alone can cause psychotic symptoms, and when a person becomes delusional or begins to hallucinate, depression could be the cause.

About two thirds of psychotically depressed people have delusions but no hallucinations, and about one quarter have hallucinations without delusions. While patients often claim that their insides are rotting, the most common delusion seen in psychotically depressed people is the that of persecution — the belief that other people are wishing the person harm. Often, the person may believe they deserve to be punished, saying they are evil and God is punishing them.

Elderly patients who express intense feelings of guilt and remorse should always be screened for psychotic symptoms.

Behavioral Interventions for Depression

1. Take a loss history and assess for unresolved grief.
2. Obtain a baseline measure of depression using a depression scale such as the Geriatric Depression Scale or the Hamilton Depression Scale. The scales provide the caregiver an easy and effective way to measure the patient's progress.
3. Help the person recognize faulty thought processes, and encourage a discussion about negative thoughts, doubts, and fears. Make a list

of these thoughts, and then ask the person to furnish evidence that the thoughts are true. Likely, the caregiver will be able to show the person that most of the negative thoughts are not based on any objective evidence.

4. Construct a *hedonic scale,* which is a list of all activities the resident used to enjoy. Using this list, have the person rate how much enjoyment, on a scale of one to ten, would be derived from each activity now. Once the rating is completed, have the person engage in one of the activities, then rate his or her level of enjoyment. Depressed people typically underrate their expected enjoyment, but when shown they actually can enjoy the activities as they once did, they become more willing to participate in them again.

5. Help the person begin a life review, recollecting past times of difficulty and how the person overcame them. These recollected strengths and successes then can be linked to current life concerns, frequently increasing the person's coping skills.

6. Teach constructive thought processes, such as problem-solving and coping skills. Help the person define problems clearly, and set goals to solve the problems constructively.

7. Help the person recognize personal strengths and abilities by listing positive qualities. If the person is unable to do this, the caregiver should be prepared to provide input as to the person's likability.

Medication Concerns

When assessing depression, it is important to consider possible complications from over-medication, drug interactions, medication side effects, and slowed or impaired metabolism. Although cognitive therapy is helpful for depression, medication is often needed to get the resident well enough to respond to intervention. When deciding to use medication to treat depression, ensure there exists:

1. Adequate indication for its use
2. A proper dosage
3. An acceptable usage duration to assess effectiveness
4. A plan for careful monitoring of side effects
5. A positive response.

Bipolar Disorder

Bipolar disorder, or manic depression, thought to have a strong biological component, is characterized by symptoms of both euphoria and of irritability.

When a person with this disorder is manic, speech is hurried, pressured, never-ending, and nonsensical The person may exhibit a condition known as "flight of ideas," a rapidly shifting conversation about a series of unconnected thoughts. Commonly, the person has delusions of grandeur, a belief of all-powerfulness, and unrealistic expectations of his or her ability. The manic person may have poor insight and judgment, making unrealistic business deals or spending money recklessly. In addition, many manic people exhibit hypersexuality.

Behavioral Interventions for Bipolar Disorder

1. Conduct a drug screening to rule out drug-induced psychosis.
2. Rule out any other medical condition.
3. Provide a safe environment.
4. Orient the resident to reality and provide maximum appropriate autonomy.

5. Assess for harm to self and others.
6. Begin a medication regimen

Chapter Eight

Anxiety

The sudden onset of an anxiety disorder is unusual in elderly people, although many have had a long medical history of anxiety disorders. When anxiety does appear late in life, it is usually either associated with a stressor, a sign of medical illness, or a medication problem. These factors should always be assessed and ruled out before a diagnosis is completed.

The root of anxiety is a malfunction of the innate human fear response system. Fear is a normal human emotion, and although no one enjoys the feeling of fear, it serves the important function of helping avoid danger. It is perfectly normal to be afraid of something never before encountered. Fear prompts a cautious approach when entering unexplored territory, and only disappears when the situation appears under control.

Fear serves another important function — it promotes social bonding. All children are naturally afraid to be alone. Because children cannot survive without their parents, fear saves their lives. A child without fear could wander off, and probably die.

Behavioral Objectives

At the end of this section readers will be able to:

Define the functions of anxiety.

Differentiate between anxiety disorders and grief reactions.

List the medical causes of anxiety.

Describe symptoms and causes of panic attacks.

Medical Causes of anxiety

Endocrine disorders
Hypo- and hyperthyroidism
Pheochromocytoma (an
    adrenalin secreting
    tumor)
Hypoglycemia
Hypercortisolism

Stimulants
* Caffeine
* cocaine
* amphetamines
* nicotine

Withdrawalfrom:
* sedatives
* alcohol
* tranquilizers

Brain Tumors
Strokes
Epilepsy
Pulmonary embolus
Chronic pulmonary disease
Aspirin intolerance
Collagen vascular disease
Brucellosis (undulant fever,
    rock fever, and Malta
    fever)
B12 deficiency
Demyelinating disease
Heavy metal intoxication
Food allergies
Balance disorder

Children instinctively run to their parents whenever they are frightened, and the parent's natural tendency is to calm the child and allay the fear. Over time, this sequence of events becomes a coping mechanism. Listening to a mother's voice saying, "It's all right, nothing will hurt you now," over and over, eventually makes these words a part of each person. This process of internalizing calming messages and feelings of being held is called *self-soothing*.

People typically spend their early years physically and emotionally attached to mothers, but as they grow and mature, and learn to self-soothe, they become able to tolerate more and more time alone, and to realize that many of the things so feared will never happen — there are no monsters in the closet.

In the elderly, anxiety disorders may occur as a result of the failure of one or both of these processes — people with anxiety disorders are afraid to be alone, and they have difficulty self-soothing.

Evidence exists indicating that this process of bonding with parents stabilizes the brain circuitry that mediates fear. Studies have shown that animals that are handled and held regularly have a stable HPA axis (the circuit of the hypothalamus, pituitary and adrenal glands are part of the "fight, flight or freeze" system). Animals handled in infancy have increased hippocampal activity throughout their lifespan, and do not show HPA abnormalities in later life. Furthermore, their levels of cortisol are permanently lower, and this decreases the risk of dementia.

In studies of older humans, HPA axis abnormalities are shown to be related to anxiety. The studies' subjects have been found to have consumed higher than typical levels of dietary fat and sugar — both risk factors for cognitive problems. They also have higher levels of plasma cortisol and a smaller number of cells in the hippocampus, the part of the brain that stores memory. These findings suggest a link among cortisol, anxiety, and increased risk for dementia

Although social bonding is a primary element in reducing fear, many elders have lost most of their social contacts, through death, illness, or relocation. Loss of social support provokes fear, while pain from losses already suffered makes elder people reluctant to form new friendships, all of which leads to isolation and increased anxiety.

Human alarm circuits prepare for threats by increasing heart rate, blood pressure, and muscle tension. When this system becomes activated, a healthy person will scan the environment for danger, identify that danger, make decisions on how to proceed, and the alarm system then returns to baseline. But when the circuit system itself goes awry, an affected person may experience a diffuse, global feeling of threat, attempt to assess the environment for danger, but see nothing external that can be identified as a threat. Because of the system malfunction, the level of arousal does not return to baseline and the person continues to seek sources for the feeling of disease

An anxious person becomes fixated on threats. Increased threat assessment causes the person's working memory to be occupied with danger, leaving no room for solutions. Lack of the ability to generate solutions keeps a person frozen in indecision.

It is understandable then, why many anxious people focus only on reducing their feelings of anxiety, rather than in recognizing, and reducing the causes. Common methods of reducing anxiety, such as isolating and substance abuse, typically cause more problems. Proper treatment must focus on reducing threats, increasing coping skills and helping with problem solving.

Anxiety disorders

Panic Disorder

Agoraphobia

Social phobia

Simple phobia

Obsessive Compulsive disorder

Post Traumatic Stress Disorder

Generalized Anxiety Disorder

Organic anxiety disorder

Causes of organic anxiety disorders

Endocrine disorders

Hypo- and hyper-thyroidism

Pheochromocytoma (an adrenalin secreting tumor)

Hypoglycemia

Hypercortisolism

Stimulants
- caffeine
- cocaine
- amphetamines
- nicotine

Withdrawal from sedatives, alcohol, or tranquilizers

Brain Tumors

Strokes

Epilepsy

Pulmonary embolus

Chronic pulmonary disease

Aspirin intolerance

Collagen vascular disease

Brucellosis (undulant fever, rock fever, and Malta fever)

B12 deficiency

Demyelinating disease

Heavy metal intoxication

Food allergies

Balance disorder

Three basic components of anxiety:
- Emotional: Restlessness, agitation, irritability, hypervigilance
- Cognitive: Worry, rumination, cognitive impairment
- Somatic: Muscle tension, aches and pains, sleep problems

Anxious people also may have another deficit — the inability to separate *realistic* fears from *irrational* fears. They may spend inordinate amounts of time perseverating over things that might happen, and whipping themselves into frenzy. This behavior tends to be more prevalent in older people with low life-satisfaction, high levels of neuroticism, and regret over not having accomplished what they wished to in life.

Older people typically suffer from many medical problems, including aches, pains, and gastrointestinal disturbances. They may conclude that these symptoms are a threat, and, becoming preoccupied with them, exhibit a condition called hypochondria, and frequently becoming high medical users. Unfortunately, being labeled a hypochondriac may mean a person will not be screened for anxiety, thus foreclosing on available and effective intervention.

Untreated anxiety disorder can manifest itself in the person becoming overly dependent on others, engaging in incessant attention-seeking behavior, or becoming overly demanding and complaining. These behaviors often are charted in care facilities as attention seeking, and the diagnosis of anxiety is frequently missed.

Older women are twice as likely to have an anxiety disorder as older men, and older adults are more likely to experience depressive symptoms along with anxiety.

Generalized anxiety disorder is the most common problem found in the elderly (followed by anxiety due to a general medical condition), affecting up to one third of older adults. Often triggered by worry and increased threat assessment, this type of anxiety also is, in part, reality-based. Older people do have more to fear.

Older people, already more prone to illness or injury, also are frequent victims of crime. Lack of mobility, decreased stamina, and waning strength contribute to feelings of vulnerability. An older person walking alone is a target for predators, so many older people, rather than exploring ways to go outdoors and still stay safe, become fearful of leaving their home. This fear, agoraphobia, is quite prevalent among the elderly in spite of the fact that phobias in general are less common in this age group.

Stressors such as retirement, disability, money problems, alienation, widowhood, and loneliness may increase anxiety. Any chronic illness (especially Parkinson's, chronic obstructive pulmonary disease and chronic pain) also can contribute to feelings of anxiety.

Panic disorders are rare in the older population, but when they do appear, they usually are tied to a stressor such as a loss or an illness. Unfortunately, many elders who have experienced a panic attack are given tranquilizing drugs, which are not effective, are addictive, and greatly increase the risk of falls.

Unfortunately, because many of these symptoms are common in older people and therefore are written off as components of normal aging rather than symptoms of anxiety. For these reasons anxiety may be present in many elders, but interpreted as part of another problem, rather than the existence of a disorder. Some of these symptoms could also be interpreted as signs of dementia. Anxiety also presents as a component of depression in the elderly — 75 percent of general anxiety patients also fit the criteria for depression.

Behavioral Interventions for Anxiety

1. Rule out medication and physical problems.
2. Explore the possibility of grief reaction.
3. Look for secondary gain.
4. Teach abdominal breathing.
5. Note any situations in the facility that trigger anxiety.
6. Eliminate caffeine and other stimulants.
7. Teach problem solving and coping skills.

Panic Attacks

Elderly people often suffer from panic attacks, which they mistake for heart attacks. Many emergency room visits are for bouts of panic.

If you have ever had a panic attack, you know that it feels awful You are overwhelmed by fear, and convinced that you are going to die.

These attacks should always be checked out carefully. If it is determined that they have no biological cause, they should be dealt with through behavioral intervention.

Intervention for Panic Attacks

1. The person should be educated about panic attacks — what causes them, what they are, and what they feel like.

    Panic attacks usually begin with the perception of an unusual physical symptom (for example, a sudden pain). This is followed by an irrational conclusion ("I have a terrible disease, and I'm going to die). The reaction to this conclusion is panic. Teach the person to recognize this process, and help them self soothe when they feel the symptoms.

2. Explain clearly that although panic attacks feel terrible, they are completely harmless.

    Often, when the person understands this, the attacks stop.

3. Teach deep breathing, This aborts the attack.

Medication for Anxiety

Medication should be considered only when all other interventions have failed. Tranquilizers are not recommended for long term use in the elderly because of their potential for abuse and because they exacerbate cognitive problems. They also have psychomotor effects that lead to adverse events such as falls, and they are addictive. I have found that it's much more difficult to get a person off tranquilizers than it is to treat anxiety behaviorally.

Grief and Trauma

Another anxiety disorder that is underdiagnosed in the older population is post-traumatic stress disorder (PTSD). Older people often face catastrophic losses, hospitalizations, surgeries, heart attacks, and strokes, all of which can result in traumatization.

Grief is the negative emotional process experienced when at least one of a person's most important relationships is ended unwillingly, through death, divorce, natural disasters, or relocation. Unfortunately, most elderly people have experienced multiple losses. Normally grief is a time-limited reaction, but sometimes grief reactions become chronic and interfere with long-term functioning. This type of problem is called *pathological grief.*

Grief may have an immediate or delayed onset. Delayed onset occurs when the person gets stuck in the stage of denial. Delayed grief reactions, therefore, are somewhat similar to the symptoms of PTSD, and should be considered an anxiety disorder. Pathological grief differs from normal grief in the development of *anxious apprehension, phobias, panic,* and *depression.*

Most societies have mourning rituals and ceremonies surrounding the death or loss of a family member or friend. creating a context in which the bereaved relatives and friends are able to experience their painful emotions and work through their loss. These rituals and ceremonies no longer exist in much of American culture, making it difficult or impossible for most people to do proper grief work. Many people in our culture are actually unaware that they must mourn or grieve. Instead, they try to escape from their pain and carry on as usual, only to have the buried feelings of unresolved grief erupt later, disguised perhaps in the form of panic attacks or anxiety.

The human grief response has its origins early in mankind's social evolution. Crying, for example, is an important survival mechanism, allowing a small child separated from the tribe to be found by listening for the cries. Children that cried the most were the ones most easily found. After thousands of years of development and evolution, crying when faced with loss has become a fundamental human instinct.

To help work through the grief of loss, traditional mourning rituals in other cultures encourage loud and sustained crying and the expression of painful emotions. After a few days, emotional exhaustion is experienced; and it then becomes possible for the bereaved person to complete the emotional and cognitive aspects of the grieving process.

Failure to mourn often results in suppression of the anger, the fear, and related emotions of the grief process. Because these emotions are never expressed, the levels of arousal in the person remain persistently high. Following the loss, the bereaved person may carry on with routine daily activities, unaware the body is still experiencing the grief reaction. Symptoms of unresolved grief, panic attacks and phobias, may not appear until many years after the loss, and then typically on or around the anniversary of the loss.

For some, the loss of one's health becomes a substitute for the loss of the person. Rather than processing the grief, the person becomes preoccupied with phobias, panic attacks, or illness. The search for the cure for the illness unconsciously represents a search for the lost relative. Feelings of anger and rage are then displaced onto the doctors and caregivers who fail to find a cure.

Even if it is suggested that an anxiety disorder is a result of unresolved grief, patients typically are very reluctant to engage in grief work. Adding to the difficulty, the spouse or family members may ridicule the idea of grief work, claiming it is irrelevant to the problem. If the patient does begin grief work, family members may interfere with the process and ridicule the patient for weeping and crying. To avoid or correct this behavior, the grief treatment must be explained thoroughly to family members, and they must be involved in the treatment process.

Chapter Nine

Suicide

I am against suicide committed by other people, but I want to reserve that option for myself.

Edwin Shneidman, suicidologist

I never met George Burns, but I admired him. And I do know his goal was to put on a performance on his 100th birthday. Although he never made it, he and thousands of fans were looking forward to this event. The important point is that at 99, George Burns was still setting goals, still making plans. This is successful aging.

Keep this in mind when working with an elderly suicidal person. Suicide is seldom a rational solution to life's problems, but it is here that our unconscious bias against age may creep in and sit on our treatment plan. When working with a suicidal person of thirty who loses their spouse, we think, "He's young, he needs to get over it. He has his whole life ahead of him." We forget that an eighty-year-old *also has his or her whole life ahead of him* — it just may be a much shorter life. George lost Gracie many years ago. There is little

Behavioral Objectives

At the end of this section readers will be able to:

Identify cues to suicidal ideation.

Name the major suicide risk factors.

Describe silent suicide.

Assess a person for suicide risk.

Factors Leading to Suicide

Acting out
Alcohol abuse
Arrested grief
Diminished life goals
Drug abuse
Conflicts with children
Chronic pain
Chronic illness
Depression
Disability
Financial problems
Fading recuperative power
Loneliness
Loss of spouse
Marital conflict
No social support system
Physical Illness
Poor physical health
Psychosis
Poor coping skills
Social isolation

doubt that it devastated him and that he grieved for years, but he never lost his lust for life.

Having suicidal thoughts is not a normal phase of life. Such thoughts come from a pathological mindset which typically disappears with time. A suicidal person feels that things will never change, but, just as a severe winter can seem bleak, cold, and never-ending, it eventually passes, and so do thoughts of suicide. Because of this, suicide often is called a permanent solution to a temporary problem. It is, in fact, a maladaptive means to escape from anguish.

Suicide is currently the seventh leading cause of death in the United States, accounting for over 24,000 deaths each year. And the suicide rate rises consistently as age increases — taking one's own life presently is the ninth leading cause of death in the elderly. White males over 65 have the highest suicide rate, at twice the rate of the general population, and six times the rate in women over 65.

Elderly people actually have a lower incidence of suicide attempts than younger people, but apparently being much more intent on killing themselves, they have a much higher success rate. Nonfatal suicidal "gestures" are uncommon among the elderly. Unlike attempts by teens and people with personality disorders, suicide attempts in the elderly are rarely done for social manipulation — they are direct attempts to die. Lethal methods tend to be used, and failure to kill one's self is most often due to poor planning, rather than any lack of intent.

Risk Factors

Major depression is the most common reason for suicide — the suicide rate among the depressed being four times higher than the national average. Agitated depression, or depression accompanied by anxiety, increases the risk. A person suffering from psychotic depression has a suicide rate five times higher than average.

Any psychotic disorder increases risk, hence, there are not many old schizophrenics. A psychotic person who has paranoid thoughts, is inappropriately fearful and subject to panic states is at very high risk for self harm. This risk is increased even more if the person hears voices commanding him or her to commit suicide.

Suicide is more common in the divorced and widowed, with elderly men who lose their wives at highest risk. Often, wives were responsible for social activities of a couple, and their death or departure means an abrupt end of the couple's social interaction.

The more closely a person is involved with others, the lower the probability of suicide. Therefore, it is important to look at the person's social support network when doing a suicide assessment. A person with no friends or family is at high risk.

There also exists a direct relationship between social status and suicide. In general, the higher one's position on the socioeconomic ladder, the greater the risk of a attempt suicide. It follows, then, that physicians and dentists have a much higher incidence of suicide than the general population.

Weakening of higher brain functions from sleeplessness, alcohol or drugs also strongly contributes to the potential for self-destruction. Half of all suicides are associated with alcohol abuse, and the suicide rate among elderly alcoholics is ten times that of those who do not drink. About 70 percent of successful elder suicides are committed by residents with previous diagnoses of alcoholism, psychosis, or organic brain syndrome.

The incidence of suicide also rises after surgery — particularly in surgeries that mutilate or change a person's appearance. The impact on the person's body image is often intolerable, and must at a minimum be grieved completely in order for the person to move ahead.

Cues to Suicide

Giving away a valued personal possessions.

Putting personal and business affairs in order.

Inquiring about how one donates his/her body to a medical school.

Planning his/her funeral shortly after the death of a loved one.

A poor adjustment to the recent loss of one or more loved ones.

A person who has always resisted suddenly composing a last will and testament.

Writing a suicide note.

A sudden unexplained recovery from a severe depression. (They may have resolved their problems by deciding to kill themselves.)

Any unexplainable change in a usual behavioral pattern.

Crying for no apparent reason.

Poor sleeping habits.

Loss of appetite.

Loss of sex drive.

Loss of ability to think.

Suicide Risk Signals

Sudden Behavior Changes:
- insomnia
- anorexia
- social withdrawal
- substance abuse
- loss of interest inactivities.

Inability to talk about the future.

Has no plans for next week or next month.

Has made suicidal threats.

Perceives life situation as hopeless.

Has no options for making changes.

Lack of family and/or peer support. (This can be either actual or perceived lack of support.)

Predictors of Suicide

Previous attempt.

Single male over 65.

Family history.

Statements of intent.

Alcohol or drug abuse.

Significant loss.

Purchase of a gun.

Stockpiling medications.

Suicide by a close family member increases relatives' suicide potential significantly. Guilt, especially over a dead loved one, feelings of worthlessness, the wish for punishment, social withdrawal, and feelings of hopelessness, anxiety, and agitation are all contributing factors.

The most important predictor of all suicides is a previous attempt. More than half of those who commit suicide have had at least one previous attempt.

Announcing Suicide

Elderly suicidal people seldom seek help from mental health practitioners, but over 60 percent of those who do commit suicide do tell others beforehand. Typical suicidal people will tell at least three people about their intent before they attempt it.

One person often told in advance is a physician. Even if they do not speak of suicide, more than 65 percent of all suicide victims seek medical attention within three months before their suicide. Among successful suicides, 75 percent have contacted their physician within one month before their death, and over one third have seen a doctor just a week before their demise.

Suicidal people almost always directly or indirectly communicate their intent to kill themselves, and do it several times and in different ways. Communication may consist of overt statements of suicide, statements of not wanting to live, or statements that life is no longer worth living. Less direct methods of communication include writing a will under unusual circumstances, changing insurance policies, giving away valued objects, or making statements of, "putting my affairs in order."

Silent suicide is the intent to kill one's self by nonviolent means, often through self starvation and resistance to care. These attempts to end one's life often go unrecognized because the depression is not diagnosed, but merely noted as resistance to care. Resistance to care should always be considered as a sign of depression and suicidal intent (more information in this appears in the section of this book called Resisting Care).

Behavioral Interventions for Suicide

1.   Ask the person about their suicidal thoughts. Suicide typically is seen as the only solution to what appears to be an unsolvable problem. Effective intervention consists of identifying the problem, and helping identify more constructive solutions.

2.   Ask if the person has a plan. A person with a plan and the means to carry it out is at extremely high risk.

3.   Get a thorough history about depression and suicide from family members and friends. If this person has a family history of suicide, antide-pressant drugs (such as Prozac) can be of great help. Studies show that suicide can have a genetic component, and low levels of serotonin are found in suicidal families.

4.   Ask a person with chronic pain about suicidal thoughts. Chronic, unremitting pain often leads to the wish to die. However, when pressed, most people with chronic pain will agree that what they really want is to stop suffering. Once this is established, all efforts should be focused on reducing the pain. A good pain management program can do wonders in these cases.

5 .   Assess a person's social support network, and the activities of a current typical day. A day spent with no friends and no joy is a day wasted. Help the person plan a day of enjoyment, and explore ways of connecting them with others who share similar interests.

6. The most effective treatment of suicide in the elderly involves cognitive therapy and group therapy, often combined with medication.

Successful treatment occurs when the suicidal person comes to see that there are other ways to deal with existing feelings and problems. The suicidal elderly person must reconnected with the world, and be given a purpose to live. Identifying this purpose is the core of cure.

Old age should be a time of enjoyment, creativity and social gratification. When the barriers of pain and suffering are removed, life regains meaning. Catastrophic losses in life do not inevitably lead to the loss of the will to live. Like Mr. Burns, the well-adjusted elderly never lose this feeling. Say good night, Gracie.

Chapter Ten

Medical Problems

Probably the biggest difference between assessing and treating emotional and behavioral problems in younger people and doing so in the elderly is that most elderly people will also be suffering from *multiple medical illnesses.*

Medical illnesses may cause stress, pain, disability and depression, but they also may cause or contribute directly to behavioral, cognitive, and emotional disorders. For this reason, medical problems should always be carefully assessed and considered before any psychological diagnosis is made or any intervention is attempted.

Medication Problems

Unfortunately most older adults will take any medication that their doctor recommends without question. The majority of the people I work with do not know the names of the medicines they are taking, and often do not know why they are taking them.

Behavioral Objectives

After completing this section readers will be able to:

Understand the role that illness plays in the problems plaguing today's rapidly growing elderly population.

Assess the effects of illness on mental health.

Recognize the causes and consequences of medical illness in behavioral and emotional disturbances in the elderly.

Use new knowledge and skills to improve the quality of life of the elderly and all who care for them.

In the elderly, over-medication is a very common problem. The average number of prescription drugs given to people over 60 years old is an astounding 15 per year. Although elderly people (those over 65) comprise only 12 percent of the population, they take 30 percent of all prescribed medications. Two-thirds of this population is taking at least one prescription drug. Thirty-seven percent are taking at least five drugs, and another 20 percent are taking seven or more medications at once. As a result, the American Medical Association (AMA) now suggests that any cognitive, emotional, or behavior problem observed in an older person taking medication should be considered to be a medication side-effect until proven otherwise. It also states if an older person is taking more than six medications, any cognitive, emotional or behavior problems exhibited could be caused by the interactive effects of the medicines prescribed.

To further complicate matters, more than a third of elderly people make serious mistakes in taking their medication, by either forgetting to take it altogether, or forgetting that they had already taken it and over-dosing.

Even worse, about 12 percent of older people taking prescription drugs are using medications that were actually prescribed for someone else. They accidently take medicine that is not their own because they can't read the label, or because they got it from a friend who said it "worked for them."

Over-the-counter medications are problematic as well. Although most people don't realize it, many over-the-counter medications interfere with memory and thinking, yet few if any of these medications indicate cognitive impairment as a side-effect.

Many prescription medications also grossly interfere with memory and cognition, but most doctors prescribing them do not explain to their patients that the drug they are prescribing may have an effect on the patients' memory or thinking.

·This clearly is a monumental problem. It is estimated that more than 200,000 people in this country are currently suffering from medication-induced cognitive problems.

It's important to realize that drugs act differently in older people. The loss of brain cells and reduced numbers of neurotransmitters in the older brain amplify the effects of many medications, and doses that are safe for younger people are often toxic in the aged.

Older bodies take much longer to metabolize and excrete certain drugs. Decreased liver and kidney function also increase the risk of drug toxicity. Drug interactions and drug side-effects also cause problems. As older people are more prone to idiosyncratic reactions to medicines, drugs should always be considered as a potential cause of observed cognitive or behavioral problems. In short, all medications need to be given with care and closely monitored. In many cases dosages need to be decreased.

In addition to the myriad problems faced by the elderly from prescribed conventional drugs, many increase their risk when they resort to alternative medicines, vitamins, herbs and other over-the-counter drugs in attempts to assuage their various or perceived maladies. This problem is exacerbated by the fact that most people don't tell anyone what they are taking.

It is imperative that a caregiver ask the person to identify everything they are taking, including prescription drugs, non-prescription drugs, vitamins, herbs, nutrients, and other alternative remedies. Have them recount any allergic reactions or adverse symptoms they have experienced in the past. If they are not asked, they will not tell.

Always tell people what medications they are about to take, why they will be taking them, and what the side-effects might be. Providing the person with as much information as possible about the medicine being

Common Side Effects of Drugs

Depression
antibiotics
ulcer medications
steroids
anti-glaucoma eye drops
cardiovascular drugs
anti Parkinson's drugs
anti-epileptic medications
Advil
Naprosyn
Indocin (for arthritis)
Antabuse
Hytrin (for benign prostatic
    hyperplasia)

Psychosis
antibiotics
urinary tract infection drugs
analgesics
  aspirin
  Darvon
cold medicines
  Actifed
  Benadryl
Albuterol (for asthma)
cardiovascular medications
antidepressants
tranquilizers
Vincristine (for cancer)
Sinemet (anti-Parkinson's)

Common Side Effects of Drugs

Confusion & Delirium
antibiotics
steroids
antihistamines
insulin
Tagamet
antidepressants,
Haldol
Thorazine
barbiturates
hypnotics
tranquilizers
analgesics
neurologic medications

Dementia
Zantac
Axid
Pepcid
cardiovascular drugs
central nervous system drugs

Insomnia
antibiotics
amantadine
Sudafed
gastrointestinal drugs
Inderal.
drugs containing caffeine
drugs containing ephedrine

prescribed can avert allergic or toxic or behavioral reactions.

Drug Abuse

Drug *misuse* (under, over or erratic use) and *abuse* (use for other than intended purposes) account for many drug-related deaths in the elderly. When misuse rather than abuse is suspected, the intervention may be one of education and simplification or clarification of the therapeutic contract. Drug education groups can be a valuable tool in these cases.

In spite of the fact that the elderly are at highest risk for substance abuse — with alcohol causing as many deaths among the age group as heart attacks — the problem is chronically under-diagnosed. It is estimated that between two and ten percent of those over the age of 60 suffer from alcoholism. In a survey of elderly patients in Washington, 9.6 percent were diagnosed with alcohol abuse, while about 5 percent were referred for prescription drug abuse.

Psychosocial factors such as loneliness and depression, and health factors related to the aging process, such as pain, disability, or chronic disease are the major contributors to alcoholism and drug abuse. Also, there is a 60 percent correlation between prescription drug abuse and alcoholism.

Misused prescription drug classes include sedative hypnotics, anti-anxiety agents, and analgesics. Valium (diazepam), codeine, meprobamate, and flurazepam are the top four drugs of abuse.

A thorough assessment is essential to detect and correct drug misuse or to diagnose drug abuse. Prior to considering any new medication, the caregiver should screen the person for potential abuse, including asking about an individual or family history of alcohol or other drug abuse. caregivers should also learn to recognize drug-seeking behaviors. When medication is prescribed, it should be with a clear clinical indication and a therapeutic end point and time limit.

Dialysis

Patients with end-stage renal disease undergoing regular dialysis are at risk of developing dementia. This may be caused by a toxic buildup of aluminum in the brain, resulting in dementia-like symptoms. Dialysis patients are also at risk of developing a thiamine deficiency, which can bring on symptoms such as confusion, abnormal movements, acute visual loss, speech disturbance, convulsions, rapidly progressing dementia, and coma. Although this is a fairly well known phenomenon, it's too often overlooked or missed. When assessing dementia, always determine whether the person is undergoing dialysis.

Post-Surgical Behavioral Problems

Elderly people undergo surgery at a fairly high frequency and usually without incident, but it is not uncommon to see drastic behavioral changes following their release from the hospital back to the facility. The trauma of surgery itself always causes a significant amount of stress, but other problems can arise as well.

The most common problems associated with surgery are:
- Adjustment disorder
- Post-surgical depression
- Post-surgical psychosis
- Biochemical and metabolic imbalances (for example, blood pressure changes after amputation)

Problems with memory and thinking after surgery mayo occur because of several factors. Caloric demand — the amount of energy consumed by the body —

Common side effects of psychotropic medications

Autonomic nervous system effects
orthostatic hypotension
dizziness
imbalance upon standing
falls
confusion
lethargy
daytime sleepiness

Oversedation & hypotension
slurred speech
staggering
fainting
dizziness or falling

Sedation
drowsiness
impaired concentration
slowed reaction time

Effects on the eye
increased sensitivity to light
strange pigmentation
increased lens cloudiness

Geriatric lab values

Enzymes
Alanine 0-22 units

aminotransferase (ALT) (to 36 units for patients under 70)

Aspartate 5 40 unitsamino- transferase (AST)

Phosphatase 19.9 83.4 units (alkaline)

Phosphatase 0.0 1.6 units (acid)

Hematology
Hemoglobin 9 g 17 g/100 ml (to 18 g for patients under 70)

Hematocrit 35% 54%

Red blood 3,000,000/mm3 - cells 5,000,000/mm3

White blood 3,100/mm3 - cells 12,700 mm3

often increases as the body tries to heal itself. If nutrition isn't adequate, the brain is most often the first organ to suffer. Occasionally, tiny clots are thrown during and after the surgery, which may result in minor strokes, and, consequently, impaired brain function. Older people may also fail to metabolize the anesthetic properly, causing the effects of anesthesia to linger for weeks after surgery, disrupting the person's ability to function. Finally, being anesthetized for hours may causes anoxia (oxygen starvation) which can lead to diffuse brain damage and cause memory and behavioral problems.

Body Image Problems

Sadly, many elderly people experience the loss of a limb or the loss of the function of a limb. Such a loss is traumatic and can be devastating, altering the person's ability to function normally and changing a person's body image and sense of self. If they no longer feel normal; they may no longer feel accepted.

Such feelings are worsened by the reactions that others have to the injury. Many people find amputations frightening, and avoid looking at a person with a missing limb. In their efforts to cope with their fear of rejection, recovering persons may become withdrawn, or lash out at others, believing that by rejecting others, they can save themselves from being rejected.

During this time of adjustment and recuperation, a person may be uncooperative, unpleasant, abusive, and difficult to work with. Keep this in mind when working with a person who has lost a limb.

It also is normal for a person to go through a period of grieving for the missing limb, although they often are reluctant to discuss these feelings with others. Addressing the issue directly frequently is the best way to open an avenue to communication. Use a statement such as, "Last year I was working with a woman who lost her leg. She told me it was a very difficult time for her. I wonder if you might be feeling that way too."

Other problems accompany amputations and must be addressed. Blood pressure may be altered. Balance and gait may be affected. And phantom-limb pain may cause discomfort and anxiety.

Post-Stroke Depression

Depression is a common consequence of stroke, particularly if the stroke has resulted in permanent disability. The patient has lost much independence, and also suffers from body image difficulties as previously discussed.

If the person has lost the ability to speak, there is even greater risk of depression. Loss of the ability to communicate is a devastating, and often results in complete withdrawal. It is vital in these cases to obtain a complete speech and language assessment before attempting intervention.

Several years ago I was asked to see a man who had been suffering from severe depression. Three years prior he had suffered a stroke that left him completely unable to speak. His ability to think, however, had been untouched. I ordered an augmented communication screening, an assessment that determined his ability to use a speech synthesizer (which in this case was a computer that contained a program to reproduce speech). When he received the device, his world changed. For the first time in years, he was able to speak again, and the depression disappeared.

Failure to Thrive

Studies show that about 15 percent of older people require professional intervention for failure to thrive. This condition includes a decline in physical health,

Geriatric lab values

Chemistry (serum)
Calcium 8.9 mg 10.9 mg/100 ml (to 11 mg for patients under 70)

Chloride 96 mEq 110 mEq/L

Cholesterol 160 mg 300 mg/100 ml (total) (150 mg 250 mg/100 ml for patients under 70)

Glucose 52 mg 140 mg/100 ml (fasting)

Phosphorus .1 mg 5.1 mgi100 mi

Potassium 3.0 mEq 5.9 mEq/L

Protein 5.3 g 7.8 g/100 ml (total)

Protein 3.0 g 5.0 g/100 ml (albumin) (to 5.6 g/100 ml for patients under 70)

Sodium 136 mEq 142 mEq/L

Urea nitrogen 7.0 mg 35.0 mgi100 mi (BUN)

Uric acid 2.0 mg 9.2 mgi100 mi

Geriatric lab values

Chemistry (Urine)
Creatinine 0.4 mg 1.9 mg/100 ml

Creatinine clearance must be calculated to take into account age related decrease in glomerular filtration rate: *140 age) X body weight (kg) serum creatinine X 72 kg

Endocrinology
TSH 0.3 6.3 IU/ml

weight loss, loss of appetite, and social withdrawal in the absence of any obvious cause.

Dehydration

Several years ago I was called in to see an 80 year old woman named Madeline. She had recently become confused, disoriented, and was beginning to show some signs of dementia. In the course of the interview, it was discovered that she was drinking very little fluids. When her fluid intake was increased, the symptoms went away within three days.

Since that time I have observed that a great many elderly people do not drink enough water. In some cases this is because they have lost their sense of thirst. But after asking dozens of people why they don't drink water, the answer I hear most is, "Because it makes me pee."

And they are right. The decreased fluid intake reduces their need to urinate, and thus reduces the likelihood of incontinence, often a source of shame and inconvenience. Unfortunately, not drinking fluids also causes fluid and electrolyte imbalances in the brain, and can cause dementia-like symptoms. Very often, correcting incontinence problems eliminates dehydration, and thus eliminates behavioral problems. Incontinence can often be treated with biofeedback.

Nutritional Problems

Another potential cause of behavioral problems in inadequate or poorly balanced nutrition. As people age, they often lose their sense of smell and taste which greatly decreases their enjoyment of food. They even may lose their sense of hunger.

Research shows that the biochemical imbalances causing anorexia in younger people and changes in the natural aging of the brain are very similar. Drug withdrawal and depression may also cause geriatric anorexia. The consequence of these changes may lead to inadequate intake of calories and essential nutrients.

Elderly people also have a tendency to narrow the scope of what they will eat, and therefore may become deficient in certain vitamins and minerals, particularly the B vitamins.

Other elders, however, may overload themselves with nutritional supplements, in the hope that taking mega-doses of certain nutrients will keep them young and healthy forever. As mentioned earlier, it is important to ask about the nutritional supplements, herbs, and other self-medicating behavior the person is engaged in, as this is very common, and will not be mentioned unless you inquire. Supplements are not an alternative to proper eating.

Sadly, failure to thrive, to drink, or to eat may also be the result of neglect at home, whether intentional or unintentional. I have worked with families that literally starved their family members to death. A typical case of neglect was described by Christine Williams-Burgess and Mary Kay Kimball

> Mr. R. arrived in the emergency room with a questionable new stroke. He was dehydrated and had lost 50 pounds. He was unable to walk and was incontinent of urine and stool.
>
> During assessment the patient confided that he felt he was a burden to his wife. He was embarrassed regarding his loss of continence and felt bad that his wife "had to clean him like a baby."
>
> Mrs. R. thought that Mr. R. was doing this on purpose. Thus, she would restrict food and fluids to decrease the frequency of the episodes of incontinence.
>
> Cases of neglect like this often come to light when a patient improves rapidly in the hospital, and again deteriorates when returned home.

Contribution of pain to benhavior problems

Phantom pain
Dental pain
Balance
Gait
Blood pressure increase
Grief reactions
Body image disturbances
Neuropathy
Depression
Cognitive impairment

Behavioral Symptoms:
Fatigue
Lethargy
Irritability
Restlessness
Quarrelsome
Intolerant
Lack of endurance

Physical symptoms:
Shoulder Pain
Generalized Pain
Fever
Headache
Vomiting
Nutrient malabsorption
Malodorous stool
Poor digestion
Faulty metabolism

Diseases of the colon:that can affect behavior
Sigmoid flexure
Fissures
Fistulas
Hemorrhoids
Diverticulitis
Malignancies
Impaction

Head Trauma

The brain is a jelly-like substance suspended in a bath of spinal fluid, and protected by rubbery membranes called meninges. Minor bumps on the head do not usually cause any damage, but getting hit hard enough to cause a loss of consciousness can cause serious injury — bruising or tearing of the brain's delicate tissues.

A *concussion* is a temporary loss of consciousness occurring after a blow to the head. The impact of the blow causes the semi-liquid brain tissue to slosh about inside the skull. Like any bruise, the injured tissue then swells. Immediately after a concussion, the victim may experience confusion, memory loss, vomiting, and blurred vision. Depending on the severity, brain function can be disrupted for weeks, causing loss of memory, and sometimes permanent brain damage.

The longer a person is unconscious following a concussion, the more severe the symptoms tend to be. As soon as possible after a person has experienced a loss of consciousness, a doctor should be consulted in order to rule out skull fracture, brain injury, or bleeding inside the lining of the brain called subdural hematoma. Subdural bleeding is a serious condition requiring immediate medical attention. Weeks after such a head injury, the person may experience headaches, dizziness, changes in behavior, drowsiness, and memory loss.

In younger people, most concussions are caused by traffic accidents, but in the elderly, they can also occur from falls, or from being hit on the head by any object. About one-third of the people who experience a concussion will exhibit *post concussion syndrome*. This syndrome includes chronic memory loss, dizziness, and changes in behavior that can last over a year. Because most knocks on the head are soon forgotten, the person usually does not connect the symptoms with the accident.

Elderly people often fall or bump their head, and later forget that the incident happened. In a younger person, these bumps may be unimportant. But the brains of elderly people are sometimes smaller, and slosh about inside the skull more easily. The decreased amount of neurons in the elderly brain makes minor damage more serious. Even minor bumps on the head in the elderly, such as a bump on the head from a cabinet door, can cause subdural hematoma. Any bump on the head should be checked thoroughly.

Repeated concussions, such as those experienced by boxers, can cause permanent brain damage, including a condition called *punch-drunk syndrome*. One study revealed that 87 percent of former boxers showed evidence of brain damage. We also know that a significant number of those suffering from dementia have a history of head injury.

Dizziness

Feeling dizzy is a common complaint of elderly people. However, typically most people don't really mean that they are dizzy. A great many people who complain of dizziness are actually suffering from Parkinsonian difficulties, that is, if they lose their balance, they cannot regain it, and they may fall. Some people also use the word "dizzy" to describe muscle weakness or damage that results in unsteadiness, and causes the person to fall or bump into things.

Others are actually feeling the results of ortho-static hypotension, a sudden drop in blood pressure upon standing. This means that when they stand up too quickly, they feel faint. This drop in blood pressure can be caused by medications or chronic low blood volume. Low blood pressure can also be a sign of internal blood loss, which is a serious condition.

Still others state they are dizzy because of vestibular disorders. These are malfunctions in the

Incontinence problemss:
Shame
Anxiety
Dehydration
Social phobias

Interventions:
Limit fluid intake at night
(no fluids after 7 p.m.)

Reduce the consumption of caffeinated beverages and alcohol (both irritate the bladder)

Re evaluate medications (some may trigger incontinence)

Elevate feet for a few hours before bed
(reduces night time urination)

Check for a urinary tract infection
(antibiotics can cure this incontinence)

Use pelvic floor exercises (Kegel exercises:) along with biofeedback to strengthen the pelvic muscles
(helps both urge and stress incontinence)

Establish a urination schedule
(for urge incontinence)

Surgery to resuspend the bladder

balance apparatus in the ear that result feelings that the room is spinning around. This condition, also known as vertigo, can cause nausea and panic attacks. This can be caused by ear infections or damage to the balance organs themselves. Because the word "dizzy" can mean so many things, always ask what the person means.

Chapter Eleven

Pain

It's 3:27 am when the phone rings. You are suddenly jolted out of a sound sleep. As you stagger towards the phone, your toe smashes against the suitcase you left on the floor. The pain is intense and immediate. As you shout something X-rated, you hop about in agony. You sit down and rub your damaged digit, and, thankfully, in a few moments, the pain is gone.

Acute pain is useful in that it is a warning the body has sustained damage. The distress accompanying pain causes a person to withdraw from the source of the pain, and learn to avoid similar situations in the future. The brain is saying, "Don't do that again!" If tissue injury occurs, pain motivates a person to seek help, and also tells us to remain immobile so that healing can occur.

Chronic pain, also called *unproductive pain,* is in no way useful, serving only to diminish the quality of life. The distress from chronic pain only causes suffering, sapping enjoyment from a day, and, over time, hampering a person's will to live.

Behavioral Objectives

At the end of this section resders will be able to:

Describe the differences between acute and chronic pain.

Define and differentiate pain tolerance from pain threshold.

Discuss the relationship between pain and depression.

Conduct a pain assessment.

Common types of pain in the elderly

headache

dental pain

back pain

arthritic pain

muscle pain

stomach pain

intestinal pain

cancer pain

post operative pain

About one out of five elderly people suffer from chronic pain, and in nursing homes, the incidence of chronic pain can be as high as 80 percent. Such pain in the elderly can impair the activities of daily living, and cause depression, anxiety, lowered tolerance for frustration, problems with thinking and attention, sleep disturbances, and irritability.

Although the elderly are more prone to painful illnesses such as neuropathy, trigeminal neuralgia, spinal degeneration, arthritis, and a variety of other degenerative diseases, little evidence exists that pain complaints are more common in the normal aged. Despite this lack of evidence, the fallacy persists that pain is an inevitable consequence of aging.

In the mistaken belief that all older people complain about pain, caregivers may ignore such complaints and thus overlook serious pathology, including life-threatening illnesses. Pain and suffering should never be equated with the processes of normal aging, but should be treated in an older person the same as it is in the young.

In reality, elderly people may actually under-report pain, either because they too expect pain with aging, or because existing communication difficulties or confusion may render them unable to make others aware of their pain.

Interestingly, although cognitive impairment may be a barrier to pain assessment, it is important to recognize that even cognitively impaired residents reliably report the presence of pain when asked.

Defining Pain

Unfortunately for caregivers, pain is a completely subjective experience — there simply is no reliable way to objectively observe whether someone is in pain. Hence, the most useful pain definition is, "pain is whatever a person says it is, and exists whenever he or she says it does." As pain cannot be observed, proved or disproved, the only basis for pain assessment is the patient's subjective report that they are in pain

In the 1986 edition of *Cancer Pain Relief*, the World Health Organization states unequivocally, "Believe the patient's complaints of pain." In other words, a report of pain by a patient should be sufficient to establish pain as a diagnosis. It is the person reporting the pain, not the healthcare team nor the family, who is the final authority on the reality of pain.

The Causes of Pain

Another common misconception among health care professionals is that all pain must have an identifiable physical cause. If the cause is elusive, the inaccurate conclusion is that the person has no "real" pain. It is important to remember that all pain is real, regardless of its cause and regardless of whether it can be diagnosed or measured.

Lack of a physical diagnosis causes some people to conclude that a person's pain is psychogenic or "all in their head." Purely psychogenic pain, however, is extremely rare and should never be assumed merely because of the lack of ability to find a physical cause.

In the face of the widespread belief that all pain should be diagnosible, in situations in which there is difficulty establishing a cause for pain, the sufferers themselves may begin to question their own sanity. They may begin to fear they will be perceived as lying or malingering, and that pain relief will be withheld because their pain is not real. It is useful and comforting to tell patients all pain is real, and it will be recognized as such.

The reality is that pain includes both a physical and an emotional component. To have pain that is purely physical, that is, to experience pain without distress, is very rare. Feelings of fear and anxiety are

Pain exists when ever a person says it exists.

appropriate reactions to pain, and shouldn't be seen a evidence that the pain isn't "real."

Lying about Pain

The reporting of pain by someone who is not actually suffering is called malingering. A true malingerer consciously fakes pain in order to get medication or to gain attention from family members or the health-care staff. Although many caregivers believe that lying about pain is common, research shows that it is actually very rare.

When a person says they are in pain, caregivers may feel the need to decide whether they should believe a person who on other occasions has been untrustworthy. There is no accurate test to detect a malingerer, and while in some instances caregivers may disbelieve a person who claims to be in pain, professional responsibility dictates that caregivers believe all patients who state that they are in pain. It is better to treat a malingerer than to deny treatment to someone who is suffering.

A professional assessment of pain should be objective, absent from personal biases, beliefs, values, or feelings about the person. Equally unacceptable is the withholding of appropriate treatment from a person in pain merely because the caregiver doesn't like or believe the person, or disapproves of the person's behavior.

This is not to say the social context in which the pain is occurring should not be considered. Secondary gain from chronic pain, that is, the rewards a person may reap from complaining of pain, includes increased attention from staff and family. In some cases, families and caregivers unwittingly encourage a "sick role," by attending to patients when they complain and ignoring them when they don't.

For some people, expressing pain may be a way to cope with loneliness, fear of physical deterioration, or fear of impending death. Focusing on pain may allow a person to avoid thinking about these unpleasant and frightening things. In these cases, behavioral intervention can be helpful.

Pain Behavior

Many health care professionals have been taught to look for visible physiological and behavioral signs that accompany pain, and therefore can be used as the basis for objective pain assessment.

With acute pain, physiological signs include elevated blood-pressure, rapid heart beat, rapid breathing, dilated pupils and behaviors such as grimacing, moaning and flailing about.

With chronic pain, physical and behavioral adaptation occurs, resulting in periods during which the person may show no overt signs of pain. As the body adapts to pain, vital signs normalize. This return to equilibrium is necessary to prevent physical harm and stress on the body, but it does not necessarily mean the pain has disappeared.

When caregivers follow the acute pain model to assess pain, there will be times when a patient's behavior and physical signs do not correlate with the patient's report of pain. Patients may experience even severe pain without behaving as though they are in pain. In other words, lack of pain behavior doesn't mean lack of pain.

A recent study shows the effect of patient behavior on pain assessment. Nurses were told to rate the pain of two patients recovering from identical surgical procedures. Although the patients both reported they had exactly the same amount of pain, during the assessments, one patient smiled while the other grimaced. Interestingly, many of the nurses underestimated the amount of pain reported by both patients, but the estimates were even lower for the smiling patient. It appears the nurses had relied on their expectations of each patient's pain, behavior and appearance rather than on the patient's actual reported level of pain.

Pain Threshold

A person's *pain threshold* is the point at which a stimulus is perceived as painful. Many caregiving professionals mistakenly believe that all people perceive pain the same. In addition, seasoned health care workers often develop their own conclusions about the range of expected pain responses for certain situations. Generalizing about pain perception is problematic, such as when a patient who experiences more pain than expected with a certain treatment, diagnostic procedure, or in a postoperative recovery period becomes labeled as exaggerating the level of pain.

For example, surveys show that most nurses expect that the most severe pain following surgery will occur in the first 48 hours and then gradually subside. However, in a recent study of post-surgical patients, 31 percent reported significant pain after the fourth postoperative day.

Tolerance for Pain

Research shows that there is no such thing as a general pain tolerance. Some people just feel more pain than others. The duration or severity of pain can't be predicted. No caregiver can can be the judge of what hurts a person, nor how long it should hurt.

Tolerance of pain is best defined as the duration and intensity of pain that the person is willing to endure. Pain tolerance, pain perception, and the expression of pain are all unique to the individual.

Further-more a person's tolerance for pain varies from one situation to another. The person's emotional state, degree of fatigue, and the value or significance of the pain for that patient all influence the level of tolerance of pain.

Many caregivers mistakingly believe that the more experience a person has with pain, the more endurance and the greater tolerance he or she will develop. The reality is that people who experience chronic pain usually have a lower tolerance of pain combined with a higher level of anxiety because they know how severe the pain can be and how hard it may be to get relief.

Attitudes about Pain

In America, many people have unrealistic and stoic attitudes about pain, believing that people should be able to cope with their pain and are weak if they ask for relief. Thus, many caregivers underestimate the severity of pain in those who report it, and adopt the attitude that the person should "just learn to live with it."

This widespread attitude results in many people in pain refusing medication that could help them so they don't appear weak. Many people have told me they don't complain about pain because they want to be a good patient, or they believe a stoic response to pain or exhaustion somehow makes them a better person

As a clinical psychologist, I have never been a strong proponent of medication, but I think many people are wrong headed and ignorant about pain treatment in this country. Too many people suffer needlessly because of pervasive negative attitudes about pain medication.

Many physicians are reluctant to prescribe pain medication out of fear of repercussions from federal oversight agencies, whose culture includes this unrealistic attitude about medicating pain. A doctor who doles out pain medication liberally often is red-flagged, or singled out for his or her "excessive" prescribing habits. This must change.

Another barrier to appropriately medicating pain is the unrealistic fear of addiction among many health care professionals, despite an abundance of evidence that narcotic drugs do not cause addiction in pain patients.

A survey of 1,781 nurses conducted in 1989 showed that 31 percent of them thought pain killing drugs should not be given because of potential addiction. Many health care professionals continue to refuse these drugs to those who need them, while others minimize the amount of pain medication a person can receive, rendering the therapy useless. These attitudes are archaic and harmful.

Effectively eliminating pain can do wonders for a person's quality of life. The priority for pain patients should always be to ensure their comfort, not to test their courage.

Many chronic pain patients, including cancer patients, refuse to take opiate-based pain medication because of their belief they will develop a tolerance, and the drugs would become ineffective. In reality, opioid drugs have no "analgesic ceiling," so the dosage level of these drugs can be increased to ensure their continued effectiveness.

It is quite common for health care workers to underestimate the severity of the person's pain, while overestimating the effectiveness of the medication they are giving. A person who received pain medication and a few hours later claims that they are still in pain, may be told, "I'm sorry, you just received a pain pill. You'll have to wait two more hours," which is not much different from hearing, "You are lying about your level of pain."

Placebos

A *placebo* is any treatment or medication that produces a response in patients because of their belief that it will work, not because it has any actual therapeutic property. The problem with placebos is that people who respond positively to them may be wrongly perceived by caregivers as malingering or fabricating their pain. While this is seldom true, I have seen staff members give residents placebos because they think the person is lying about their pain, or because "They don't know the difference."

The use of placebos is never justified to determine the existence of pain. Since most people have some response to a placebo, no conclusion other than that the patient believes in the intent and efficacy of the treatment should be drawn from a placebo response. While placebos have a place in research trials, using them for diagnosis is unwise.

Depression

In the elderly, pain and depression are closely linked — pain can be exacerbated by co-existing depression, while many who experience chronic pain often become depressed and anxious.

Studies show that up to 59 percent of patients requesting treatment for depression also complain of recurring pain, and conversely, 87 percent of patients coming to chronic pain clinics exhibit the symptoms of depression.

Even when a person denies being depressed, they may exhibit the symptoms. In fact, most people are unaware of the common symptoms of depression — sleep disturbances, early morning awakening, psychomotor retardation or agitation, anorexia and weight loss — and do not realize that depression can worsen pain.

In some cases of unrecognized depression, complaints of pain may be the person's way of explaining a loss of interest in life, low energy, poor concentration, and guilt. In cases where pain complaints are accompanied by the symptoms listed above, behavioral interventions can help. (For more on depression, see chapter 7 in this book.)

Pain and Cognition

Several studies that have shown that chronic pain can cause cognitive problems. In fact, in one recent study, the central processing speed (the time it takes to think) in chronic pain patients was significantly slower than in head injury patients. Pain interferes with attention, concentration, and endurance, and can preoccupy a person to the degree that they cannot think clearly. This should always be taken into consideration when undertaking cognitive assessments.

Pain and Activity

Arthritis and muscle pain does not improve with rest. In fact rest can make the pain worse. Furthermore, a person loses one percent of his muscle mass for each day he remains inactive. Inactivity can lead to *disuse syndrome,* and *may result in the person losing the ability to walk.*

Pain Assessment

A pain assessment should include:
1. A complete medical and psychological history
2. A thorough physical examination
3. A complete neurological examination
4. A description of the pain's location
5. Conditions that make the pain worse or better

6. The effect of the pain on the person's mood and behavior.

7. A screening for cognitive impairment

8. A screening for depression

9. A vision and hearing examination to screen for sensory deprivation

10. A review of the person's activities of daily living

11. A gait and balance assessment

12. Pain measurement completed by the patient

   A pain scale is an efficient and simple way to measure pain intensity. It consists of a horizontal line, with two end points labeled "no pain" or 0 and "worst pain ever," or 10. Ask the patient to mark the line that corresponds to existing pain intensity.

13. Pain description completed by the patient

   Tools such as the McGill Pain Questionnaire provide information about the quality of the pain experienced.

Also evaluate how the patient responds to treatment and relates to caregivers, to help assess possible secondary gains. The probability of pain-related behaviors is higher in people who have difficulty establishing a trusting and secure relationship.

Chapter Twelve

The Aging Senses

Hearing

It was a winter day in 1994, I was visiting with a lovely 86-year-old woman named Gina, who lived in a retirement home in the southern part of Orange County, California. It was the week before Christmas, and the facility was holding a Christmas party. The meeting hall was filled with the aroma of cakes and cookies, and the room danced with the sounds of holiday music, tinkling silverware, and casual conversation.

But Gina sat alone in her room.

I found this odd because I knew how much she loved the company of others. She had lost her husband two years before, had no family, and craved social stimulation.

When I asked her why she was not at the party, she told me some very important things. "I would love to be in that room," she said, "but you see, I am hard of hearing. People don't know it. They just think I'm ignoring them. When somebody walks up and says hello and I don't hear them, they think I'm stuck up."

"But you have two hearing aids," I said.

"Sure," Gina replied, "but you don't realize that when you wear a hearing aid in a crowded room, the noise is overwhelming. Everything gets amplified. All I

At the end of this section readers will be able to

State the incidence of hearing loss in the older population:

Describe the common causes of hearing loss.

Explain the social and emotional consequences of impaired hearing.

Communicate effectively with hearing impaired adults.

Signs of hearing impairment

Certain words are misunderstood.

Another person's speech sounds slurred.

The person cannot hear when there is background noise.

Speech can be hard to understand.

Certain sounds are overly loud or annoying.

Constant hissing or ringing in the ears.

Certain voices cannot be heard.

> hear is a jangled, jumbled roar. I can't tell the voices from the background noise. It's unpleasant and overwhelming.
>
> So, I'm faced with a dilemma. I can go to the party and be blasted with noise, turn my hearing aid down and be accused of being stuck up or stupid, or stay in my room and be lonely. I love being with people, but I hate going to gatherings because people treat me like I'm retarded or something."

Since that time I've heard similar complaints by many elderly people. Sadly, many cope with their loss by isolating, withdrawing, and sinking into loneliness and depression, rather than working to fix the problem. To prevent this from happening, do the following:

Interventions for Hearing Loss

1. Determine whether the person can hear in the environments in which they live.

   Have a conversation in the dining room, the bedroom, and outdoors. Turn on the television or radio with the volume adjusted to the person's liking, then have a conversation.
2. Explore methods of hearing improvement.

   A significant portion of hearing-impaired adults refuse to use hearing aids, complaining that the device does not work properly, or is uncomfortable, or that the person does not know how to put the device in, or operate it correctly. They may say they forget to put it in, or keep losing it. Another common complaint is that the hearing aid is ineffective in noisy environments, being unable to filter out unwanted sounds.

   In clinical settings such as hospitals and long-term care facilities, amplifiers may be a good alternative to a hearing aid. These devices are worn around the neck and are larger than a hearing aid, making them harder to lose and easier to operate. Also, the person is able to adjust the volume to fit the environment, making the amplifier more user friendly.

3.   Have the person's hearing checked regularly.

About 30 percent of adults aged 65 to 70, and about 50 percent of those over age 70 suffer some degree of hearing loss. Hearing impairment ranges from having difficulty understanding words or hearing certain sounds to total deafness.

Because hearing loss usually occurs gradually, people are often unaware their hearing has changed. Rather, they believe others are talking too quietly, or mumbling. Undetected hearing loss often triggers social isolation, suspicion and paranoia.

Hearing loss may be caused by viral infections, vascular disorders (heart conditions or stroke), head injuries, wax buildup, tumors, certain medications, or age-related changes in the ear. These factors need be considered when making a hearing loss diagnosis in an elderly person.

Conductive hearing loss involves the blocking of sounds that are carried from the eardrums (the tympanic membranes) to the inner ear, and may be caused by ear wax in the ear canal, or fluid, abnormal bone growth or infection in the middle ear.

Sensorineural hearing loss involves damage to parts of the inner ear or auditory nerve, and often occurs in older people. An audiologist is able to make an accurate diagnosis of this type of hearing loss.

4.   Tell friends, family, and all caregivers about the person's hearing loss.

Many people try to hide a hearing problem because they are self conscious or ashamed.

They may refuse to have their hearing checked, and refuse to wear a hearing aid.

Instead of admitting they can't hear, some people may pretend to understand what others are saying. As a result, they fail to reply — making them appear rude — or they misunderstand and make nonsensical or out-of-context comments — making them appear out of touch with reality. These behaviors can frustrate other residents and staff members, causing them to avoid talking to the hearing impaired person who then feels hurt and isolated. It is better all around that everyone know about the person's hearing problem.

5.   Educate others about hearing loss.

Ask the person to tell people around them what they can and can't hear, and the details of the problems presented by noisy environments.

6.   Ensure the person wears the prescribed hearing aids.

Many people refuse to wear their hearing aids because they are in denial about their problem, or their pride prevents them from using them. Often, they simply forget they have hearing aids. A sign on a person's door or mirror stating, "put in your hearing aids" usually corrects this problem.

7.   Don't allow people to use hearing loss as a tool for hearing only what they want to hear.

My grandmother was hard of hearing for most of her adult life, and often would fail to respond when she was asked a question. I noticed, however, she never, ever, failed to hear the words, "dinner's ready." People can use their hearing problem as an excuse for ignoring things they don't want to hear — a phenomenon called "selective hearing."

Vision

While changes in vision are universal, visual impairment often is unrecognized and misunderstood in elderly people. In 2004, researchers found that more than 28 million Americans over age 40 have eye ailments serious enough to put them at risk for vision loss and blindness. This number is expected to soar as the U.S. population continues to age. Visual impairment is also related to higher risk of death in older people.

Cataracts are the leading cause of blindness worldwide, and affect an estimated 20 million American adults, with the number of cases is expected to reach 30 million in the next 20 years.

Macular degeneration, glaucoma, and diabetic retinopathy are also major causes of blindness and vision loss and are strongly linked with aging.

In the clinical population the numbers are higher. It's estimated that 30 to 50 percent of nursing home residents are visually impaired to a sufficient degree to interfere with daily functioning, and greater than 90 percent of those over 70 have some form of cataracts.

People who experience vision loss not only have trouble seeing, but they also lose much of their independence, their ability to function, and their self-worth. They may have trouble doing even simple tasks, such as getting dressed, and may begin to view normal parts of their environment, such as staircases, as dangerous and to be avoided. Bumping into furniture may cause bruises and broken skin, while missing a chair altogether may result in a painful fall. Some people may have trouble finding their rooms, and simple pleasures like reading a newspaper, magazine or book become impossible. Watching television or even having a conversation with a friend both may become more difficult as the visual component of communication is lost.

Signs of vision problems

Performing Daily Activities

Exhibits changes in reading, watching television, walking, or performing hobbies.

Squints or tilts the head to the side to get an object in focus.

Has difficulty identifying faces.

Has difficulty in locating familiar objects, even in a familiar environment.

Reaches out for objects in an uncertain manner.

Has difficulty identifying colors and selects clothing in unusual color combinations

Reading and Writing

Can't read mail or a newspaper.

Holds reading material close to the face or at an angle.

Writes less clearly and precisely and has difficulty writing on the line.

Finds lighting in the room inadequate for reading and other activities.

Signs of vision problems

Brushes against the wall while walking.

Consistently bumps into objects.

Has difficulty walking on irregular or bumpy surfaces.

Goes up and down stairs slowly and cautiously, even with no other physical limitations.

Has difficulty getting food onto a fork.

Has difficulty cutting food or serving self from a serving plate.

Spills food off the plate while eating.

Pours liquids over the top of the cup.

Knocks over liquids while reaching across the table for another item.

Needless to say, people suffering vision impairment begin to suffer frustration and anxiety as well.

Visual impairment not only is frequently overlooked by others, but often goes unrecognized by the person suffering it. The gradual progression of visual loss allows the person to adapt to it slowly, without being aware that the visual world is fading.

As people age, two types of visual problems occur — reduced color discrimination and the inability to tolerate glare. Colors with short light waves — such as green, blue, and violet — become much more difficult to see than red, orange, and yellow. All colors dull, and pastels become indistinguishable. Dark colors, which easily blend into the shadows, become nearly impossible to see, and danger lurks where dark floors, doors and walls blend together.

The behaviors in the box on this list the most common indicators of vision problems. Elderly people who experience five or more of these signs and symptoms should have a thorough eye examination from an ophthalmologist. In many cases, surgical procedures, glasses, medications, and adaptive devices can correct or improve the person's vision.

Caregivers should always be alert for signs of vision loss, and can employ a variety of techniques to better communicate with persons who are visually impaired.

Behavioral Interventions for Visual Impairment

1. When walking into the person's room, identify yourself and anyone else accompanying you. When leaving, announce your departure.

    Older adults with low vision often find it difficult to identify facial features, but readily recognize voices.

2. Explain to the person exactly what you plan to do.

Tell them in advance if you are going to touch them, give them something, or remove something.

3. Avoid using the pronouns "he" or "she" when referring to someone in a group.

Identify each person by name, thus allowing the visually impaired person to know who is present, and whom is being talked about.

4. Always be sure to include the person in a conversation.

Visually impaired people are not able to pick up the subtle social cues of a conversation, so take special care to include them.

5. When speaking to a visually impaired person, always address them by name, so they know you are speaking to them.

6. Don't automatically assume that the person would like to be helped.

Never force help on a person. Older adults with vision impairments are still able to do many things independently and might feel patronized by caregivers who offer too much assistance.

7. During personal care activities, allow the person to feel the items to be used.

Be sure to describe size, shapes, and colors. Explain each task step-by-step. Encourage the person to complete a task independently, offering praise when appropriate.

8. Communicate with the person face-to-face and within close range, thus allowing the person to see you clearly and to read body language.

9. When offering seating, be sure to place the person's hand on the back or arm of the chair so they can orient them selves and not risk a fall.

10. When leading, have the person hold your arm above the elbow and follow half a step behind you

Be precise when giving directions. For example, say, "There is a curb two feet away, directly to your left." When entering an unfamiliar setting, describe it in detail to the person, and point out such things as tables, chairs, and rugs.

11. Reduce glare

Soften glare from windows by using adjustable blinds, shades, and curtains. Glare from glossy paper during reading can be reduced by using an overlay of clear yellow plastic. This also makes the print on the darker.

Caregivers should avoid positioning themselves in the path of a bright light from a window or lamp, because the glare will prevent the patient from seeing them properly.

12. Provide adequate lighting

Older adults with fading vision require two to three times more light than the general population in order to see properly. Put chairs near windows to take advantage of natural light. Light should be provided throughout a room with additional light from floor and table lamps near activity areas.

Provide the person with the ability to adjust the light in their room. Use three-way bulbs, high-low switches and dimmers. Gooseneck lamps and other adjustable lamps allow the person to focus the light where it is needed most. Use lamp shades of heavy, dark material to help concentrate light on an activity. Lights should be placed so that they shine on the task at hand.

13. Use night lights in bedrooms, hallways, and other dimly lit areas to orient and guide the person, and prevent falls.

14. Avoid sudden changes of light intensity.

Older eyes have difficulty making the adjustment to a sudden change from dark to light, and the person may actually experience a temporary vision loss.

15.   Use Color Contrast

Colors that are too similar can blend together and become indistinguishable. For example, a person with poor vision may have difficulty seeing a white toilet or sink against a white wall or floor. Paint doorsills, doorknobs, and door borders a contrasting color from walls. Ensure that furniture contrast against walls, and accessories contrast against furniture. Use brightly colored vases and lamps to make furniture easier to locate.

Use contrasting colors for the tops and risers of steps. The handrail should contrast against the wall. Ensure there is adequate lighting throughout the stairwell.

In the bathroom, the toilet seat should contrast with the bathroom walls and floor. Put contrasting-colored tape around the edge of the toilet seat and sink if necessary.

Make toiletries brightly colored to promote visibility. Consider painting the walls in the bathroom a contrasting color to the floor.

In the tub room, drape a dark-colored bath mat over the side of the tub to promote visibility.

16.   During meals, use light-colored dishes against dark-colored tablecloths.

Clear glasses or dishes may not be visible.

17.   Serve milk or other light colored liquids in a dark cup, and coffee or other dark-colored liquids in a white cup. This allows the person to assess the level of the liquid in the cup.

18.   Food should contrast against the plates.

Servings should vary in color. For instance, avoid placing white rice, white meat chicken, and cauliflower on the same plate.

19.   Structure the environment.

Familiarize all persons who have visual impairments with their environments.

Make sure doors open flush to the wall and push chairs and other objects out of traffic paths. Keep the placement of furnishings constant. See that chairs are pushed up tightly to tables and that cupboard and dresser drawers are not sticking out.

Keep closets consistently organized to help persons low vision more easily locate clothes. Color code dresser drawers with tape and put dividers in the drawers to help them identify items. Mark or label drawers so items can be returned to the same places.

Chapter Thirteen

Hallucinations

A *hallucination* is an internally generated experience interpreted as external. Although most people don't admit to hallucinations, over half of us will experience them at some time in our lives. The most common hallucination is hearing one's name called.

Hearing your name called, hearing voices, or other sounds are all *auditory hallucinations*. This type of hallucination generally occurs in people suffering from schizophrenia, but also occurs in people with organic conditions, such as epilepsy, brain tumors, or drug intoxication.

The most prevalent type of auditory hallucination is *running commentary* — the experience of hearing one or more voices commenting on and critiquing everything the hallucinating person is doing. These hallucinations often are composed of thought fragments and endless loops of sentences, which may be repeated hundreds of times a day. Even when the person is able to recognize that the voices are hallucinations, the problem is truly maddening.

Behavioral Objectives

At the end of this section readers will be able to:

Define the types of hallucinations.

Discuss the causes of hallucinations.

Recognize the effect of hallucinations on the well being of older people.

Discriminate between psychotic and non-psychotic hallucinations.

A *command hallucination* is the phenomenon of hearing a voice compelling the person to do or not do a certain act. People experiencing command hallucinations may feel compelled to themselves or others.

Some auditory hallucinations have been found to be caused by sub-vocalization, that is, the hallucinating person is actually speaking without knowing it. Having the person stick out his or her tongue can actually stop the voices.

Visual hallucinations are less common than auditory ones, but can be very frightening. People with brain damage sometimes hallucinate snakes, spiders, and other frightening creatures.

Visual hallucinations have been observed in elderly patients with diffuse Lewy body disease, a common type of dementia. There is also a three percent prevalence of visual hallucinations among patients with macular degeneration.

Seizures in the occipital lobe (the part of the brain that processes vision) may cause visual hallucinations but these are rarely complex and fully-formed hallucinations. Instead, the person usually sees flashes of light or colors in the half of the visual field on the opposite side of the seizure focus. Frontal lobe seizures, on the other hand, may cause complex, violent visual hallucinations without an alteration in consciousness.

Seizure-related hallucinations sometimes are caused by strokes. One of my patients described her experience in the hospital after suffering a stroke which affected her visual cortex.

> "I thought I was fine until the nurse came into see me. She had these horrible, huge, distorted eyes. I was feeling sorry for her until my husband walked in. To my horror, his right shoulder was missing. This is when I realized something was wrong with me."

Charles Bonnet syndrome is a type of visual hallucination characterized by the lack of psychosis. In 1769

Charles Bonnet noticed that his grandfather was having visual hallucinations, but, other than the hallucination, he showed no evidence of mental illness. Since that time, many cases of this type of hallucination have been reported.

Nursing consultant Dr. Kathleen Buckwalter has described a classic case of both visual and auditory hallucination caused by loss of vision, a phenomenon that she likens to phantom limb experiences and which she calls *phantom hallucinations.*

> The nursing home staff had initially asked me to see Mrs. C. because of her "visual hallucinations." When I queried her about "seeing things." She described the following scene in vivid detail. The image would come and go unexpectedly, and had become more frequent as her eyesight became progressively worse.
>
> Over the past year it was almost always the same scene — a World War I French battleground where her former fiancee (who had been killed in the war) was stationed with his battalion. Mrs. C. described in exquisite detail the landscape (which she had never seen), the soldiers' khaki uniforms. And even noted how the horses' lips curled when they whinnied, as if to laugh at her for being so startled by the sight of the vision.
>
> "Can't you see them — the horses and men over there on the wall?" she would ask. "Oh, they seem so real to me."
>
> Although somewhat amazed by her vision, Mrs. C. was not particularly frightened or troubled by it and clearly understood that she was the only person able to see it.

Olfactory hallucinations are hallucinated smells, most commonly rotting flesh or something burning. This type of hallucination is rare but important, as it is often the first sign of a brain tumor.

A *misidentification* hallucination is the experience of hearing voices coming from machinery, running water, and other external sounds. Often the voices coming from these places make comments about the person, or gives them information. Misidentifications are quite common, but often go undiagnosed because they are not widely known.

Several years ago I was called to see an elderly gentleman who was living in a nursing home in Long Beach, California. The staff was concerned because he was spending hours each day with his ear pressed to the Pepsi machine. He was hearing the voice of his stock broker coming from the machine. This was not a psychosis, but a classic misidentification hallucination.

Tactile hallucinations involve the imagined experience of being touched, or of having something crawling on the skin. This type of hallucination sometimes occurs during a toxic reaction to amphetamines or other drugs. It also may be a sign of psychosis.

Another common type of hallucination is that of *widowhood* and *bereavement*. People who have recently lost loved ones may see them in the house, hear their voices calling to them, or hear their footsteps in the hall. A great number of people have had vivid dreams of the lost person coming into the bedroom at night to speak to them. It is important to inquire about when such hallucinations are occurring when a resident has suffered a loss, as discussing them can relive a great deal of anxiety.

Often, in order to find out if a person is experiencing hallucinations, you must ask. But Dr. Steven Dubovsky, professor of psychiatry in medicine at the University of Colorado School of Medicine, points out that people are afraid of their hallucinations, are reluctant to admit having them, and often deny having them when asked.

A patient I saw recently, when I asked him if he had ever seen things or heard things, told me "Well, no I don't"

I said, "Well, are there ever any times when you think you might hear someone call your name?"

His answer was, "Well, sure, that happens all the time, isn't that normal?"

I said, "Do you ever hear the phone ringing when it's not?"

He said, "Yeah, but everybody has that happen."

I asked, "Do you ever hear a high pitched sound or a buzzing sound or an odd sound of any kind?"

He said, "Well, sometimes, but that's just a ringing in my ears."

"Does it ever sound like it might be a voice?" I asked.

"Oh, sure, but everyone hears that."

Then I asked him, "Do you ever notice movement out of the corner of your eye and then you look again and there is nothing there?"

"Well sure," he replied.

Does it ever look like anything that you think you might recognize?"

The patient said, "You mean, like a bat?"

I said, "What about a bat?"

He said, "No, I don't see bats."

I said, "Well, what else don't you see?"

He said, "Well, I don't see animals, and I don't see a dog lying in the road."

I said, "Why don't you see these things?"

He said, "Well, If I paid attention to them I'd be crazy."

As mentioned earlier, sensory deprivation can often lead to hallucinations. Residents who do not get enough environmental stimulation sometimes create their own by hallucinating. Helping them to be more socially active can correct this problem.

Chapter Fourteen

Delusions

A *delusion* is a belief with no externally verifiable evidence, not shared by culture or context. As bizarre and beyond reality as these beliefs may be, they are often unshakable to those who hold them.

Symptoms of paranoia, clinically called *delusional disorder*, are common in the elderly. About half of elderly people with delusional disorders have an underlying brain disease, usually a vascular disorder. Other patients may suffer from *late-onset psychosis* which often includes delusions.

As sense organs deteriorate, some elderly people develop a condition called *sensory paranoia*. When this condition is present, impaired hearing may cause people to misinterpret what is said to them, to hear, for instance, an innocent statement as an insult. Impaired vision may cause a person to misinterpret an innocuous movement as a threat, prompting him or her to strike out in perceived self-defense.

There are other causes of delusional disorder. As people age, they may begin to lose their feelings of power and control. A person who has had to accept

– 139 –

Common delusions

Concerns over money
Contest winning
Somatization
Phantom Boarder
Persecution
Theft
Pathologcal jealousy
Hoarding

daily caregiving has relinquished much autonomy, becoming dependent on others for survival. Power turned over to caregivers may be replaced by feelings of helplessness and unimportance. Reacting to these intolerable feelings, some people may begin to manufacture false beliefs. These beliefs center around reactions to their loss of independence. To maintain a sense of importance, the person may come to distrust and devalue his caregivers.

Delusions often begin with misinterpretations of a single incident — a casual comment or an innocuous event taken as a personal attack. As delusions become more fixed, however, the facts of the original incident become so changed and distorted that the original situation is unrecognizable. Soon the incident can develop into elaborate, rigid systems of ideas.

Symptoms of Delusional Disorder

Below are the most common symptoms associated with delusional disorder. A person suffering from a paranoid condition may exhibit some or all of them.

Suspiciousness

In the early stages, people may come to erroneous conclusions that can be corrected. These delusions are called *over-valued ideas*. A person with an over-valued idea may often be dissuaded using reason and logic.

However, as delusions become more solidified, no amount of confrontation or logic is effective. At this stage a person may come to believe that all conversations pertain to him or her, and may believe that people on radio and television programs are talking about or giving him or her secret information. Ordinary events, such as watching others talking and laughing together, are misconstrued as being about the delusional person. The phenomenon of hearing personal content in unrelated information is called *ideas of reference*.

Suspicions may focus on one person, a particular group, or everyone. The paranoid person may actively search for clues, no matter how farfetched, to confirm his or her suspicions, and ignore any evidence to the contrary.

Delusions of persecution

As cognitive functions deteriorate, people develop delusions based on their feelings of vulnerability. These delusions of being harmed or mistreated are called *delusions of persecution.* The most common delusion of this type is the belief that someone is stealing from the person. Sufferers may believe their food is poisoned, that caregivers and family members are conspiring against them, or that their caregivers want to kill them. Other common delusions include being cheated, being spied upon, followed, or harassed by a secret group of people.

As the condition progresses, the person's list of grievances may grow longer and become more complicated, and new people become included in the delusions as enemies. This growing group of conspirators is known as a *paranoid pseudo-community.*

Jealously and possessiveness

Alois Alzheimer's first case, a 51-year-old woman named Auguste D., suffered from cognitive deficits and delusions of jealousy. A person suffering from this delusion becomes convinced that their mate is unfaithful, and seemingly insignificant occurrences are blown out of proportion and used to confirm this belief. The person will unceasingly accuse their mate of cheating, and may harass innocent people believed to be the offending parties.

Paranoid people who accuse their mates of having illicit love affairs frequently tell them that they will stop questioning them if they only will "tell the truth." Because of this, the spouses of paranoid people

Hoarding is seen in:
Schizophrenia
Obsessive-compulsive
    disorder
Anorexia Nervosa
Dementia

80 percent of hoarders
    grow up in a house with
    someone who hoarded.

In psychotic hoarding
    dopamine blocking
    drugs decrease the
    behavior.

Hypochondriasis

Despite numerous reported symptoms, the person does not appear to be suffering significantly.

Hostility is directed outward.

Social interaction is frequently decreased but not dysfunctional.

Insist on discussing their physical ailments to the exclusion of intrapersonal and interpersonal issues.

Frequent episodes of somatic difficulties in mid-life.

Condition tends to be consistent over time.

Do not tolerate the side effects antidepressants.

Suicidal thoughts are rare.

sometimes actually confess to affairs they did not commit, only to discover that accusations escalate rather than diminish.

Grandiosity

A common form of delusion is the *delusion of grandeur.* People with this type of delusion amplifies their own importance — they are no longer mere people, they own the hospital. They may believe they are powerful political figures, or royalty. They may suffer from *paranoid illumination,* in which they believe they have been chosen by God for a special purpose.

Paranoid individuals usually have inflated views of their own abilities, believing they are all powerful or exceedingly brilliant, and deflated views of others. They may believe that everyone else is incompetent, and act toward others in rude and condescending manners. This type of delusion often is seen in dementia and in manic-depressive illness.

Curiously, although many patients have these delusions of grandeur, none of them actually attempts or plans to leave the facility. It seems at least part of them knows they need to be taken care of.

Phantom Boarder Syndrome

Another common delusion often seen in dementia patients and people with vascular problems is the *phantom boarder syndrome,* or the conviction that a stranger is inside the person's room or somewhere in the house. Dr. Sowmya S. Mikkilini and colleagues describe a case of this delusion in the *Annals of Long term Care.*

An 82-year-old woman was brought to the clinic by her family for evaluation of her auditory hallucinations.

Three months prior to her visit, she began to hear noises on the second floor of her house. She believed that a homeless person had begun residing upstairs. She heard him come into the house, usually at night, walk up the stairs, and move objects around. She had never actually seen this person, and they had not spoken.

On a few occasions, she summoned up enough courage to walk upstairs and found everything as she had left it. She had her locks changed twice and called the police on two occasions; the police thoroughly searched the grounds without finding any evidence of the intruder.

Neuropsychological testing revealed significant cognitive deficits, especially in the area of verbal memory, executive functioning, and a depressive reaction congruent with her psychotic experience.

The overall profile was consistent with a dementing process, most likely Alzheimer's disease, although Lewy bodies dementia and vascular dementia were in the differential.

Less common delusions are those of denial. These delusions include denial that the person is ill (*anosagnosia*), and denial that the person is blind (*Anton's syndrome*).

Behavioral Interventions for Paranoid Delusions

As previously mentioned, delusional persons often complain that people are stealing from them, or that their food is poisoned. All complaints should be investigated, then sorted into realistic verses delusional. Realistic complaints need to be dealt with, and the delusional ones modified therapeutically.

1. Learn the person's idiosyncratic food preferences.

    Many paranoid people like their food from sealed cans, because they believe that sealed food could not have been poisoned.

2. Do not talk about the person in their presence or within their earshot. Do not engage in whispered conversations near them.

    Paranoid people think every conversation is part of the conspiracy against them. Take precautions against reinforcing this belief.

3. When taking an object from them, explain why you are taking it and what you are going to do with it.

4. Pay attention to the content of the delusions.

   Determine what environmental, historical, or social factors may be contributing to the present problem.

5. Every time the person complains, have them fill out a complaint sheet.

   This makes them feel someone is recognizing and validating their complaints. It also creates a record of their complaints for reference and resolution. This helps to keep the person reality-oriented, and also discourages them from making too many complaints and having to work to fill out the form.

6. Discuss and encourage healthy activities and attitudes.

   Reinforce any positive behavior, and point out constructive efforts.

7. Do not dispute paranoid delusions.

   People may be talked out of over-valued ideas, but not delusions. If you dispute the delusions, you will be seen as the enemy.

8. When the person begins to talk about paranoid material, remain calm and friendly.

   Do not agree with statements that are false or actions that may be harmful to the person or others. If the person trusts the caregiver, and is not too set in the delusions, a caregiver may be able to express a different view. However, if this results in the person becoming angry, stop immediately. Redirect the conversation to a neutral subject, or refocus the person by through involvement in some activity or interest.

9. Limit the time that spent talking about paranoid complaints.

Convey caring to the person, but emphasize the lack of productivity in endless talk about the complaints.

10. Talk to the person in a clear, straight-forward manner.

Paranoid people are mistrustful and look for hidden meanings. Ask direct questions and offer reasons for requesting certain information.

11. Always keep your word.

Paranoid people are extremely sensitive to dishonesty. Do what you say you are going to do, and you will keep their respect.

12. Avoid surprises and unannounced changes.

Most paranoid people are rigid by nature and need a structured, predictable environment. Surprises, even pleasant ones, may create confusion and hostile behavior.

13. Encourage the person to follow through with treatment.

If the person is upset about some aspect of treatment, suggest that the person discuss it with the doctor or therapist. A paranoid person may respond more favorably to someone perceived as an authority figure.

14. Do not force control. Use persuasion to get the person to do things.

People who need daily care have little control in their lives. They will see forced control as part of a conspiracy to take away their power. If they perceive you are ordering them to do something, they will prepare for battle. Help the person see the practical advantage of what you asking, offering evidence of the benefit that will come from the change. If the person becomes angry or misunderstands the need to change, stop and try again later.

15. Do not tease or make jokes about paranoid people.

People suffering from paranoia have no sense of humor. They view jokes or attempts at humor as demeaning, and will react with hostility.

16.   Do not react to sarcasm, irritability, accusations or blame.

Caregivers should not take accusations personally. Most paranoid people think that their caregivers are stealing from them. Recognize that a paranoid individual's remarks and behaviors are not actually prompted by you, but by their disorder.

17.   Beware of the paranoid who keeps written records of everything, has an enemies list, or stockpiles weapons.

These are the cardinal traits of the type of dangerous paranoid who will kill perceived enemies. This type of person also may have a history of calling the police on neighbors, and filing lawsuits about perceived transgressions.

Chapter Fifteen

Strokes

A *stroke* is the destruction of brain cells caused by an interruption of blood flow to the brain. The number of strokes in the United States has decreased almost 50 percent in the last thirty years, a decrease attributable primarily to advances in the medical control of high blood pressure. Even so, over two million people a year suffer from strokes.

Strokes are the leading source of adult disability, afflicting about 500,000 Americans each year, and the number three cause of death after heart disease and cancer.

Eighty percent of stroke victims survive, often suffering permanent loss of function, such as the ability to speak (called *aphasia*) or paralysis of part of the body. Strokes also are called *cerebral vascular accidents* (CVAs) a misnomer as, to a great degree, they can be predicted and prevented.

Researchers have found that a brain chemical called *calpain* may cause brain cell damage after a stroke. Normally calpain cleans up blocked receptors in neurons and facilitates memory transfer, but too much

Behavioral Objectives

At the end of this section readers will be able to:

Describe the major types of strokes.

Discuss the problems associated with brain damage.

Discriminate between signs of left vs right hemisphere strokes.

Recognize post-stroke depression.

calpain in the system kills neurons. A stroke also is followed by the release of *glutamate*, a chemical that causes brain damage. This phenomenon is called a *glutamate cascade.*

Strokes occur in three major ways. A blood clot that completely clogs an artery and causes a stroke is called a *thrombus*, and the incident is called a *thrombic stroke.* About 80 percent of strokes are of the thrombic type.

When a bit of plaque, the debris that blocks arteries in atherosclerosis, breaks off and clogs a smaller vessel or capillary, it causes what is called an *embolic stroke.* If an artery in the brain bursts, and blood spills into the brain, the incident is called a *hemorrhagic stroke.* This type of stroke usually occurs from a combination of atherosclerosis and high blood pressure, and accounts for about 10 percent of all strokes.

The Arteries

The blood vessels that supply oxygen to the body are called *arteries.* The wall of an artery consists of several layers of smooth muscle. Blood is supplied to the human brain by four major arteries. The two *internal carotid arteries* supply about 85 percent of the total blood flow to the brain, with the *vertebral arteries* supplying the remaining 15 percent. If these vessels become blocked or clogged with plaque, blood flow to the brain is diminished. This condition must be corrected to restore proper brain nourishment.

The Carotid Arteries

The two large *carotid arteries,* one on each side of the neck, supply blood to the cerebral hemispheres. A small branch of each carotid supplies blood to the artery of the eye. If this branch becomes narrowed by atherosclerosis, and part of the plaque breaks off and travels to the brain, the afflicted person may experience a temporary loss of vision to one eye. People who have experienced this, describe it as like having a curtain drawn in front of the eye. Such episodes may occur several times a day.

People over 40, particularly those with diabetes or high blood pressure, should have their carotid arteries checked regularly. If narrowing of the carotid artery has occurred, a murmur (called a *bruit)* can be heard through a stethoscope. More sophisticated testing includes X-rays with the use of dye, and computer analysis. The most recent technique for diagnosing carotid narrowing utilizes sonar.

Blockage of the carotids is serious. If the carotid artery becomes so blocked that blood flow to the brain is impaired, surgery may be required. The procedure, known as an *endarterectomy,* is similar to "roto-rootering" the artery. If the damage to the artery is severe, doctors may replace a portion of it with a vessel from another part of the body, usually the leg. If the blockage is not too severe, aspirin can sometimes be used as a substitute for surgery because it impedes the formation of blood clots. Aspirin, however, may cause other problems, such as internal bleeding, anxiety, and confusion.

Many doctors believe that neurological deficits and cognitive functioning improve after a carotid artery cleaning procedure, because of improved blood flow to areas of the brain which were previously impaired.

The Basilar Artery

At the base of the brain is the *basilar artery.* This artery furnishes the brain stem and the merging cranial nerves with blood.

Atherosclerosis in the basilar artery often causes sufferers to complain of vertigo and nausea. Vertigo is the very unpleasant feeling of uncontrollably spinning around in space, and can be accompanied by vomiting.

Patients with blockage in the basilar artery frequently experience tingling sensations around their mouth, difficulty pronouncing words, and also may have swallowing problems.

When the blood flow through this artery is interrupted, the person may suffer a brief loss of consciousness, or may fall down. Other indications may be loss of equilibrium, staggering, and behavior mimicking drunkenness. Some people with this problem are not able to walk at all.

A severe stroke in this part of the brain results in a condition called *locked in syndrome*, characterized by complete paralysis in the entire body. Often the victims are able to move only their eyes. The devastating consequences of this type of stroke dictate that caregivers should take basilar artery symptoms seriously and seek immediate medical attention.

Many of the symptoms described above can be caused by an inner ear infection, and should not be confused with basilar artery problems. Also, a rare congenital disorder called *Arnold-Chiari's malformation* has been known to cause similar symptoms. Rule out these potential problems before seriously considering basilar artery damage.

Transient Ischemic Attacks

Transient ischemic attacks (TIAs), mimic strokes in their symptoms, but unlike actual strokes, which can cause permanent disability, TIAs, caused by a temporary decrease in the blood flow to different parts of the brain, last only up to 24 hours. There may be a loss of motor ability and thinking capacity, but these symptoms lasts several minutes to a day and then disappear.

The major cause of TIAs is atherosclerosis of the arteries supplying the brain. Other less common causes include episodes of irregular heartbeats, low blood pressure and brain tumors.

If the blood flow to the part of the brain called the hippocampus is blocked during a TIA, memory loss will occur. Repeated episodes of TIAs over time may cause dementia. Other symptoms of TIAs include nausea, dizziness, brief flashes of numbness in the face and arms, or sudden weakness of an arm or leg.

Experiencing a TIA can be a terrifying, but soon after the episode, the person feels fine. Consequently, people often fail to seek help, and may even neglect to tell anyone about the episode. This is unfortunate, because, as the Mayo Clinic reports, one-third of patients with a TIA will suffer a stroke within five years of the first attack. Twenty percent will suffer stroke within one month of the initial attack, and 50 percent within a year.

People experiencing TIAs may have no signs of heart disease but should nonetheless receive a thorough cardiac workup. Many are found to have hardening in the arteries of the heart — in fact, the cause of death in people with TIAs is usually heart attack.

Injections of a clot-dissolving drug called *tissue plasminogen activator* (TPA) has been shown in recent years to dramatically improve the chances of stroke patients recovering with few lasting effects. In a study of 624 stroke patients, victims were randomly assigned to get either TPA or a placebo. After three months, doctors judged the patients' conditions on four scales of stroke symptoms. Depending on the measure used, those receiving TPA were between 30 to 50 percent more likely to have full or nearly complete recoveries.

On the most conservative of these scales, the doctors found that 31 percent of the patients receiving TPA showed no permanent disability, or were left with minor symptoms such as slight weakness in one arm. By comparison, only 20 percent of those in the untreated group were as fortunate.

Symptoms of a right-hemisphere stroke

Left side paralysis or weakness

Impulsive behavior

Difficulty performing daily tasks

Problems with perception

Left side neglect

Problems with visual memory

Incessant talking

Poor judgment

Short attention span

Time disorientation

Loss of the left visual field

Impairment in abstract thinking

Emotional outbursts

Lethargy

To be effective, TPA must be administered within the first three hours of the onset of symptoms. Caregivers must be well-educated in recognizing the symptoms of stroke, so they can quickly make an emergency call when one occurs. Since prompt treatment is essential to recovery, strokes are now considered emergencies by ambulance crews and hospitals. Prior to administering TPA, however, a stroke victim must be given a CAT scan to confirm the stroke is from a blood clot in the brain rather than from a broken blood vessel.

Complicating the situation is the fact that giving TPA too late in the course of a stroke may trigger bleeding in the brain and cause further damage. In a major study in which European doctors gave TPA to patients six hours after stroke symptoms began, the drug increased the risk of death by two-thirds. Even when the drug is used properly, there is a concomittant increase in bleeding in the brain in 6 percent of patients. The study concludes, however, that this hazard is offset by the reduction in symptoms among stroke survivors. When given to the right person at the right time, TPA can prevent lifelong disability.

Behavioral Problems Resulting from Stroke

People with right hemisphere strokes may exhibit a syndrome called *neglect*. They may be completely unaware of things that occur on the left side of their body. In a condition known as *anosagnosia*, sufferers may have lost function in the entire left half of their body and be completely unaware that anything is wrong. Others exhibit a condition called *somatophrenia* and are unable even to recognize their own arm or leg as theirs. If asked them about the arm, they may say, "Yes, I see that arm, but it's not mine." In rare cases, the person may even come to hate the useless limb, and may try to damage it. This condition is known as *misoplegia*.

All of these conditions can be dangerous as well as disconcerting because the afflicted person, being unaware that they are paralyzed, may attempt to stand, walk, or engage in other behaviors that can cause them harm.

Some right-brain stroke victims may exhibit a condition known as *Capgras Syndrome*, characterized by the belief their family members and friends have been replaced with exact duplicates — impostors who involved in some conspiracy, such as a plot to steal the stroke victim's money.

Language is located in the left side of the brain in most people, so people with left hemisphere strokes often lose their ability to speak, a condition called *expressive aphasia*. A person may have lost language function, but, as singing seems to be a right hemisphere task, still be able to sing. Because of this, it is sometimes possible to teach people who cannot speak to sing their requests.

Post -Stroke Depression

It is normal for stroke victims to go through bouts of depression and mourning. For those with permanent losses of function, the losses must be grieved. The treatment for post-stroke depression is the same for any depression and is discussed in chapter seven of this book.

Dementia and Stroke

Evidence exists that stroke victims are at higher risk for dementia, as they have already suffered brain damage. Also, the fact they had the stroke indicates they already suffer from high blood pressure, heart disease, or arteriosclerosis — all of which are contributing factors to dementia.

Symptoms of a left-hemi-sphere stroke

Paralysis or weakness on the right side of the body

Partial or complete loss of understanding language

Partial or complete loss of the ability to speak

Impaired attention

Impaired thought processing

Decreased problem-solving ability

Poor judgment

Poor insight

Impaired voluntary movements

Confusion between left and right

Lack of insight

Loss of the right visual field

Memory problems

Low tolerance for frustration

Impulsive behavior

Slowness

Depression

Section Three

Managing Behavior Problems

Caregiving Activities Rated by the Elderly and their Nurses

Statement	Elders Rank	Nurses Rank
See that the bed pan or urinal are provided when needed	1	11
Relieve my anxiety by explaining reasons for my symptoms	2	23
Notice when I am in pain and give me medications if ordered	3	3
Observe the effects of treatments ordered by the physician	4	5
Give prescribed medications on time	5	17
Carry out doctor's orders	6	10
Help me to assume a comfortable or appropriate position	7	15
Encourage me to take more responsibility for my own care while in the hospital	8	31
Check on bowel functioning and report problems to the doctor	9	12
Make me feel you are happy to care for me	10	25
Take time to listen to me	11	7
Notice changes in my condition and report them	12	1
Provide me with a clean, comfortable bed	13	37
Provide a comfortable, pleasant environment (proper temperature, free from odors and disturbing noises)	14	40
Teach me about the medications that I will be taking at home	15	6
Take my temperature and pulse	16	21
See that my food is served properly	17	41
Give me pamphlets to read and/or talk with me about my illness in order to help me understand how to care for myself	18	28
See that the unit is clean and tidy	19	48
Provide privacy during my bath and treatments	20	16
Be sure that I have necessary equipment – glass, towel, soap, blanket, etc.	21	38
Help me maintain or restore normal elimination	22	9
Take special care of my skin so it does not become sore	23	2
Help me in and out of bed	24	27
Discuss with me the amount and type of activity I should have at home	25	39
Help me understand how to plan the diet I will need at home	26	32
Assist me with meals	27	18
Be understanding when I am irritable and demanding	28	30
Help me get necessary exercise while I am in the hospital	29	35
Be sure I have a copy of my diet	30	43
Arrange for a public health nurse to visit me at home	31	26
Explain about diagnostic tests ahead of time so that I will know what to expect	32	8
Give or assist me with a daily bath	33	42
See that I have food and/or fluids between meals	34	33
Ask the dietician to serve me soft foods that I am able to chew	35	24
Make me comfortable by rubbing my back	36	44
Allow me to make decisions about my care	37	20
Plan my care so that I will be able to rest while in the hospital	38	36
Tell my doctor that I am worried about my condition	39	29
Change my position frequently	40	13
Consider my personal preferences when caring for me	41	22
Take time to talk with my family and answer their questions	42	19
Help me make arrangement for my care at home	43	14
Talk with my family about my illness and the care I will need at home	44	4
Help me with grooming, such as care of my nails, hair, end/or shaving	45	49
Arrange for my priest, minister, or rabbi to visit me	46	45
Assist me with care of my mouth and teeth	47	34
Talk with me about topics unrelated to my illness, such as news, hobbies, other interests	48	47
Make it possible for me to observe my religious practices in the hospital	49	46
Plan some diversion or recreation for me	50	50

Adapted from Hudson & Sexton: Perceptions about Nursing Care Journal of Gerontological Nursing Dec. 1996 22(12):41-46

Chapter Sixteen

Behavior Problems

In 1987, in order to establish higher quality health care standards for the long-term care industry, the federal government implemented sweeping nursing home legislation known as the *Omnibus Budget Reconciliation Act* (OBRA).

The intent of this legislation was to create a legal means to eliminate substandard and poorly-managed facilities, to upgrade marginal facilities, and to bring all facilities into compliance with the newly mandated levels of quality care. In short, the legislation was designed to ensure residents received better treatment.

The new OBRA guidelines, required every care facility to develop a quality assurance plan and quality assurance procedures.

Enforcement of the act consists of frequent observation of the facilities, followed with severe sanctions for non-compliance. By law, failure to meet the standards of quality care may result in every person connected with a facility facing civil and criminal liability.

Behavioral Objectives

At the end of this section readers will be able to:

Understand the purpose of treatment guidelines.

List the common behavioral problems found in older adults.

Name the goals of OBRA guidelines.

Discuss the reasons that behavioral interventions should precede medical interventions.

The new health care standards have been enforced by periodic surveys — a major source of anxiety and frustration to many long term care facility owners who believe the fulfilling of these requirements greatly increases the cost of long-term health care.

In reality, better care means fewer problems, less paperwork, more customer and staff satisfaction, and an improved public image. Taking better care of the people a facility is responsible for has no down-side. Significantly, surveys show that the quality of care has vastly improved since the legislation went into effect.

The OBRA Guidelines are designed to:
1. Minimize environmental stressors, including room noises, facility disarray, staff and room-mate problems.
2. Minimize psychosocial stressors, such as family and loss issues.
3. Eliminate behavioral problems caused by medications and illness.
4. Decrease the use of psychotropic medications, using them only when behavioral interventions have proven unsuccessful.

OBRA requires that a patient who is having problems be assessed, diagnosed, and treated following an interdisciplinary treatment plan. The treatment plan has as its goal to obtain quality care for the full complement of emotional and behavioral problems, and typically begins with behavioral and psychotherapeutic treatment, as well as interpersonal and social intervention.

Within these clearly delineated plans of psychological and behavioral intervention for all emotional and behavioral problems, psychotropic medication is to be used only after all other avenues of intervention have been explored. Medications are deemed appropriate only in cases of major psychosis, Huntington's disease, Tourette's syndrome, for people with dementia who are experiencing psychotic symptoms, and for short term amelioration of problems such as nausea and intractable hiccuping.

Behavioral Problems

Research shows that about three fourths of the people in retirement, assisted living, or long-term care facilities will exhibit problem behaviors at some time. These behaviors can be damaging to the person and to others, may interfere with care, and may upset other residents, the resident's family, and stress the care-giving staff. These problem behaviors add to the already heavy workload of the caregivers.

Many problems in the elderly originate from their perceived lack of caring from the staff and other care-givers. These can arise in part because of differing perceptions about what is important to patients. The table on page 156 displays the results of an interesting and valuable study which showed clearly that care-givers frequently may misunderstand the needs of their clients. I encourage caregivers to read this table carefully.

The elderly present with a multitude of behavioral problems, the most common of which are listed in the margin of this page. In the past, many of these problems were addressed through psychotropic medication, seclusion, and restraints. The problem was that these methods usually didn't work, often doing little more than preventing the resident from engaging in the problem behavior. In addition, many of the medications used for these problems had undesirable side-effects, and some actually made the symptoms worse.

Ongoing research has revealed that a great many of these problems could be more effectively corrected through the use of psychotherapy and environmental or

Abusive behavior
Agitation
Anger
Arguing
Anxiety
Attention Seeking
Biting
Combativeness
Complaining
Crying
Cursing
Difficulty dressing
Eating problems
Entering other's rooms
Fighting
Grabbing
Hallucinations
Hitting
Hopelessness
Impulse control
Isolation
Manipulation
Medication compliance
Memory problems
Moaning
Muttering
Pacing
Paranoia
Psychosis
Resisting care
Rummaging
Screaming
Sleep problems
Spitting
Sexual inappropriateness
Undressing
Unsafe movement
Wandering
Yelling

behavioral intervention. Such findings led to the new guidelines now used for the care of the elderly.

As mentioned earlier, emotional and behavior problems occur in the elderly for the same reasons they occur in any age group — presence of stress and or grief, and lack of coping skills. The major difference in working with the elderly results from the frequent presence of two other major contributing factors, medical problems and cognitive impairment. Once these have been assessed, intervention can proceed.

Chapter Seventeen

Assessment

A comprehensive assessment always should be done before intervention or treatment begins. It is invaluable to begin as soon as possible to identify cognitive, emotional or behavioral problems. Proper assessment and intervention will improve the quality of life of the person and significantly reduce caregiver burden.

If the problems identified are those normally handled by the staff, intervention should begin immediately. If the presenting problems indicate that additional psychiatric or medical assessment is needed, notify the primary care physicians who can order further consultations, lab tests and psychological testing.

Assessments typically begin with a social and medical history. While much of this data might come from the person being assessed, families are often the best resource for this type of historical information. Also, previous physicians and/or previous facilities are often able to provide historical information as well as rationales for previous treatments. Unfortunately, in the

Behavioral Objectives

At the end of this section readers will be able to:

Describe the value of a complete assessment.

List the components of defining the causes of problem behaviors.

Perform a brief cognitive assessment.

Assess higher cognitive functioning.

world of long-term care, there are too many cases in which no medical history is available other than a discharge summary from the last hospitalization.

A significant proportion of psychological and behavioral problems in the elderly are actually caused by undiagnosed medical illness, medication side-effects, interactive effects of multiple medications, or nutritional deficiencies. Establish that the symptoms are not the result of and of these before initiating the assessment.

A comprehensive assessment examines every facet of a persons life, including a

- complete physical exam,
- medical history,
- psycho-social history,
- mental status exam,
- medication review (including all medications and any changes in medications),
- loss history,
- nutrition assessment (including caloric intake, nutritional deficiencies dietary preferences, and all vitamins, minerals and other supplements),
- complete environmental assessment.

Begin assessments only after answering the following questions:

- What is the problem?
- Whose problem is it?
- What could be causing it?
- What can be done?

What Is the Problem?

Identify the problem behaviors. Begin by asking the person what problems he or she is experiencing. The person's own view of problems always takes precedence over the family's and caregiving staff's view.

"For many older adults who have entered the formal service system for help, the reality of their lives — their wishes, beliefs, history, likes and dislikes — is reduced to whatever is revealed by the measurement tools used to assess them."

Taking the Measure of Assessment Scott Miyake Geron

I like to approach this by asking these questions:

a. *What do you like best about this place?* Asking this question first often starts the process on a positive note. It also supplies information that can help solve problems.

   For example, if Mr. Johnson tells you he likes Joanne, the CNA who cares for him, Joanne can be a valuable asset for problem solving. This answer also tells you two important things: Mr. Johnson is saying something positive, and he has established a relationship with another person.

   The inability to make any positive comments often results in a person's being identified by caregivers as a "grumpy old person." More often, however, this negative abruptness is a sign of depression.

b. *What do you dislike the most about this place?* Asking this question likely will result in hearing the person's biggest complaint. Remedy this complaint first, and the person will be much more cooperative when tackling subsequently identified problems.

c. *What other problems are you having?* After addressing the number one problem, continue to identify and record all other problems and frustrations the person is experiencing. Read them back to the person to ensure they have been recorded accurately. Help the person objectively identify each problem. For example, if Mr. Johnson says, "I hate my roommate," ask him, "What does your roommate do that you don't like?" Or, if he says, "The food here is terrible," ask, "What changes would you like to see?"

Observe the person in several settings. Look at the quantity and quality of their social interactions, and record what you see as problem behavior.

Assessment team

Family
Physician
Nurse
Social worker
Psychologist
Audiologist
Dentist
Nutritionist
Occupational therapist
Optometrist
Consulting pharmacist
Physical therapist
Podiatrist
Speech pathologist
CNAs
Clergy

Domains of an assessment:

Socioteonomic status
Personal history
Loss history
Persoanl preferences
Functional status
Environment
Environmenal history
Mental health history
Previous diagnoses
Resolved mental health
    problems
Physical history
Previous diagnoses
Resolved medical problems
Smoking and substance
    use/abuse
Current
History
Medications and supple-
    ments history
Current medications and supplements
Do current medications
    match current
    diagnoses?
Potential side-effects and
    interactive effects
Current diagnoses
Ongoing medical and
    psychiatric conditions
    and treatments
Current symptoms
When symptoms first noted
Change or progression of
    symptoms. Are current
    symptoms related to
    current diagnoses?
    Current health status,
    health promotion and
    disease prevention
    activities, health
    behaviors, exercise,
    nutritional status and
    risks.

Whose problem is it?

Problem behaviors are a matter of perspective. What caregivers may see as a problem may be an enjoyable experience for the person engaging in the behavior. Conversely, the person may see normal staff caregiving behaviors as bothersome and unwanted. Families may be uncomfortable with certain behaviors which are not seen as problematic to caregivers or patient.

Share the recorded list of the person's problems and difficulties with family members and caregivers to determine what they see as problem behaviors. Look for a connection between the resident's problems and the caregivers' problems.

When Mrs. Johnson was asked what she disliked most, she promptly replied, "I'll tell you what I don't like! I need help getting out of bed to go to the bathroom, but the staff doesn't respond to the call light when I press it. Sometimes I press that button five or six times, and no one comes.

Eventually I wet the bed. This is stupid. It takes the staff three times longer to change my clothes and put new sheets on my bed than it would take to just answer the call light."

I asked the staff why they didn't always respond to Mrs' Johnson's call light, and they replied, "She rings that light about thirty times a day. If we answered it every time, we wouldn't have time to do anything else."

After pondering this dilemma for several minutes, I came up with a possible solution. Mrs. Johnson was angry with the staff, and the staff was angry with her. I talked to the administrator about moving her from station one to station three. She said this could be done. We found a resident on station three who had a good relationship with Mrs. Johnson, and then asked Mrs Johnson if she would like to move in with her.

After the move the call light problem promptly disappeared. The problem was long-standing anger between Mrs. Johnson and the staff at station one. Each blamed the other for being difficult. The staff at station three were not angry at Mrs. Johnson, and answered her call light immediately. Once the emotional climate was changed, the problem disappeared.

What could be causing the problem?

Look for any medical conditions or medications that could be causing the problem. Without a thorough screening for these conditions, all behavioral intervention will be ineffective. Common medical problems include anemias, thyroid and parathyroid problems and infections.

a. *Clearly define each target behavior.* Each problem must be defined in terms of person, place and situation.

b. *Observe the behavior over time.* If the behavior is not dangerous, observe it for several days, and record when, where, and how often it occurs. All behaviors occur in a particular environment, and most problem behaviors occur at specific times of day. Note any recent environmental changes such as

A recent room change

A change in roommates

A change in the room (painting, furnishings, lighting, etc)

A change in staff or caregivers

A change in daily routines

What was happening right before the problem began?

Can the behavior be tied to any external trigger?

c. Identify the causes or antecedents to the behavior. Is there any medical condition that could cause this behavior? Has there been a change in medication or treatment? Could it be a medication problem?

For suspect medication problems, refer to a consulting pharmacist. Consulting pharmacists

Assessment of Activities of Daily Living (ADL)

- Bathing
- Eating
- Dressing
- Combing hair
- Brushing teeth
- Urinating
- Defecating
- Speaking
- Writing
- Seeing
- Typing
- Hearing
- Grasping
- Lifting
- Tactile discrimination
- Climbing stairs
- Walking
- Sitting
- Standing
- Lying down
- Driving
- Flying
- Riding
- Sexual function
- Participation in usual sexual activity

Environmental Changes:
• Room change
• New roommate
• Remodeling
• Furniture moved or replaced

Recent Social Changes.
• Family visits
• Personal loss
• Activity schedule

Signs of Depression.
• Sadness
• Crying
• Anxiety
• Irritability
• Apathy
• Feelings of worthlessness
• Withdrawn
• Physical complaints

specialize in the side-effects and interactive effects of medications and medication-related problems. A good source for locating a geriatric consulting pharmacist, is www.seniorcarepharmacy.com.

d. *Log the consequences of the behavior.* What happens after the behavior occurs? How is the patient being rewarded for the behavior?

e. *Assess the person's level of cognitive functioning.* What portion of the behavior could be caused by dementia, the result of a pre-existing personality trait? What portion could be responsive to psychotherapy or behavior management?

What Can Be Done?

a. *Is the person aware of the behavior?* Determine if the person is aware that he or she is engaging in a problem behavior.

b. *Assess the meaning of the behavior.* Does the person engage in the behavior for a specific reason, and is he or she able to explain the reason?

c. *Is the behavior reality based?* Ask the person why he or she is doing the behavior. Behaviors based on delusions or psychosis are handled differently than reality-based behavior.

Mental Status Exam

The mental status examination is a global assessment of a person's level of functioning that will allow the matching of proposed interventions to a person's ability. Most mental status exams include evaluation of orientation, thinking, memory, judgment, and insight.

Appearance and Level of Functioning:

The first step is to get a picture of the person's overall appearance. Observe the following:

1. Is there any evidence of visual or hearing impairment?

    Establishing the person's ability to see, hear, and respond to external stimuli will help determine the person's ability to respond to the rest of the assessment.

2. Is the person clean and neat, or sloppy in appearance?

    Poor hygiene can be a sign of apathy, dementia, depression, or psychosis.

3. Does the person appear older than his or her stated age? Physical deterioration often accompanies mental deterioration. Substance abuse, smoking, and hyperthyroidism may cause a person to look older than expected.

4. Is the person able to sit still? Restlessness can be a sign of thyroid dysfunction, dementia, anxiety, or mania, but it can also be caused by medications.

5. Does the person exhibit any involuntary movements? Unusual or involuntary movements may indicate an unwanted response to antipsychotic medications, usually in the form of a condition known as *tardive dyskinesia*. This neurological condition results in unwanted limb movements, lip smacking, and Parkinsonian-like symptoms. Antidepressants may cause *akathisia*, a sense of inner restlessness that makes it impossible for the affected person to sit still.

6. Is there any evidence of paralysis or other restriction of movement? Paralysis most often is caused by stroke, and may be accompanied by depression or cognitive problems.

7. Are there any abnormalities of speech? Loss of articulation — slurring of speech or inability to

pronounce words — usually indicates loss of brain function. Pressured speech, a rapid unending stream of talking, is indicative of mania. Tangential speech, in which ideas ramble and focus is missing, is a sign of psychosis. Profanity, yelling, and verbal abuse are often signs of dementia. Difficulties with word finding can be a sign of fronto-temporal dementia, which also can be responsible for personality changes.

Orientation:

Establish the person's awareness of the environment by asking:

1. Were are we?
2. What year is this?
3. What state are we in?
4. What is today's date?
5. Where have you been for the past twenty four hours, and what did you do there.

Asking "Can you tell me where you are?" will provide two important pieces of information. First, if the person does not know where he or she is, check for further evidence of disorientation. Second, if the answer to this question is merely, "Yes," check for dementia, as people with cognitive impairment often answer questions very concretely.

Personal Information:

Asking the following questions will provide information about the person's history, level of education, and remote memory function.

1. What year were you born?
2. Where were you born?
3. How old are you?
4. How much schooling do you have?
5. What did you do for a living?
6. How many children do you have?

An inability to precisely answer these types of questions indicates a profound loss of intellectual ability.

General Information:

Ask the following questions to ascertain the person's general fund of knowledge and remote memory function:
1. Who is the president of the United States?
2. Who was president before him?
3. How many states are there?
4. Where to you keep your money?
5. Please count backwards from 30 to 1.

Speech and Language:

This segment of the assessment evaluates the speech centers of the brain.
1. Have the person say, "No ifs, ands, or buts." People who cannot pronounce this sentence correctly may have brain damage to the speech centers of the brain.
2. Have the person write a sentence and read it aloud. This provides information as to how well the person can construct a thought, how well he or she can read and write, and whether any motor problems are present. The contents of the sentence is also of value, as it provides inside into the person's thoughts and concerns.
3. Name three objects such as a pen, a watch, and a ring, and ask the person to repeat the names back without pausing. Inability to name common objects is a strong sign of dementia.
4. Ask the person to name ten cities, colors, fruits and animals. Inability to do this is indicative of dementia. People who cannot do this will often confabulate.

The best answer I ever received to the request to name ten animals was, "A crane and nine loons." Another woman told me, "Sarah Johnson." When I said I thought Sarah Johnson didn't count as an animal, she told me, "Oh yeah? I guess you don't know her."

5.   Ask the subject to spell the word "world" backwards. People with even minimal brain problems usually cannot do this because it requires the use of higher brain functions in the language hemisphere that are easily disrupted.

Motor Functions:

1.   Ask the person to put his or her right hand on his or her left ear. People with severe abnormalities in the language center of the brain often cannot accomplish crossover tasks. Deep lesions in the midbrain structures can produce a similar syndrome.

2.   Ask the person to complete simple tasks, such as hair-combing or shoe-tying. Inability to accomplish these simple tasks likely indicates the presence of apraxia, which is the inability to perform meaningful skilled movements, and may involve abnormalities of both language and motor parts of the brain.

Higher Brain Functions:

To test the function of the frontal lobe, the part of the brain controlling executive functions, give the following test of hand movements.

1.   Ask the person to make a fist with one hand and use it to strike a table or armrest.

2.   Ask the person to open one hand, and then hit the table or armrest with the open palm of the other hand.

3.   Ask the person to alternate between using the fist with one hand and the palm with the other ten times in rapid succession.

4. Ask the person to reverse the hands. Try this twice. If the person fails at both tries, cognitive impairment may be present.
5. Ask the person to subtract 7 from 100.
6. Ask, "What is 12 times 13?" To correctly answer this problem, the person must be able to manipulate numbers in his or her mind.

Proverb Interpretation:

Ask the person the meaning of "A rolling stone gathers no moss," and "People who live in glass houses shouldn't throw stones." People in the beginning stages of cognitive impairment often will interpret the proverbs literally, as in, "If you throw stones at a glass house, you'll break the glass." (Be aware that proverbs are culture-bound, and people who did not grow up in the United States may not understand them for cultural rather than cognitive reasons.)

Clock Test:

Have the person draw the face of a clock, and put the hands on ten-minutes-after-eleven. Assess the person's ability to comprehend and execute this task. All the numbers drawn on one side, for example, may indicate neglect. The inability to put the hands in the proper place suggests mental impairment.

Figure Drawing:

1. Have the person copy or reproduce drawings of increasing complexity. For example, give the person a sheet of paper that has drawings of simple shapes on the left side and ask them to copy the shapes on the right side of the page. Evaluate the person's drawings for accuracy.
2. Ask the subject to draw a three dimensional picture of a house. (Be aware that artists, architects, and others who may draw for a living may do well on these tests even if they are mentally impaired)

Long Term Memory:

Tell the person three unrelated words and ask him or her to repeat the words, in their exact order, immediately, and after four minutes. During the four-minute interval, have the person do a few math problems. People with normal memory function usually are able to repeat back three out of the three words. Two out of three is acceptable. Inability to recall the words indicates processing and memory problems.

Insight:

The data gathered thus far should provide a good assessment of the person's thought processes and memory function. Evaluating insight goes a bit further.

Ask the person, "Do you have any problems with memory or thinking?" If their answer does not fit the assessment, the person has impaired insight. People with moderate memory problems will usually be aware that they are having trouble, while people with severe problems will usually insist their memory is fine.

Judgment:

Ask the person. "If you broke a friend's favorite vase, what would you do to prevent the person from becoming angry?" The answer will provide information about the person's sense of judgment and coping skills.

Social Appropriateness:

Ask the person what behaviors are appropriate for certain social situations. For example, ask, "What would you do if you saw a person drop their wallet?" A person who cannot give a socially-appropriate answer to this type of question displays impaired judgment.

The information gathered from this complete assessment will help determine if psychotherapy or behavioral intervention are likely sufficient to solve the presenting problems.

The Mini Mental State Exam was developed in 1975 by Marshal and Susan Folestein and Paul McHugh. It is a brief test of mental status and cognition function. The authors of the instrument were very clear that it cannot replace a complete clinical assessment, and should never be used to make a diagnosis.

A shortcoming of the exam is that, although it is designed to give a snapshot of a person's mental status, it is often used to show cognitive decline. It is impossible to show cognitive decline in a person unless you have earlier data showing their previous mental status.

For example, some people have always had problems with memory and cognition, and a low MMSE score is an indicator of their normal mental status. Conversely, people with above average mental abilities may score high on this test, even though their mental status is declining.

As the MMSE has become more popular, clinicians realized that factors such as premorbid condition, age, and education have an impact on the test scores. For this reason an age and education correction grid was created to correct the scores which resulted in a more valid score. However, the grid is seldom used in the clinical setting today, and therefore scores may not accurately reflect the person's cognitive state.

On the next page is an example of the correction grid:

Mini Mental Status Cutoff
score corrections for age and education

Age	Education			
	4th grade	8th grade	High School	College
18-24	23	27	29	29
25-29	25	27	29	29
30-34	25	26	29	29
35-39	23	26	28	29
40-44	23	27	28	29
45-49	23	26	28	29
50-54	23	27	28	29
55-59	22	26	28	29
60-64	23	26	28	29
65-69	22	26	28	29
70-74	22	25	27	28
75-79	21	25	27	28
80-84	20	25	25	27
>84	19	23	26	27

Chapter Eighteen

Interventions

Assessment is useless unless there exists consistent communication and documentation among all members of the care giving staff regarding the evaluations and findings. Document and disseminate the behavioral assessment once completed, and move immediately to the formulation of an intervention plan.

Although the intervention techniques in this book have proven to be effective, every person is different, and what works for one may not work for another. Also, what works at one time of day may be ineffective at another time. Finally, as some people may deteriorate over time, what once worked eventually may become ineffective.

The Intervention Plan

Begin with one of the identified problem behaviors, and formulate goals for its modification.

1. List the probable and possible causes of the problem behavior.

Historical Events

1904 Teddy Roosevelt
  elected
1905
1906
1907
1908 Ford builds Model T
1909 Taft elected
1910
1911
1912
1913 Woodrow Wilson
  elected
1914 World War I begins
1916
1917
1918 World War I ends
1919 Prohibition begins
1920
1921 Harding elected
1922
1923 Coolidge elected
1924
1925
1926
1927
1928 Herbert Hoover
  elected

2. Assess what potential goals are within the person's ability to attain.
3. Describe the specific interventions to be used.
4. Define treatment goals and time limits for the intervention plan.
5. All staff on all shifts must be aware of and involved in the treatment plan. Notify them in writing, and follow up verbally.
6. Implement the plan for the stated time period, and assess the results.
    • If current treatment goals have been met, set new goals that approach the criteria for termination of treatment.
    • If the treatment goals have not been met, assess the reasons.
    Has the treatment team carried out the plan in a consistent and conscientious manner? Are the goals within the resident's current capacity or must they be modified? (if yes, return to step two.)
7. When treatment goals are achieved, the intervention is complete.

Elements of Intervention

All behavioral interventions should contain the following elements:

- *Acknowledgment:* Tell the person that you recognize he or she is having a problem. One of the most common complaints of elderly people is that their problems are discounted or ignored.
- *Validation:* Confirm the person's right to feel as he or she does, whether or not these feeling are reality-based. If the person is delusional, agree with the delusional statement, and attempt redirection.
- *Problem-solving:* Assist the person in identifying some solutions to the stated problem. Document all attempts at problem-solving, so the person has a

record of what has been done, and others will not waste time trying what has not worked.

- *Reinforcement*: Reward any behavior that resembles or approaches the goal.
- *Consequences:* Inform the person of the logical consequences of unwanted behavior, and ensure there are no rewards for such behavior.

Know the Person

To accomplish effective interventions, you must get to know the person with whom you are working. Before you begin, obtain the person's medical history. If the person is in a hospital or skilled nursing facility, review the chart thoroughly. Ask caregivers and staff members what they know about the person. If possible, talk to the family members, and gather as much background information as you can.

Ask about the person's education, job, hobbies, religion, political affiliation, likes and dislikes. Ask about their personality, their temperament, their pet peeves, their skills and their shortcomings. Become as familiar with them as possible before attempting the implement any behavioral intervention. Match interventions with the person's level of functioning.

Acknowledge Age Differences

The tendency to group elderly people into the general category of "old" is so prevalent, caregivers often fail to make generational distinctions among older adults. It is easy to see that a twenty-year-old is from a different generation from a forty-year-old, but a sixty-year-old is frequently not differentiated from an eighty-year-old. An eighty-year-old is, in fact, from a different generation than a sixty-year-old, and these substantial differences must be acknowledged.

Historical Events

1929
1930
1931
1932 Roosevelt elected
1933
1934
1935
1936
1937 Chinese Resist Japanese
1938
1939
1940
1941 Pearl Harbor attacked
1942 Manila captured by Japan
1943
1944
1945 Japan Surrenders Truman elected
1946 Philippine Independence
1949 China Occupied
1950 Korean war begins
1951
1952 Immigration and Naturalization Act of 1952 is signed
1953 Korean war ends Eisenhower elected
1954
1955 Advent of TV
1956
1957 Desegregation at Little Rock
1958
1959 Explorer I, the first U.S. satellite, successfully orbits the earth
1960

Steps to behavioral intervention

1. Get a thorough history
2. Assess & rule out medical problems
3. Assess & rule out medication problems
4. Assess cognitive functioning
5. Identify problem behaviors log:
   • frequency
   • severity
   • antecedents
   • consequences
6. Formulate intervention plan
7. Implement plan
   • change antecedents
   • change consequences
   • educate
   • psychotherapy
8. Assess effectiveness of intervention
   If not successful:
   • re-assess goals
   • re-assess capacity to respond to goals

If successful, terminate intervention.

To gain a clear perspective of the person with whom you are working, it is helpful to look at the year the person was born. A person born in 1900 will have had a much different life experience than someone born in 1930.

Consider what year it was when the person graduated from high school, and entered the world of work. Things were immensely different for a worker in 1920 than they were in 1950. Post-war America was economically and socially a different place than it was prewar. The culture, values, beliefs and preferences of each generation are unique, and must be considered in caregiver communications, evaluations, and plan development.

Approach

How you approach a person is the most important factor in determining how the person will respond to you. People with dementia, often have severe cognitive deficits, but are still quite able to recognize and react to emotions. Hence, they will respond to your emotional tone even if they cannot understand what you are saying. When you display impatience and irritation, those feelings will be imparted to the resident, and he or she will respond in kind.

Approach a person slowly, from the front, and with a positive, friendly attitude. Don't take negative responses personally, and don't over-react to unusual behavior. Be responsive, not reactive.

Ask the person how they wish to be addressed. Some people prefer to be formerly addressed. Researcher Barbara Wilson illustrates why this can be important.

C.W. was a patient who became densely amnesic in 1985. The staff members are always seen by him as strangers, no matter how long they have cared for him.

A formal greeting was less unnerving to him than demonstrable affection from people he perceived as strangers.

Verbal Instruction

People with hearing problems or dementia often have difficulty understanding and comprehending what is said to them. Dementia may prevent them from understanding words, or recognizing common objects and people. They may also have a difficult time separating reality from delusion.

1. Always use a calm, soothing voice and gentle touch.

2. Identify yourself by name, role and function. For example, "Hello, Mrs. Stevens. My name is Dr. Matteson. I'm here to help you with any problems you are having."

3. Speak slowly and clearly, and give the person ample time to respond. Older people may need a longer period of time to comprehend and respond to what is being said.

4. Use simple language, concrete terms, and concepts that the person can understand.

5. Use positives, not negatives. Tell the person what you want them to do, not what you don't want them to do. Avoid negative commands like, "Don't do that," which infantalizes people and may provoke anger.

6. Match your tone of voice, posture, and demeanor to what you are saying. People understand messages more clearly if your actions correspond with what you are saying.

7. Do not offer choices or ask questions when it's not necessary. For example, say, "It's time to go to dinner," not, "Would you like to eat now?"

8. Help a person complete a thought or sentence when it is apparent that they are stuck.

9. Respond to the person's emotions, and do not attempt to correct misperceptions. It seldom is helpful to point out to patients they are deluded. If they have memory problems, they will soon forget anything they are told. If they do not, they will include you in the delusion and come to see you as an enemy. A better tactic is to validate the person's feelings, and not worry about the reality of what is being said. For example, if they tell you, "I'm the Captain here," say something like, "That must make you feel important," rather than, "You're not the Captain."

Non-Verbal Interventions

When helping a person master a new task, consider the non-verbal component of the intervention by using the following steps.

1. Stand directly in the person's line of sight, assuming an equal or lower stance.
2. Make eye contact.
3. Move slowly, as quick movements may scare some people.
4. Break down all tasks into simple steps.
5. Implement the beginning of each task by showing the person how to begin. Give behavioral cues, such as putting a hair brush in the resident's hand and beginning to brush. The person's motor program should then take over the task. If the tasks are too difficult, however, the person may become agitated and resistant. If so, re-assess the person's abilities.
6. Provide opportunities for the person to succeed at tasks. The primary goal of all activity is to build confidence and self esteem. Reward and reinforce any success.
7. Do not do things for a person simply to save time. While tempting because of a busy

schedule, doing this infantalizes the person, and will lead to more demands for caregiving.

8.   Do not rush a or pressure a person to complete a task. Instead, observe how long it takes him or her to do something, record this information, and plan to allow ample time for completing the task in the resident's schedule.

9.   Give the person as much control of his or her life as possible. Assist, guide and educate, but do not dominate.

10.   Limit distractions in the environment. When teaching a skill, turn off televisions and radios. Close the door. Give instructions to other staff not to interrupt.

11.   Use distractions to refocus and redirect the person during any caregiving task that may increase unwanted behavior.

12.   Do not force a person to do anything against his or her will. Leave the area and return to try again later. When you return, explain once more what you are going to do.

13.   Anticipate the person's needs based on your knowledge of her or him. Take the time to learn the person's schedule, needs, and personal preferences, and you will greatly increase cooperation.

Chapter Nineteen

Specific Behavior Problems

Catastrophic Reaction

A *catastrophic reaction* is an uncontrolled emotional outburst, a response to feelings of overwhelming helplessness. Catastrophic reactions include crying, yelling, outbursts of anger, flailing arms and legs, and hitting.

Brain-injured people (particularly with left frontal hemisphere damage) often respond to cognitively demanding questions or tasks with catastrophic reactions. Sixteen percent of people with dementia exhibit this behavior, and it's also frequent in acute stroke, particularly after subarachnoid hemorrhages and cerebral infarcts. Catastrophic reactions also are also strongly related to post-stroke depression.

In most instances of this behavior, the person will be unaware of why they are becoming agitated, possibly because of disconnection syndromes or implicit memory problems. This is most common in patients with aphasia.

Behavioral Objectives

At the end of this section readers will be able to:

List common behavior problems.

Diccuss the causes of these problems.

Assess the antecedents of these problems.

Intervene to correct or decrease the incidence of the problems.

Causes of Catastrophic Reactions

Organic variables
Brain damage
(especially in the amygdala, temporal lobes, hypothalamus and frontal lobes)
Neurotransmitter dysfunction (decreased serotonin levels in the brain)

Psychological variables
Encountering a new environment
Realization that one is forgetful or ill
Reduced ability to communicate
Acting out psychotic distress
Accentuation of premorbid personality traits
Problematic relationship to caregiver in the past

Environmental variables
Unidentified noise
Inadequate lighting
Moving to unfamiliar places
Adversarial patient management style

Catastrophic reactions occur most often in the morning, when care activity is the highest, and when caregivers are most pressured to stay on schedule and complete their activities. Getting ready for the day consists of a complex set of behaviors, and can be taxing for both the caregiver and the person being assisted. The physical contact and intrusiveness of grooming or getting dressed may be unwanted and unpleasant. The best way to avoid these reactions is to work within the person's capacity to cope with stimulation.

When catastrophic reactions do occur:

1. Respond to them; do not react to them. If you see a person becoming upset by your activity, stop what you are doing. If the person attempts to hit you, realize the behavior is not directed at you, but occurs because the person is frightened and is acting in perceived self-defense. When responding to an outburst such as this, ask yourself, "What's my goal?" not, "Omigod, what do I do now?" Do not yell at the person something like, "What's the matter with you? I'm only trying to do my job!" Remember, the goal is to help the person calm down.

2. Allow the caregiver with the best relationship with the resident to respond to the reaction. Rapport with a recognized caregiver can do a lot to calm a person down.

3. Approach the person calmly and speak softly.

4. Do not attempt to talk the person out of the reaction.

5. If appropriate, use touch to establish contact.

6. Give reassurance.

7. Refocus the person with an object or another topic.

8. If necessary, guide the person to a quiet place for a time out.

9.   Do not call attention to the behavior.

10.   If all else fails, leave the room and return later.

Resisting Care

Patients who resist care cause problems throughout their environment, upsetting both caregivers and other residents alike. When a person consistently resists care, schedules are disrupted, and tempers may flare. Caregivers become frustrated when their efforts to be helpful are rebuffed.

Studies show that people are most likely to resist care when they are approached by more than two people at a time. Resistance to care also occurs when caregiving activities are too rapid or rough, or when the caregiving is undertaken according to caregivers needs, rather than those of the residents.

Some people resist care because they fear being hurt, or they may resent the fact that they can no longer care for themselves and project those feelings of resentment at the caregiver. Much like a young child, whose greatest power is to be disruptive, an elderly person may see the refusal to accept care as the only power he or she retains.

People with dementia may resist care because they no longer comprehend the meaning of daily activities like bathing or taking medication.

Resisting care, refusing to eat, and refusing to take needed medication also may be signs of *silent suicide,* an unstated attempt to end one's life. This resistance is called *indirect self-destructive behavior* (ISDB).

Behavior Interventions for Resisting Care

1.   Identify one staff member to establish rapport and be the primary caregiver.

2.   Avoid situations that are antecedents to resistant behavior.

Types of Resisting Care

Noncompliant Eating
eating foreign objects or materials
refusing to eat
choking due to bolting food down
eating foods not permitted on diet
eating excessively

Noncompliant Drinking
the use of alcohol
refusing to drink liquids
drinking toxic liquid (shaving lotion, etc.)
excessive intake of liquids
drinking liquids not permitted on diet
not drinking liquids on one's own

Noncompliant Smoking
smoking excessively
careless use of cigarettes
careless use of matches
smoking against medical advice
smoking in unauthorized places

Abuse of Medication
refusing medications
hiding when medications are given out
hoarding medications
overdosing
taking unauthorized medications
using illicit drugs

The most common fears about bathing

Being naked in front of strangers

Being lifted into the tub

Getting in and out of tub

Noises that the tub makes

Water in the tub

The tub itself

Mechanical devices on the tub

3. Distract the person when engaging in a behavior that has caused resistance in the past.
4. Allow the person as much autonomy as possible.
5. Put something in the person's hands to occupy them.
6. Assess them for depression and suicidal ideation.

Bathing Problems

As a child, I was taught to take a bath each night before bed. After the bath, I was often rewarded with hot chocolate and a story. This was always a special time of day for me. For many of us, bathing is still one of life's special pleasures.

Unfortunately, this is not true for many elderly people who need help with bathing. What might have been a pleasure in the past is now fraught with issues of privacy, independence, and personal space.

Bathing an elderly person can be a time-consuming and difficult task. In fact, researchers Philip Sloane and Laura Mathew found that bathing elderly people required more time and more supervision than any other activity of daily living. Professional care-givers report that the amount of time spent bathing patients equals or surpasses the amount of time spent on any other job assignment.

Some residents, interpreting bath time as a time during which they are stripped naked in order to be harmed become agitated and fearful.

Keeping in mind that elderly people need not bathe every day — as frequent bathing can dry and crack aged skin — do the following.

1. Ask family members about the person's bathing habits, preferences (such as baths or showers), and usual time of bathing. If at all possible, develop a bathing schedule that resembles the person's preferences.
2. Give baths only when necessary. Ensure bathing

frequency is within the care guidelines of your state, but don't over bathe a person.

3. Be cognizant of the person's self-consciousness about nudity and need for dignity. Allow them as much privacy as possible. Use same sex caregivers whenever possible. Research on bathing shows that patients become most resistant when stripped of their clothing, seated on a cold, metal, mechanical chair, and restrained with a safety belt

4. Do not ask the person to undress until they are in the bathroom.

5. Ensure the room temperature and the water temperature are comfortable to the person, not to you.

6. If the person is demented, gradually introduce them to the idea of bathing. Many problems associated with bathing result from a lack of understanding by caregivers of the behavior of people with cognitive impairment and dementia. The bathing task goes better if — rather than perceiving bathing as a single activity — it's seen as a series of independent steps, each requiring specific instructions and attention to each exhibited behavior as it occurs. For example:

   Take the person into the bathroom just to hear and see the running water.

   Allow the person to undress.

   Help the person into the tub or shower.

   Give the person a washcloth and let him or her begin to wash. This engages motor programs that do not involve working memory.

7. Do not get in arguments about bathing. Proceed slowly, step-by-step. If the person resists, don't argue — try again later. Negative experiences during bathing have an undesirable effect on the relationship between the patient and caregiver, which can last throughout the day. Repeated

Common behavioral problems during bathing

Resisting care

Yelling or screaming

Restlessness

Verbal aggression

Talking to self

Physical aggression

Catastrophic reaction

Throwing things

Factors affecting taste and smell

Alzheimer's disease

Parkinson's disease

Renal failure

Upper respiratory infection

Smoking

Bronchial asthma

Diabetes mellitus

Certain medications (antide-
    pressants, valium)

Zinc and niacin deficiency

Vitamin B12 deficiency

negative bathing experiences can result in permanently alienating the caregiver from the patient.

8. Take personal items such as favorite soaps, bath oils, towels, and wash cloths into the bathroom to make the surroundings more familiar and inviting. People experience discomfort entering a room that does not resemble a bathroom or a home-like bathing area.

9. Shampoo the person's hair last, to minimize the chance for soap to get in the eyes, and to avoid discomfort from dripping hair.

10. When all else fails, use sponge-baths. the goal, after all, is to keep the person clean, not to get them to obey you.

Eating Problems

Lost in uncongenial surroundings, fed on unfamiliar food, they sickened, became inefficient, and were then allowed to crawl away and rest.
    – Joseph Conrad, *Heart of Darkness*

People have eating problems for a variety of reasons. Nearly half of all people between the ages of 75 and 80 have lost much or all of their sense of smell, and consequently, their flavor and odor perceptions are diminished. This decline in the smell and taste senses is a normal result of aging, but can it can also be made worse by disease, dementia and medication side-effects. When a person is having problems with food intake, taste and smell should be assessed.

Dietary analysis of people with taste and smell problems show that their food intake differs significantly from those without such problems. For example, those with sensory deficits had a lowered preference for strongly sour or bitter foods, and ate fewer vegetables and citrus fruits.

Researchers also have found that women with reduced functioning of the senses of taste and smell eat more saturated fat, while men, who have less acute senses of taste and smell than women throughout their lives, may respond differently to the age-related decline.

Some people do not eat well because they have difficulty chewing and swallowing food, as a result of dental problems or neurological damage. Still others may have no appetite because they are depressed.

Furthermore, there is evidence that dementia may actually damage the parts of the brain that regulate hunger, rendering the person unable to feel the need to eat. People with advanced dementia may no longer be able to comprehend the complex task of eating.

Although all of these factors affect appetite or cause eating problems, the most common reason for people refusing to eat is simply because they do not like the food — either because they have certain food preferences that are not being considered, or because the quality of the food is bad.

Complaints about food is one of the most common grievances regularly heard from long-term care residents, not surprising considering the resident's situation. Imagine no longer being able to enjoy any of your favorite foods. Every day of your life, three times a day, you are served something you didn't ask for and don't like. It's understanding that food is at the root of many problems that exist in a long term care facility.

Eating is an important part of life, and being served consistently poor food can lead to a great deal of unhappiness and disruptive behavior. Fortunately, this is a relatively easy problem to correct, and usually well worth the effort. Even something as simple as giving residents two options at a particular meal can greatly increase satisfaction.

Taste and aging

Taste buds decrease from 345 per papilla at 20 years old to 88 at 80 years.

Loss of taste and smell decreases appetite and increases poisoning risk.

Sweet is the taste that stays the longest.

Flavor enhancement increases eating.

Behavioral Interventions for Eating Problems

1. Experiment with various food textures. Deficits in smell and taste may leave texture as the only enjoyable part of eating.

2. Enhance the flavor of the food. Adding flavor to food can improve food intake. A group of elderly men and women living in a retirement home ate more food and improved their immune function when several foods at each meal were enhanced with either meat, cheese or maple flavoring.

   Bacon flavor also increases food consumption, especially when added to vegetables. Fruit flavors and sauces increase the consumption of chicken and pork. The ability to detect the aroma of cooked carrots falls dramatically in the aged, and concentrated carrot essence increases the amount of carrots they will eat.

   Butter flavoring and extracts such as almond and lemon aid in food consumption also. Twice the amount of extract called for in a given recipe enhances flavor for the aged palate. Herbs and spices are better if doubled as well. Lifting the cover from the food just before the person begins to eat releases concentrated food aromas and increases the appetite.

3. Be aware of the resident's cultural and ethnic food preferences, and honor them as much as possible.

4. Learn about the resident's prior eating habits and food preferences. Ask the person or family members about idiosyncratic eating habits. Not everyone eats three meals a day.

5. Minimize all noises and other stimuli that distract the residents from focusing on eating.

6. To minimize confusion, limit the number of foods served at one time, and the number of utensils present.

7. Stroke the resident's arm gently while he or she

is eating, Several studies show that this simple intervention increases food intake in people with dementia.

8. Assess poor eaters for paranoia. Paranoid people often refuse to eat because they think their food is being poisoned. Giving them canned food sometimes helps, as they think it is less likely to have been tampered with.

9. Sometimes it is necessary to feed the person.

Sleep Problems

As people age, the quality and quantity of sleep decreases. Sleep problems in the elderly include problems falling asleep, problems staying asleep, and early morning awakening.

The most common reasons for sleep problems in the elderly are too much napping, pain, and the need to go to the bathroom. Older people who wake up during the night are at high risk for injury. Sleep problems are disruptive to caregivers and other residents.

Behavioral Interventions for Sleep Problems

1. Become aware of the resident's sleep habits and sleep difficulties.

2. Ask the resident and family members to describe the resident's sleep habits.

3. Establish a regimented bedtime, and bedtime routine.

4. When a person awakens during the night, re-orient them to time and place, and calm them. A gentle touch and soothing voice are effective methods of calming.

5. When a person repeatedly gets out of bed and disturbs others, guide the person to a place where disturbance is minimized.

6. When a resident is not able to return to sleep, place the person near the nurse's station and give

Fall prevention checklist

Gather data from all sources – the resident, family, all nursing shifts, and other staff.

Occurence
Is there a pattern to the resident's falls?
Same time of day
Same place
Same situation (e.g. fails out of bed)

Check for
Medication problems
Orthostatic hypotension
Delirium
Confusion
Infection
Weakness.
Blood sugar abnormality
Urine test abnormality
Occult blood
Blood pressure changes

Activity
Was the person:
Doing anything new or unusual
Standing
Walking
Getting in or out of wheel-chair
Getting in or out of bed
Responding to a bowel or bladder need
Reaching for food or water
Reaching for a call light

him or her something to do.

7. Provide plenty of activity during the day. This improves sleep quality and reduces napping.

8. Eliminate caffeine and other stimulants. Elderly people metabolize caffeine very slowly. One cup of coffee a day can cause sleep problems, as it may take up to six hours for an elderly person to eliminate the caffeine in that one cup. Check to confirm that none of the medications a person with sleep problems is taking contain caffeine. Antidepressants potentiate caffeine, and the antibiotic *Cipro* can increase caffeine levels drastically.

9. Have residents go to the bathroom just before bedtime.

10. Furnish bedtime snacks to alleviate blood sugar problems.

11. Do not set bedtime too early.

12. A good proportion of sleep problems are caused by minor aches and pains. A simple analgesic, like aspirin, can improve sleep quality.

13. Make sure the person gets at least one half hour of morning sun every day to increases the body's melatonin level. If there is no sunlight, use light panels.

Falls

Falls and injuries can be deadly to frail and elderly people. In fact, half of the hospital beds for trauma patients are occupied by people suffering hip fractures caused by falls. At least 20 percent of elderly women suffering hip fractures die within one year of the accident as a result of complications of the injury, making fractures from osteoporosis the 12th leading cause of death in the United States.

Injuries in the elderly also occur because of general weakness, degenerative muscle disease, balance disorders, impaired motor function, medication problems, impaired judgment, memory loss, sensory loss, and problems with depth-perception.

Victims of strokes in the right hemisphere are often paralyzed on the left side of the body — unable to move the left arm, leg and foot, and unable to walk. However, they may exhibit — temporarily or permanently — a *complete denial* of any disability whatsoever. The denial of paralysis is caused by the loss of a particular brain system that allows them to have awareness of their internal body map. The difficulty with such patients is that, lacking any awareness of their paralysis, they often attempt to stand, walk, or engage in other activity that can result in falls or injuries.

In some cases, people may hurt themselves by actually attempting to throw the unwanted, paralyzed limb out of bed. Others may attempt to injure the limb in order to get rid of it. These patients need to be confronted frequently with the reality of their disability, so they come to know there is something wrong. Even frequent reminders don't work in some cases.

Transitions from wheelchairs to beds are often sources of unsafe movements and injury. Many people with physical limitations insist on getting out of bed unassisted, risking a fall. Poles by the side of the bed can be helpful in cases such as these, so the person, who cannot get in or out of the bed safely, can slide down the pole without injury. The use of alarms can warn caregivers when a person at risk of falling is attempting to get up.

Physical restraint often has been considered the only recourse in the prevention of unsafe movement, but because it is so restrictive, restraint can lead to other problems such as agitation. In addition, it has also been shown that in many cases, restraint actually *increases* the number of injuries, because caregivers use

Fall prevention checklist

Environment
Was the person:
In a crowd
In a noisy place
On a wet floor
In an unfamiliar place
Stumbling on an object in his path
Restrained

Personal impairments
Was the person:
Having vision or hearing difficulty
Uncomfortable in any way (e.g. in a wheelchair, bed, chair, walker, etc.)
Wearing shoes properly fit and tied
Wearing clothing properly
Agitated, frightened, or angry
In any pain
Suffering from motor or gait difficulties
Suffering from neurological damage
Cognitively impaired
Dizzy, weak or faint

restraints as a substitute for careful observation and protection. Restraint always should be used as a last resort, not as a replacement for monitoring unsafe movement.

Behavioral Interventions for Falls

1. Assess the person's potential for self-harm and falling.
2. Observe the person to determine the degree and type of unsafe movements exhibited.
3. Determine if the person can walk and talk at the same time. People who have to stop walking to talk may suffer from a condition known as *walk and talk* syndrome and are at increased risk of falling.
4. If a person is observed about to do something unsafe, do not yell at or run towards him or her. This can frighten the person and cause injury. Approach calmly and remove the person from the potential harm.
5. Refocus the person as you attempt to defuse the danger. For instance, offer an enticing object so the person loosens his or her grip on a chair or bed-rail.
6. Never rush or pressure a person to do something.
7. Ensure shoes are on properly, and shoelaces are tied.
8. Use non-skid shoes.
9. Ensure clothing is put on properly. Eliminate ties, scarves, and belts.
10. Clean up spills immediately.
11. Do not move objects in the resident's room.
12. Use night lights.
13. Use position-change alarms and wander-guards when necessary.
14. Teach safe transfer methods to all caregivers. Unsafe and uncomfortable transfers are a not only one of the most common complaints of

people receiving care, they are also one of the major causes of injuries.

15. Place banners or ribbons across door-ways to unsafe and off-limit areas.

16. Install handrails in all hallways.

Self Harm

People with dementia may harm themselves by biting, scratching or rubbing. As this often is done as a means of self stimulation, it is useful to refocus them on another less harmful behavior. Following is an example.

> An 82-year-old female resident of a nursing home diagnosed with advanced Alzheimer's disease had been biting her finger incessantly for the past year. On examination, her digit was found to be bitten to the bone.
>
> Attempts at wrapping her finger and placing mittens on one hand and then both hands were unsuccessful.
>
> Various pharmacologic agents, including clonazepam, thiothixene, thioridazine, trazodone, propranolol, carbamazepine, and buspirone, were administered with no success. After observed that some patients with Alzheimer's disease appear to make chewing movements without food in the mouth, we offered chewing gum to the resident in an attempt to distract the patient from chewing on her finger. Within 24 hours of introducing the gum, the finger-biting ceased. Over the next 6 months there were no recurrences of finger-biting, and no episodes of swallowing the gum or aspiration were noted.

Complaining and Attention Seeking

Every one has complaints at one time or another, but unwarranted complaining — complaining that has little basis in reality — is bothersome, irritating and disruptive. And when a patient and caregivers develop a negative relationship as a result, everyone suffers. When caregivers become irritated with a person, it affects the quality of care. In addition, like the boy who cried wolf, the incessantly complaining person soon becomes shunned and ignored, creating the potential for legitimate complaints to be missed.

Chronic complaining usually consists of constant concerns about health, quality of care, and dissatisfactions with other residents. Most complaining, however, is the result of depression, low self-esteem, under-stimulation, and inadvertent reinforcement of negative behavior.

Attention-seeking occurs when patients constantly requests that they talk to caregivers about something they perceive to be vitally important

Behavioral Interventions for Complaining and Attention-Seeking

1. Listen to and assess the validity of a person's request or complaint. If the complaint seems valid, find a remedy.
2. Ensure that complaints about pain and discomfort are checked out thoroughly.
3. Set limits on complaining, and attention-seeking, and inform the resident of the limits.
4. Don't ask a complaint-prone resident how he or she feels.
5. Reinforce positive behavior.
6. Increase the resident's social stimulation.
7. Make a list of the positive things that the person is willing to talk about. Give the list to all caregivers and encourage its use. When the person begins to complain, start talking about one of these topics.
8. Do not reward complaining with special attention.
9. Give the resident a complaint form to fill out. Keep a file of the person's complaints and the actions taken to remedy them. When a complaint reoccurs, show it to the person, and remind him

or her of what has been done to help remedy the problem.

10.   Set aside a specific time to listen, and inform the person, you will be available at that time.

Manipulation and Splitting

People with emotional and personality disorders are often manipulative, dishonest, and devaluing. On the other hand, people with dementia, though difficult at times, usually are not deliberately manipulative. Therefore, it's important to know the resident's cognitive status when assessing for manipulation.

A resident showing manipulative behavior and minimal signs of dementia, should be screened for personality disorder. Most commonly, manipulative behaviors are symptoms of *narcissistic, borderline,* and *antisocial* personality disorders.

There are many types of manipulative behavior, but the most common and most disruptive is *splitting.* Splitting, often used to disrupt treatment, involves a resident assessing the defenses and weaknesses of each caregiver, and systematically playing them against one another. Caregivers soon find themselves fighting with each other about things they have been told by the resident, undermining the sense of teamwork, and diverting attention away from the person.

In one of the facilities in which I was consulting, an elderly gentleman named George actually caused three staff members to be fired. Over time, George would gain the confidence of one staff member, and then tell them that other staff members were complaining about them. He would then do the same thing with other staff. Soon he had the staff talking behind one another's back, gossiping, and sabotaging each other's work. Before long, fights would break out, and someone would eventually get fired. This behavior continued for almost a year before I was called in to develop an intervention plan.

Although each situation must be handled differently, here are some general guidelines to prevent manipulation and splitting.

Behavioral Interventions for Manipulation

1. Give the person as much independence as possible. People often become manipulative when they believe they have no other power.
2. Be very clear about non-compliant behavior, manipulative behavior, and their consequences. Tell the resident what the results of their actions will be. For example, say, "Mrs. Gibby, you do not have to come to lunch, but there will be no food available if you get hungry later."
3. When a person begins to complain about another caregiver, involve that caregiver and work out the problem among the three of you. This is very effective in reducing splitting.

Yelling and Screaming

Yelling and screaming disturbs other residents as well as staff. These behaviors may occur because of over-stimulation, or in response to demands made that are beyond the person's capacity. However, these behaviors also occur as a result of under-stimulation and boredom. Some residents may yell and scream for self-stimulation, or to get attention, while others do so because of genuine pain, discomfort, hunger, anxiety or depression.

Behavioral Interventions for Yelling and Screaming

1. Assess the cause. Determine the time, place, and frequency of the behaviors, and look for a pattern.
2. Ask the person what is wrong.
3. As an immediate intervention, give the person something to eat or suck on.

4.   Distract the person by talking about something that interests them.

5.   Provide comfort through physical touch.

6.   Play soothing music.

7.   Provide the person with a comforting or stimulating object such as a stuffed animal.

8.   If it is determined that the cause is over-stimulation, relocate the person to a quiet room.

9.   If it is determined that the cause is under-stimulation, increase the person's opportunity for social contact.

10.   Break the reinforcement cycle. Give the person attention when they are not yelling or screaming, and ignore the behavior when it occurs.

11.   When all else fails, move the person to a place where the disruption to others is minimized.

Verbal Aggression

Verbally aggressive behavior includes arguing, threatening, swearing, and demeaning others. This behavior may be a result of resisting care, fighting, or may be a component of a catastrophic reaction. Anything that exceeds the resident's coping ability may trigger verbal aggression.

In some cases, verbal aggression may be a person's only form of expressing anger and frustration about his or her condition. Verbally aggressive or abusive behavior may also be used as a defense against loneliness and emotional pain. The person may feel that being abusive will distance others, and therefore save them from having to deal with their true feelings.

Mrs. Nickerson had a reputation in the facility for being cranky, abusive, and generally unpleasant. Many of the staff avoided working with her because of her abrasive manner. However, it was discovered that this was her way of distancing people to protect herself

The most common forms of agitation

Restlessness

Pacing

Complaining

Perseveration

Repeating the same words

Chronic negativity

Chronic attention seeking

Swearing

Verbally abusive language

from her feelings of worthlessness, loneliness, and fears of abandonment. Inside she was thinking, "I'll reject you before you have a chance to reject me." Ignoring her initial abuse and confronting her feelings of loneliness ended the problem.

In people with dementia or other forms of cognitive impairment, impulse control is impaired. Because they no longer have the means to prevent themselves from acting on impulse, anger is immediately and bluntly expressed.

Behavioral Interventions for Verbal Aggression

1. Don't attempt to settle an argument or reason with an angry person. Angry people are irrational, and are poor problem-solvers. Talking to them when they are raging will escalate their anger, and worsen the problem. Instead, talk about the behavior when it is not happening, and constructive solutions can be discussed.

2. Distract the person. Ignore the abusive behavior and ask a question about an unrelated subject.

3. Approach the person calmly. Touch is usually calming, but be aware of the resident's capacity for assaultive behavior. Don't put yourself in harm's way.

4. If the verbal aggression is directed towards you, do not take it personally, and do not react to it. Ignore the behavior, and reflect an attitude of caring. If this does not work, and the abusive person is in no danger, leave the room.

5. If a person is consistently being verbally abusive towards you, look for ways you may be inadvertently reinforcing the behavior. Some residents get satisfaction out of upsetting caregivers. If you are visibly upset by the abusive behavior, you may be encouraging the resident to repeat it.

Agitation

Agitation is the most frequent reason for a behavioral consultation. Agitation may be caused by many things, but it's usually a by-product of cognitive impairment related to brain damage or dementia.

Agitation may also be caused by over-stimulation, or the person's inability to comprehend what is required of him or her.

Often, agitation is a result of frustration felt about the loss of freedom and choice experienced by the elderly when living in a group environment. Put yourself in their shoes for a moment. Think of checking in to a hotel. As soon as you arrive, you are assigned a room, but when you open the door to the room, you see two other people you've never met before. You are told they are your roommates, and you should get ready for bed. The next morning, you are told to get out of bed or you will miss your breakfast. When you reach the dining room, you are given a meal you didn't order, and don't want. You try to send it back but are told it's your only choice. Getting irritated yet?

Keep this scenario in mind when working with agitated patients. If you believe they are in a receptive state, validate their feelings and protect their self-esteem. For example you might say, "I can see that you are frustrated, and I understand why. This would be aggravating to anyone."

Although agitation is a common problem in dementia, most negative behavior occurs because it is inadvertently reinforced by others. Negative behavior attracts attention. Elderly patients who feel alone and neglected will do anything to get attention, and agitation is a very effective way to accomplish this.

When you see someone becoming agitated, your best response is to leave at once or provide the person access to a quiet place. People with memory impairments soon forget what disturbed them.

Use verbal and nonverbal communication to enhance feelings of safety and minimize fear. When supportive, empathic verbal skills are combined with active listening, most patients, even those who are demented or psychotic, respond, and anxiety or hostility can be defused.

The agitated person should be encouraged to express his or her feelings, but also be refocused as a distraction from anxiety.

Keep communications short and simple. Interactions should be directed at validating the person's feelings, and increasing self-esteem while decreasing anxiety.

When agitation is reduced, channeling anxiety in positive ways will facilitate continued de-escalation. Every stage and step are critical because patient behaviors can escalate rapidly to assault, or de-escalate to calmness if effectively managed. If the patient begins to de-escalate, nurses need to constantly monitor patient's behavior until it is stable.

Aggression is also a way to overcome feelings of vulnerability and powerlessness. The aggressive response is primitive and instinctive, with the same origin as a cat arching its back and making its hair stand on end. The message is, "Leave me alone."

Like the angry cat, agitated people need more personal space because of their heightened perception and increased vigilance. Respecting personal space promotes feelings of safety and security.

Be aware that the more agitated a person becomes, the less ability they have to concentrate, think clearly, or consider the consequences of their actions. Threatened people think about survival, not consequences.

Behavioral Interventions for Agitation

1. Ask the person what is agitating him or her. This is often the most direct route to intervention,

even if answers are not forthcoming. If the person is able to explain the problem, take steps to remove the its source , or help the person cope with the difficulty. If they cannot tell you, complete the following steps.

2. Do a complete assessment to establish the person's cognitive skills, memory function, and emotional state. This will allow you to assess what kind of intervention would be most effective.

3. Check to see if there have been any recent medication changes, or a change in the person's health.

4. Observe and record what happened immediately before the problem behavior. This might allow you to assess what triggered the behavior, and possibly eliminate the triggers.

5. Withdraw all reinforcers for the problem behaviors. This often means removing the person from the area in which the agitation occurred. It is sometimes necessary to move the person to a quiet room for time out. This also may require ignoring the agitation, as it is sometimes used to get attention.

6. Provide the person with structured daily activities. People with cognitive impairment do not tolerate change well. Because thinking and memory are impaired, new surroundings and new events are confusing and upsetting.

7. When all else fails, implement negative consequences for problem behaviors. Explain to the person that the behavior is unacceptable, and that certain privileges may be withdrawn if it persists. Negative consequences work in people with mild to moderate dementia, but are ineffective in those with serious cognitive impairment.

Chapter Twenty

Assault

Mrs. Donner had just arrived at the inpatient unit when I was called in to do an evaluation. When I looked in her admission notes, they read "Reason for admission: assault." I asked her, as I always do, "Why are you here?" To which she quickly replied, "Well, the damn nurse or whatever she is was trying to make me eat, and I wasn't hungry. She tried to grab my hand, so I hit her."

Assault is the targeted use of physical force that may harm other people. Assaults include hitting, grabbing, pushing, slapping, stabbing, or throwing things at another person. Unacted upon threats of assault and verbal abuse should also be considered part of assaultive behavior, as they significantly change the climate of caregiving. Unfortunately, as Mrs. Donner pointed out, many assaults occur when caregivers are in the process of working with residents.

The Incidence of Assault

Assault is an all too common problem in care facilities. While over a third of geriatric patients in

Behavioral Objectives

At the end of this section readers will be able to:

Define assault.

Describe the causes of assault.

List factors that contribute to assaultive behavior.

Intervene in or prevent assault.

Factors that contribute to Assault

Physiological Factors
physical illness
infections
electrolyte imbalances
epilepsy
temporal lobe abnormalities
medical toxicity
reactions to drugs
paradoxical drug reactions
substance abuse
drug withdrawal
dementia
fronto-temporal dementia
hallucinations
dehydration
constipation
sleep-deprivation

Psychological factors
history of assault
restlessness
agitation
disorientation
low frustration tolerance
impulse control problems
personality disorder
mental instability
schizophrenia
delusions
restrictions on behavior
recent significant loss

nursing homes will engage in verbal assaults, physically assaultive behaviors occur in about 10 percent. But in geropsychiatric hospitals, where patients are more acutely disturbed, over 20 percent of the patients commit assault.

Unfortunately, even though assaults can be harmful to patients and caregivers, most assaults are never reported. In fact, in a year-long study in a nursing home, researchers found that out of 1,108 incidents only 203 were actually reported. Surveys of nursing staff have shown that many of these events go unreported because caregivers have become habituated to assaults, that is, the assaults happen so frequently that caregivers begin to accept this behavior as unavoidable and routine.

Some caregivers believe if they report assaults, they will be seen as the perpetrators, not the victims. Many nurses have stated that they don't feel that the administrators at their facilities would support them if they reported being attacked.

Even so, the most common reason that assaults are not reported is the desire to avoid the hassle of extra paper work. Overworked and over-stressed staff and administration see assault reports as one more thing to add to the pile. The problem with this is that *not reporting assault prevents adequate prevention and intervention,* and can lead to more serious problems later — problems that could affect everyone in the facility. Preventing or circumventing assaults now is a prudent move to avoid injuries, complaints, and litigation later.

Rather than implement intervention programs for assault, too many facilities consider assaultive residents as nuisances, and quickly refer them elsewhere. Mrs Donner was a prime example. The facility had referred her to the hospital because they could not deal with her behavior, and wanted her relocated.

The Consequences of Assault

Violence in a facility has profound effects on the caregiving staff — physically, emotionally and behaviorally. Physical injuries from assaults can result in black eyes, swollen jaws, scratches and bruises, ringing in the ears, hearing loss, headaches, back injuries, and in extreme cases loss of consciousness and broken bones. While most physical injuries heal, the emotional and behavioral scars linger on.

Researchers report that caregivers who have been assaulted exhibit a variety of long-term emotional reactions. Although their immediate reactions are usually shock, disbelief, and self-blame, long-term reactions include feelings of helplessness, irritability, resignation, sadness, and depression.

Caregivers often fear returning to the scene of the assault and develop general fear of the residents. This leads to avoidance behavior, including an avoidance of any reminders of the assault.

Some caregivers become preoccupied with the assault, and play the incident over and over in their minds. The trauma of assault also causes some caregivers to change their relationships with co-workers — they may become defensive, withdrawn and short tempered. Some caregivers may attempt to cope through an increased use of alcohol, cigarettes, or drugs, or through increased absenteeism from work, or loss of interest and involvement in their work. Others become so traumatized they consider or actually make a career change.

It has been my experience that caregivers deal with these feelings in one of two ways — blaming themselves or blaming others. A better approach is to to put blame aside, take an objective look at the incident, and learn how to prevent it from happening again.

Factors that contribute to Assault

Environmental factors
environmental load
violation of personal space
crowding
agitated or provoked by
    others
excessive stimulation (e.g.
    noise, light, temperature
    and activity level)
transfer to another facility
the use of seclusion or
    restraints
medications without
    consent
family visits

Milieu Problems
staff angry at patient
staff angry at doctor
differing beliefs
differing agendas
poor documentation
failure to carry out orders
doctor doesn't respond to
    calls
problems with power-
    structure
staff conflicts
shift change problems

Factors that contribute to Assault

Caregiver factors
staffing allocations
rigid routines
poor relationship between
   caregiver and patient
caregiver stress
making derogatory remarks
the use of smoking as a tool
   for control or punish-
   ment
belief that residents need to
   be taught something
poor training
lack of tools
poor problem solving skills
projection: "He shouldn't
   do that"
control issues: "He can't do
   that"
punitiveness: "I'll teach
   him"
power problems: "I'll get
   him"

The Causes of Assault

Environmental Factors

Robert Bigelow, author of a 1972 paper entitled *The Evolution of Cooperation, Aggression, and Self Control* concluded that, "the crowding of strangers, especially near such valuable resources as food..." was one of the major causes of human aggression. Anthony Storr, while researching the causes of aggression, found that violent behavior is most likely to occur in conditions of territoriality and social posturing. Residents often feel one-down and resentful that others are controlling their fate, and aggression is a face-saving behavior in these situations — a way to exert power and maintain control.

It appears that Bigelow and Storr were right, because most assaults occur when there are many people in one place, when food is present, and when caregivers are most actively involved with their patients. Most assaults occur when caregivers physically prompt the patient to eat, dress, shower, or move from one position to another.

In fact, assaults are most likely to occur during three peak activity periods — between 7 AM and 10 AM, usually during morning preparation activities, between 12 noon and 2 PM, during and after lunch, and between 4 PM and 7 PM, during and after dinner.

Environmental Load

In his interesting book *Public Places and Private Spaces,* Dr. Albert Mehrabian explains that environments are best be described by the amount of information they contain. The rate at which this information must be processed is called *environmental load.* A *low-load environment,* such as an uncrowded private beach, is one in which the amount of information to be processes is small.

High-load environments include elements such as crowding, unfamiliarity, movement, and noise — just the type of environment found in many care facilities. High-load environments are known to cause a great deal of stress — they are the reason we long for that private beach so much.

As described above, the three peak activity periods of the day — or the three highest-load environments — occur when strangers and food are present together. Of these three high load time periods, centered around breakfast, lunch and dinner, morning is the worst.

Morning is a difficult time for many people, but for the old, frail, and cognitively impaired person, it can be hell. Reeling from the residue of two sleeping pills that have not yet metabolized, the person is rousted from bed, prodded to get up, get dressed, and start the day. While still in a fog, the person is greeted with a flurry of activity. Caregivers do their best to be helpful (while also being attentive to their daily schedule), but their efforts typically are uninvited and unwelcome. It is no surprise that assault is often the crime of the cranky.

In many facilities, residents are deprived of much of their personal space. They are often asked to share rooms and recreational space with people they do not know, and may not like. Strangers frequently enter their rooms. Residents are subjected to medical and care-giving procedures that involve unwanted physical contact. Crowding is constant.

Nursing home residents are often unwillingly placed in close proximity with a group of strangers, many of whom are loud, intrusive, inappropriate, unpleasant, or unsavory. Put too many such people in a room for an extended period of time, and tempers are bound to flair.

Limited personal body space can create intolerable anxiety for people with impaired coping skills. While each person's "buffer zone" varies — in cognitively

The body buffer zone in most people sufferng from schizophrenia is four times larger than in a normal population.

impaired people it is larger than in healthy people, and in most schizophrenics is four times larger — any activity that involves the invasion of perceived personal space — whatever the dimensions — increases the risk for assault. The majority of assaults in long-term care facilities occur because a resident is attempting to defend his or her personal space.

In addition to crowding, familiarity also affects environmental load — most people are more comfortable in a room with twenty others whom they know well than in a room full of strangers. For people with memory impairments, *the environment is always unfamiliar, which increases the load significantly.* A person with severe memory problems may have been in a facility for a long time, but will continue to see caregivers and other residents as strangers.

Noise

As people age, their ability to filter out unwanted noise decreases. While the average teenager can move into a trance-like state, eliminating all outside stimuli other than his Ipod, elderly people are easily detracted, irritated, and overwhelmed by too much noise. In cognitively impaired people, excessive noise or motion may overload their coping level and cause them to "snap." I have seen people run from the day-room because of too much noise and activity.

Structure

Routines are important to the elderly. Change requires much more thought than does habit, therefore cognitively impaired people find change frightening and confusing. Thus, disruption of daily routines often increases agitation. Assaults more than double between Sundays and Mondays, probably because of different activity schedules, different staff, and the after effects of weekend visits from friends and family.

The more emotional conflict there is in the staff of a facility, the more assaults will occur.

At Atascadero State Hospital in California, researchers Harold Carmel and Melvin Hunter found that the transition between the relatively low level of activity on weekends and the higher level of activity on the weekdays may contribute to assaults.

While routine and structure is good, too much structure is not. In an effort to impose structure, some caregivers put great emphasis on the maintenance of institutional rules and routines. When patients do not cooperate with the pre-ordained routines, caregivers over-react with harsh, punitive behaviors which trigger assault-provoking cycle. Residents also may become angry about schedules and treatment regimens that are contrary to their wishes.

Gerontologist Marilyn Lewis Lanza and her colleagues found that strict rules and limit setting lead to an extreme level of provocation, and that physically setting limits on patient behaviors caused many assaults, particularly among patients with organic brain syndrome or dementia.

Emotional Climate

While environmental factors play an important part in the emotional state of the individual, milieu factors set the emotional tone for the environment. Simply stated, the more emotional conflict there is in a facility, the more frequently assault will occur.

Under-staffing means over-worked caregivers are unable to give residents the attention they need. While the staff becomes frazzled trying to meet the needs of everyone, the residents become agitated when needed help does not arrive. By the time the caregiver is able to attend to the resident, both are already in a high state of agitation.

Staff Conflict

The amount of conflict within the staff, between the staff and administration, and between the staff and

The amount of conflict within the staff, between the staff and administration, and between the staff and the doctors all have a profound effect on the amount of agitation and assault in a facility.

For people with memory impairments, the environment is always unfamiliar, which increases stress significantly.

the doctors all have a profound effect on the amount of agitation and assault in a facility. When a staff member is angry at a doctor or a superior, they may displace this anger unto the resident. This "kick the dog" behavior creates a poor relationship between the caregiver and residents, and sets the stage for behavioral problems.

Psychological Factors

The most potent predictor of assault is a *history of assault.* So, the more often a person has been assaultive, the more likely it is the person will continue to be that way. When informed that a particular person has been assaultive, gather as much information as possible about the person's assault history, including how frequently the person has been violent, with whom, and under what circumstances. Give this information to all caregivers.

People with histories of assault and those with disorders that include loss of impulse control (like organic brain syndrome and borderline personality disorder) should be considered as at high-risk for assault behavior, and need an immediate clinical evaluation for their assault potential. A prevention and management plan should be implemented as soon as the person arrives at the facility. All staff needs to be aware of the plan measures.

In a study of geropsychiatric state hospital patients in North Carolina, Christopher Colenda and Robert Hamer reported that elderly patients with schizophrenia or bipolar disorder committed 20.8 percent and 10.4 percent respectively of all assaultive behaviors on the unit.

People with schizophrenia have, in addition to an increased personal space as described earlier, an acute sensitivity to questions. Already possessed of a fragile sense of self, they see questions as intrusive and overwhelming. Many years ago one of my patients told me, "When you ask a question, it feels like a knife cutting my arm off." To this day, I remember that statement, and respectfully avoid questions as much as possible.

Demented people also don't like questions, which often put them in an embarrassing situation of trying to think or remember. They frequently react with anger in an effort to cover up their disability.

Physiological Factors

Despite the profound effects the environment has on those working and living in it, people differ in their reactions to these effects. What a person brings to a situation is as important as what the situation brings to the person.

Figure 1 illustrates how two people in the same environment may have differing abilities to cope with environmental stress. Any one person's normal level of coping skills, however, may also depend on how that person is feeling physically at any given time.

Physical illnesses such as colds, flu, or infections lower a person's tolerance for frustration. Grumpiness typically accompanies illness, but for a cognitively-chal-

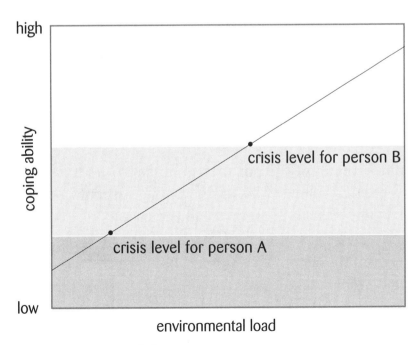

Figure 1 Coping and the environment

Preventing Assault

1. If a person has a continuing negative reaction to a staff member, assign a new primary care giver.
2. Reinforce behavioral limits frequently.
3. Assess the person's need for personal space and privacy.

   Allow ample space between you and the patient. Place personal items in their room, including furniture if possible.
4. When it has been determined that violation personal space causes fighting, stay out of the person's personal space.

   Knock on their door before entering their room

   Stay a few feet away and talk to them in a calm manner. Avoid interventions in a small room.
5. Provide appropriate opportunities for the person to be assertive instead of aggressive.
6. Give the person as much control as possible.

   Autonomy and power lessen the need for aggression. The more control a person has in decisi ons pertaining to them, the more cooperative they become.

lenged person, whose biochemistry is already askew, even a minor illness or infection may cause delirium, confusion, and aggression. Elderly people require a much longer recovery time following an illness, and their frustration tolerance may remain impaired for weeks.

Medical toxicity may also trigger aggression. Drugs metabolize much slower in the elderly, and weakened livers and kidneys are unable to excrete toxins rapidly. For this reason many medications should be given in low doses initially to ascertain tolerance.

Drug reactions may cause aggressive incidents, as some elderly people may exhibit paradoxical reactions to drugs. For example, recent studies show that rage reactions can occur in elderly patients who recently started taking benzodiazepines. Diazepam (Valium), especially when given in low doses, can cause extreme agitation and assaultive behavior. Violent behavior occurring as a reaction to various psychotropic drugs has been documented as well.

Seizure disorders, especially temporal lobe seizures, can cause violent outbursts.

Dehydration, a relatively common occurrence in the aging population, can lead to electrolyte imbalances, confusion and aggression. Water balance decreases with age, with body water level typically falling from 62 percent at age 25 to less than 50 percent at age 55. Older people actively may further restrict their water intake because of incontinence, or because they lose their sense of thirst.

Advertisers of laxatives often point out that "occasional irregularity" leads to irritability. While these ads are comical, they speak truth in that particular point. Constipation can and does lead to feelings of discomfortableness, making sufferers edgy, irritable, and unpleasant. High fiber diets can do wonders for a person plagued with this problem.

Sleep deprivation also can put a person on edge. In fact, chronic sleep problems not only can increase aggression but can lead to confusion and hallucinations.

Damage to the brain may have a noticeably effect on aggression. Seizure disorders, especially temporal lobe seizures, can cause violent outbursts. During a seizure, a person is capable of carrying out complex, goal-directed violent behavior of which they have no memory following the incident. Studies report that as many as one-half of temporal lobe epileptics regularly experience aggressive behavior.

Brain damage to structures affecting perception and inhibitory control, especially frontal and temporal lobes, results in *disinhibition* — the inability to control impulses. Patients with *fronto-temporal dementia* are especially prone to aggressive behavior, and should be approached with caution. A person with frontal lobe problems loses the capacity to make conscious decisions about the consequences of his or her actions. Impulses are acted upon without any thought of their outcomes.

Consequently, even though people who commit assault may feel remorse following an episode, their impaired impulse control may cause them to repeat the behavior. People with impulse control disorders do not learn from experience, making behavioral interventions such as imposing consequences or setting limits often ineffective. In such cases, preventing the reoccurrence of the conditions that led to the assault is the best intervention.

Those with cognitive impairment often misinterpret the actions of others, and may see caregiving activities as threats. They may also become reactive to being touched. Elderly patients with dementia or schizophrenia may panic when caregivers approach. Behavior researcher Phill Jones reported that aggressive responses occurred most often when the patient could not understand the intentions of staff.

Demented patients commit nearly two-thirds of recorded assaults on caregivers and other residents. The severity of the assaultive behavior is related to the

Elderly patients with dementia or schizophrenia may panic when caregivers approach.

severity of the dementia. It's always a good idea to inform a person with dementia what you are about to do, and to ask permission before you begin.

Caregiver Factors

In studies of assaultive behavior in nursing homes, many incidents of assault occurred when two or three caregivers approached a patient at one time. The team approach created a panic response from the patient, who felt attacked and invaded, and struggled in self-defense.

Sixty-five percent of assaults are against the nursing staff and nursing aides — the people who have the most frequent contact with residents. Unfortunately, they also are the least likely to have been trained to deal with aggression.

Although assaults happen frequently, few patients behave aggressively in the absence of aversive stimulation. Richard Whittington and Til Wykes investigated the frequency with which violence by psychiatric inpatients was preceded by a negative interpersonal encounter. *Fifty-four of 63 assaults — 86 percent — were immediately preceded by the assaulted caregivers having caused frustration in the patients, by placing an unwanted activity demand on them, or engaging in some form of unwanted physical contact.*

Even more interesting is the finding by Margret Baltes and associates that much of the caregiving going on health care facilities was unnecessary. Baltes noticed that when caregivers receive a set of general caregiving instructions, they tend to adhere to them regardless of the competence level of the resident. Thus many residents who were capable of self-care behaviors were treated in the same manner as those who were unable to help themselves. The study indicated that in some facilities, *almost 80 percent of care-giving behaviors on the units were the result of*

Assaults in long term care more than double between Sundays and Mondays.

compliance with staff instructions, rather than requests for help from the residents. In addition, the residents stated they were fully aware they were not doing things that they actually were able to do.

The clear conclusions — most assaults occur during caregiving, and a great deal of care giving is unnecessary — lead to the most effective resolution of assaultive behavior: obtain a valid assessment of a resident's ability to care for him or herself, give them as much autonomy as fits that assessment, and intervene only when necessary.

Interpersonal Skills

Interpersonal factors play a significant role in assault, and a poor relationship between a resident and a caregiver is a major warning sign of trouble to come. Caregivers who have personal problems with patients develop unhealthy relationships with them, characterized by disagreements, anger, and aggression.

I commonly observe situations in which residents provoke caregivers by making derogatory and racist remarks about them. It takes great skill and experience on the part of the caregivers to shrug off this abuse.

Poorly-trained caregivers who feel unable to control violence, may in some cases actually scare patients into acting aggressively. The caregivers' inability to contain their own anxiety results in escalating agitation in already unsettled patients.

Caregivers who are most concerned about patient violence have been found to be those who feared they would not be able to contain their own violence if provoked.

The presence of male caregivers increases the risk of assault, perhaps because of an assumption by residents that males are more threatening and provocative. It also has been noted that male staff tend to use confrontation as a means of resolving conflict, a method frequently resulting in increased agitation.

People with impulse control disorders do not learn from experience, and behavioral interventions such as giving consequences and setting limits are often ineffective.

Confrontation has been found to be counterproductive in most episodes of agitation and assault.

Researchers Pauline Levy and Peter Hartocollis found that violence decreases in aggressive patients when the caregivers are female. They believe this is both because female caregivers are less likely to act in aggressively, and because some patients perceive male caregivers as authority figures threatening their sense of autonomy. Many assaultive patients actually stated they were less likely to hit a woman. Consequently, it may be a good idea to have female caregivers initially intervene in tense situations in order to de-escalate looming conflicts.

System Overload

As we have seen, people differ in their capacity to cope with environmental load. Individuals become aggressive when their socially-sanctioned coping skills break down. For example, if a person cuts in front of you in a line, you may politely point it out to them. If they respond in an insulting manner, you might get angry. If they become belligerent, you might forget politeness and begin to act aggressively. All of us have a coping limit. As Mehrabian points out, *aggression occurs when the environmental load exceeds a person's ability to cope with it.*

For a cognitively impaired person, this coping limit can be very small. Too much stimulation, unwanted activities, and violations of personal space, as mentioned earlier, are the most common causes of overload.

Prior to resorting to assaultive behaviors, most people display increased anger and agitation. They may begin to pace in an agitated fashion and verbally express irritation. Other behaviors include fist pounding, pressured speech, repeatedly requesting assistance from others and repetitive questioning. The earlier a caregiver can identify these precursor emotions and behaviors, and intervene, the less likely it is that an assault will occur.

Preventing Assault

The first step in preventing assault is to obtain a thorough history of the person. An initial assessment should be performed immediately after a patient's admission to measure his or her assault potential — including any a history of assault, aggression, or general unpleasantness. Special precautions need to be taken when new patients are found to have a history of assault. It is important to promptly determine what circumstances tend to precipitate such attacks, and to avoid these events when possible.

Become aware of the person's personal buffer zone, and provide that information to all caregivers. Respect of personal space promotes feelings of security in the patient.

When a patient with a history of assault is not angry, limit-setting technique can be used to control verbally assaultive behavior. Setting clear limits on patients' behavior informs them about what is and is not acceptable. Caregivers must also calmly but clearly describe the consequences of unacceptable behavior

Behavioral Interventions for Assault

Start simple.

1. When fighting or assault occurs, separate the participants immediately.
2. Remove all participants to quiet rooms for time out.
3. Tell the participants the behavior is not acceptable, but do not scold or shame them.
4. Be respectful, calling each participant by name, expressing concern and asking how you can help.
5. Ask the person who initiated the assault to explain why he or she did it.

6. Determine whether the explanation is valid. Assault is never justified, but the events leading up to it may form a valid complaint. If the person has a valid compliant, explore constructive solutions to the problem.

7. If two people fight frequently, take steps to keep them separated. Re-assign rooms when necessary.

8. If a person cannot be managed without restrictive measures, the use of seclusion may be necessary to protect that individual as well as others. It is important to keep other patients safe by removing them from a tense situation.

9. Restraints should be used only as a last resort. Studies show that in most cases use of restraints increases agitation. But if a person is out of control to the degree that he or she may harm the self or others, restraints may be necessary. In these cases, the person should be told the restraint for his or her own protection and safety.

10. After an assault has occurred, caregivers will need to reassess the milieu, which needs to be non-threatening and calm in order to facilitate the assaultive patient's successful re-entry. Caregivers should explore all patient and caregiver factors that may have precipitated the assault, and take appropriate steps to prevent a re-occurrence.

Chapter Twenty-One

Wandering

Kirk: What could possibly be the purpose of this madness?

Spock: Madness has no purpose or reason, but it may have a goal.

— Star Trek, *Lazarus*

Pooh, who felt more and more that he was somewhere else, got up slowly and began to look for himself.

— A.A. Milne, *The House at Pooh Corner*

Remember the last time you entered a room only to realize you had no idea why you were there? After a moment of frozen confusion, you probably scanned the room, searching for a cue as to why you came, then, throwing your hands in the air in frustration, returned empty-handed to your starting place. To make things worse, as soon as you got back, you immediately remembered the purpose of your journey.

For most of us this happens infrequently, but for people with dementia or other cognitive problems, this experience is the norm. A demented person's journey, as with a normal person, begins with a clear goal, but

Behavioral Objectives

At the end of this section readers will be able to:

Describe the causes of wandering.

Discuss the definitions of wandering.

Compare and contrast the benefits and risks of wandering.

Provide opportunities for wandering in a safe enviornment.

because their memory is failing, that goal is quickly forgotten. Mere moments after the brain has sent the message to the motor system, the reason for the journey disappears. And because motor programs run without conscious awareness, the person will continue to walk long after he has forgotten why he departed.

Unlike a healthy person, demented people have no way to recover the memory that prompted their journey. Returning to the place of origin doesn't work — in fact, they cannot remember the place of origin. They can't even recall where they were a moment ago. This lack of continuity causes them to experience a frustrating, never-ending series of desires without destinations.

This problem is called *wandering*. It is a common problem in the demented, and is potentially harmful to the sufferers as well as to those around them. Unfortunately, as wandering is one of the most difficult behaviors to manage, wanderers are often excluded from nursing homes because of the potential disruption, the disturbance of other residents, and the risk of injury.

The Incidence of Wandering

According to researcher Lawrence Snyder, there is one wanderer in every ten skilled nursing facility residents, and six in every one hundred residents in intermediate level care facilities.

Among those living at home, hundreds of elderly people wander from their homes every day, and about 40 percent of them become lost when they wander. Fifteen percent of these people are lost for more than 6 hours, and the police become involved in one third of the cases. The average time between the first time a person gets lost from wandering away from his or her home and that person's institutionalization is eight months.

The Causes of Wandering

Wandering has been described as aimless movement — a behavior without an aim or a goal. However, although wandering looks purposeless, it has meaning when viewed through the eyes of the wanderer.

People who pace around a room randomly are drawn to various environmental cues — like dishes, clothing or personal items. They may be acting quite purposefully, but as they pick up an object, they forget their purpose. Each act is disrupted because of the inability to hold a goal in long-term memory, making these these behaviors appear meaningless when they are, at least for the moment, both purposeful and important. Interference with the behavior of a wanderer often results in anger, agitation, and even catastrophic reactions.

I'm a morning person, but a few weeks ago I stayed up late to finish a project. I woke the next morning in a fog, staggered to my coffee pot, and, semi-conscious, scooped the ground coffee from the container, and poured them directly into my coffee cup.

Obviously this was not the result I was looking for. Although I have made coffee thousands of times, in my confused condition I had left out several important steps — putting the coffee in the pot, adding the water, and turning on the pot.

This is just what happens in dementia. Motor programs are often left intact, but what is missing is the proper *sequencing* of these programs. Like with my fumbled attempt to make the morning coffee, behaviors of a cognitively-impaired person may be executed out of sequence. in a series of unconnected, random acts. Purposeful actions do occur, but the *plan* is missing, the actions occur at random, and the person's behavior appears confused and pointless.

Other Reasons to Wander

While much wandering results from sequential confusions, there are other causes as well.

Discomfort or pain can cause anxiety and agitation. When agitated, most healthy people become more animated, and many pace when angry. For the cognitively-impaired person, with little control over his life and poor problem-solving skills, wandering may be the only outlet to work off this energy and it may be the only way they can express discomfort.

And this may be an old habit. Researcher Noel Monsour found that even before the onset of cognitive impairment, patients exhibiting wandering behavior had a history of relieving stress by physical means such as walking.

It has been suggested that wandering may be a means of alleviating loneliness or a substitute for social interaction. Regardless of a person's freedom of movement, the social interaction of the wanderers is much less than that of non-wanderers. As people become more cognitively-impaired, they spend more time alone than do the non-demented. Because they have difficulty carrying on conversations, they are often excluded from social activities. Researchers suggest that reducing wandering might be accomplished by increasing the opportunities for social interaction.

Wandering may be triggered by environmental and emotional aspects of the milieu. Each patient has a biological drive for stimulation that includes the need for a certain amount of varied, meaningful activity. Problems arise when the patient's drive for stimulation and the stimulation level in the facility do not match. leaving a person either over- or under-stimulated. The quantity and quality of environmental stimulation and the subsequent impact on sensory overload or deprivation contribute to the patient's need to escape to a more comfortable place.

As a person's spatial deficits increase, wandering increases. The person becomes increasingly confused about his environment, and may begin a quest to find something or someone familiar. In this case, wandering results from the inability of the person to make sense of his or her environment.

Wandering also has been associated with "sundowning." This type of wandering appears to be associated with the onset of darkness and is caused by the person's loss of spatial orientation in the dark. People with dementia are less able to maintain orientation in space without the need for visual scanning than are healthy individuals.

Medical Conditions Associated with Wandering.

Several studies have found that low blood pressure is related to frequency of pacing. Low blood pressure can result in hypoxia, which is often associated with restlessness.

An increase in the dosage of psychotropic drugs appears to equate with more frequent standing and pacing behaviors. Psychotropic medications have little effect on modifying problem behaviors such as agitation, and actually can promote wandering behaviors in some people.

Confusion can be caused by many drugs, including diuretics, sedatives, antihypertensives, analgesics, anti-anxiety drugs, and drugs that affect the gastrointestinal system. Diuretics, for example, can cause an electrolyte imbalance, reflected in a low potassium and/or sodium level, which results in gross confusion. A sedative given at bedtime is often metabolized slowly in an elderly person and produces morning grogginess and disorientation. And a patient who receives a sedative at bedtime may be unable to find the bathroom in the middle of the night because of grogginess, resulting in incontinence.

The Definition of Wandering

In 1989, OBRA mandated that all nursing homes indicate in their MDS (minimum data set) if a resident is a wanderer. However, the law did not provide a clear and exact definition of wandering, probably because it *is* difficult to define.

As illustrated in this chapter, wandering can include a variety of behaviors. In general, it is a tendency to move about in a seemingly aimless or disoriented fashion, in pursuit of an indefinable or unobtainable goal, but also has been defined as any change in a person's physical location which results in his/her inability to return to the point of origin. Still others have defined wandering as extended periods of movement without a full awareness of the behavior.

Wandering behavior may include following others around, imitating others' behavior, attempting to leave the facility, tampering with doors, windows or machinery, or entering others' rooms.

Lawrence Snyder has found that wanderers were in motion a higher percentage of time than non-wanderers and, in fact, were in motion a full 55 percent of the time. The study found that wanderers had more problems with recent and remote memory, orientation to time and place, ability to respond appropriately to a given conversation topic, and overall psychosocial skills. Other studies found a strong relationship between the frequency of wandering and severity of dementia. In people who have dementia and are mobile, those with the greatest cognitive impairment are more apt to wander. An analysis of wandering behavior showed that two components — cognitive impairment and hyperactivity — differentiated wanderers from non-wanderers.

David Thomas studied the continuity of personality to wandering, and found there were two general types of wanderers: *continuous wanderers* who wander more than 50 percent of the time, and *sporadic wanderers* who roam intermittently and in bursts of time. Thomas suggests that the first step in intervening with wanderers is to ascertain whether their behavior is continuous or sporadic.

Richard Hussain developed another way to define wandering, identifying four types of wanderers. *Exit seekers* are those who repeatedly attempt to leave their physical environment, generally stating they are looking for someone or something, or they need to go somewhere. They may be obsessed with returning home, because they cannot remember why they are not there. Exit-seekers' wandering may also be a remnant of a previous work role or attempts to put some meaning and purpose into their life.

Akathesiacs exhibit restlessness and pacing behavior, often as a result of prolonged use of psychotropic medications. Other drugs also may cause restlessness. Certain people have a paradoxical reaction to opiate-based pain-killers (like codeine), causing them to become restless rather than sedated. Acetaminophen or non-steroidal anti-inflammatory drugs (NSAIDs) help akathesiacs.

Self-stimulators are those whose focus is the desire to turn the knob on a door. They do not care necessarily about actually leaving, but want the physical stimulation of opening the door. Others may wander out of the need for sensory stimulation — wandering gives them something to do. These residents may wander down a hallway, touching everything repeatedly. This type of wandering is often a sign of on-going under-stimulation or lack of structure.

The last type of wanderer is the *modeler*. Because of cognitive deterioration, they become caught up in following someone else. If the people they are with leave, they too want to leave. This behavior is a type of *echopraxia,* the involuntary mimicking of another's behavior.

The Benefits of Wandering

Within a safe environment, wandering can be beneficial. Wandering stimulates circulation and cellular oxygenation, promotes exercise, and decreases contractures. Consequently, one of the goals of managing the wandering patient is to provide a safe level of wandering without putting the patient at risk for injury.

Wandering allows a person to cope with stress and find security, and is a way to channel excess energy and anxiety. Overall, controlled wandering is viewed as having a beneficial effect for the wanderer because it fulfills a particular need.

The Hazards of Wandering

Despite its potential benefits, wandering frequently is associated with negative outcomes for both the wanderer and caregiver.

Researchers have categorized problems caused by wandering as either *safety-* or *nuisance-related,* with the most significant safety problem being a wanderer's attempts to leave the facility. Unless a facility is locked, people suffering from dementia or other forms of confusion frequently will attempt to leave the facility, usually placing themselves in peril. Approximately 20 percent of the caregivers at long-term care facilities have reported at least one incident in which wandering resulted in serious injury or death.

A number of factors may prompt wanderers to walk out of a facility. Some are attracted to the view outside the door or the light at the door, both which enhance the attractiveness of leaving the unit. Others may be cued to attempt exiting behavior by the protrusion or shape of a door knob or the shininess of a bar on the door. These attractive cues may cause residents to touch the door and trigger the alarm, even when they did not intend to exit.

Wandering behavior, besides being potentially dangerous, also is disruptive to other residents and to caregivers, as wanderers frequently intrude into other people's rooms, hop into their beds, or rummage through their belongings.

Persistent wandering eventually takes its emotional toll on patients and caregivers alike. As care-givers attempt various creative ways to restrict or control wandering, the patients often become more agitated, restless and determined. The caregivers may become frustrated as they try to protect the patient from falls and other potential dangers of the incessant and seemingly aimless activity. This frustration sometimes leads to counterproductive methods such as physical or chemical restraint, which be more dangerous to the patient than the wandering.

Many nursing homes have established special care units designed to accommodate wanderers. However, since most of these facilities were not originally designed for dementia patients, they may result in the placement of the wanderer into an environment that is not suited for their other needs.

Behavioral Interventions for Wandering

While wandering may pose a safety risk to the patient, it is important to remember there are beneficial effects of wandering. Intervention should focus on understanding why the behavior is present, and, if it appears to be therapeutic, allowing it to continue at a controlled and safe level.

The use of physical and chemical restraints should not be used, as such restraints tend to promote agitation and injury and do little to reduce falls.

1.   Approach the person from the side or from the front and gently redirect him or her away from

Wandering checklist:

Has the person's amount of social interaction decreased?

Does the patient have a history of relieving stress by physical means?

Does this person have a history of the wandering behavior?

Can this person find the bathroom unassisted?

What time of day is the wandering most prevalent?

What type of wandering is usually exhibited?

Does the person return after he wanders?

Does wandering increase after family visits?

exits and other residents' rooms. Walk the person back to the common area. If you know this person will not react negatively to being touched, gently take a hand or elbow and walk the person in the desired direction.

2.   While you are guiding the person back, provide distractions by talking about something he or she likes. You may also re-focus the person with an object, such as a stuffed toy. By focusing attention on some object such as a toy, a set of keys or a wristwatch, patients forget that they were attempting to leave. Another means of diversion is providing patients with simple activities such as organizing magazines.

3.   Remember the behavior a person is engaged in may be based on a delusion, and therefore usually of short duration. In these instances it may be best to allow the person to finish the behavior before redirecting him or her. If so,

4.   Comment on what you think the person may be trying to do, and what he or she is feeling. If the person says, "I've got to get back to work," respond by saying, "I know work is important to you," as you redirect him or her.

5.   Use verbal commands that focus on what the person should do, not what the person should not do. It is much more difficult for a demented person to understand the inhibition of action required by the command, "Don't go out there" than the prompt to action command of, "Stay in the building."

6.   Always look around before exiting the area.

7.   Use visual barriers and disguises. Doorknobs and push bars are cues for the hand to touch, even when the person does not intend to leave the unit. A beige cloth secured across the doorway with Velcro will hide the doorknob and bar, and stop this problem. Another visual barrier

that has worked well consists of a painted grid on the floor in front of doorways. Capitalizing on cognitive deficits, the grid gives the appearance of an unstable surface, and the patient refuses to walk near the door. Similarly, a mat or differently patterned piece of carpet placed in front of exits. with cause patients to avoid the area.

8. Use wander-guards when appropriate. Electronic monitoring of patients using patient monitoring arm bands or electronic monitoring devices at selected doorways have been used in some facilities. Similar to department store security systems, an alarm is activated when a monitored patient goes through the doorway. This technology serves to help caregivers know where the patients are, rather than acting as a deterrent inhibiting the movements of the patients.

9. Use large name and address tags to help people return the wanderer home. If possible, inform the local police of wanderers.

10. Keep outdoor clothing such as hats and overcoats out of sight. These items often trigger wandering behavior.

11. Schedule a time period when wanderers are encouraged to walk and engage in other physical activity. Provide a wide variety of short-term, structured activities to reduce anxiety and help wanderers believe they are spending their time in a constructive, meaningful way.

12. Gather all the wandering patients together, and take them for a walk. This accomplishes several things. First, it will remove them from the environment where they may be disrupting others. Second, it will allow them to do what they are already doing, but the behavior now becomes prescribed and structured. Third, it will increase their quality of life. Fourth, it will allow them to expend energy so that they are less agitated at

other times. Finally, the daily exercise will improve their sleep.

13. Ensure the wanderer has access to windows, which allows the person to view the environment and be aware of the weather, season, and time of day. Windows also expose the person to light, which helps regulate their biological clock, which in turn improves sleep and reduces nocturnal wandering.

14. Ensure the person has eye-glasses and hearing aids if they need them. Loss of vision and hearing can result in decreased stimulation, and lead to wandering as a stimulus-seeking behavior.

15. Use behavior modification. In a recent experiment, food rewards such as applesauce. chocolate, candies, or a sip of cola, were used as the primary reinforcer for desired behavior. A loud hand clap near the patient's ear served as an aversive stimulus. In 3-minute training sessions, a reward was given to the patient in the presence of a large orange rectangle, and the hand clap was administered while the patient was looking at a blue circle. The orange rectangle became associated with good times ahead while the blue circle was associated with an unpleasant experience.

Orange cards were then posted in places that were safe for wandering, such as the patient's room, the lounge and the hall, while blue circles were posted near hazards like staircases, closets, or exits. This arrangement decreased wandering significantly.

In one special care facility for dementia patients, several patients were former POWs of World War II. They often attempted to escape by climbing over the walls surrounding the outdoor area of the facility. When an "OFF LIMITS" sign, which was commonly used in the military, was put on the wall, there were no further attempts to escape.

In another facility, establishment of a men's club, with meetings held two evenings a week, resulted in calming its members. Folding clothes, gardening, supervised walks, or cooking activities to provide social contact, and helping residents participate in activities in which they have a high chance to succeed both decrease the desire to leave.

16. Monitor the person frequently to insure that all physiological needs are being met. A person who is hungry, uncomfortable or in pain is more prone to wander. A resident who wanders into another resident's room is usually in search of a bathroom.

17. Decrease nighttime wandering. Environmental factors associated with nocturnal wandering such as excessive background noise should be reduced to ensure the room is quiet and comfortable.

Providing a steady background noise such as a ticking clock, an aquarium pump, or headphones with relaxation tapes or special music also can help keep residents calm and in their rooms at night. The use of 'white noise,' any low intensity, continuous, rhythmic sound such as a window fan, reduces nocturnal wandering and promotes sounder sleep.

Establish a bedtime routine and move physical activities to the afternoon. Toilet the resident before bedtime and frequently throughout the night. A confused resident frequently attempts to crawl out of bed and wander because he or she is wet or has a full bladder.

Chapter Twenty-Two

Groups

Regardless of age, a person may be grossly immature in certain facets of life. Like younger people, many elderly people may lack coping skills, communication skills, problem-solving skills, or a strong sense of self-worth.

Problems frequently attributed to old age actually may have existed throughout a person's entire life. The grumpy and abusive old man in room 3 may actually be that way because he never learned a better way to communicate. Old people do not automatically get grumpy, but grumpy people do get old.

Groups can provide an effective place to work on these behaviors or skill deficits, but many elderly people are reluctant to participate, or be self-disclosing in groups. While a younger person may be more eager to connect socially, elderly people often state they have no interest in bonding with anyone. Their fear that getting to know other people on an intimate basis will result in further loss must be considered when examining resistance to care and group participation.

Behavioral Objectives

At the end of this section readers will be able to:

Discuss the goals of group activity.

Explain the reluctance to participate in group activity.

List the common types of groups and their purposes.

Use tools to conduct successful groups.

People with cognitive problems may find groups confusing and overwhelming, so potential group members should be screened individually to determine if they are likely to benefit from group experience.

Group Goals

The immediate goals of group participation are

1. To improve participants' self esteem through success-oriented interactive experiences.
2. To improve participants' ability to talk about thoughts, feelings, fantasies and ideas in the presence of others.
3. To foster in participants concern and caring for the self.
4. To teach participants' empathy and demonstrate concern for others.
5. To maximize the participants' ability for self-expression.
6. To teach participants to listen and respond, rather than react.
7. To provide a supportive, non-critical environment in which participants may express fears, losses, anxieties, and problems.
8. To provide participants with social stimulation.
9. To teach participants problem-solving and planning skills.
10. To help participants become more responsible for themselves.
11. To maximize participants' personal autonomy.
12. To teach participants how to problem-solve in socially appropriate ways.
13. To develop in participants awareness of the consequences of their actions.
14. To integrate participants into society, incorporating feelings of being worthwhile and loveable.

15.   To develop in participants the awareness that other people share similar fears, anxieties and disturbing thoughts.

Types of Groups

Assertiveness Training

The purpose of assertiveness training is to learn the differences between non-assertive, assertive and aggressive behavior, to become aware of the ways that people are manipulated, coerced, or made to feel guilty by others, and to learn, practice and develop assertive behaviors.

Communication Skills

The purpose of a communication skills group is to explain the differences between effective and ineffective communication, to learn to recognize the barriers to communication, and to teach specific listening and expressive skills.

Specific skills include:

- Writing down the problem to be solved.
- Discussing only one issue at a time.
- Staying focused on solving the problem rather than winning the argument.
- Making statements instead of asking questions.
- Being assertive, not abusive.

Emotional Education

The purpose of an emotional education group is to teach group members about the eight primary emotions, to recognize their own emotional reactions to specific situations, and to learn ways for controlling or coping with their emotional reactions. Group members should be educated in recognizing the basic emotions and labeling them when they occur, and be taught when it is appropriate to express these emotions, and how to do so clearly and constructively.

Popular songs

1901 Chocolate Creams Cake Walk
1902 Bill Bailey, Won't You Please Come Home
1903 St. Louis Rag, Ida (Sweet As Apple Cider)
1904 Red Devil Rag, The St. Louis Tickle
1905 My Gal Sal
1906 Dill Pickles Rag
1907 Kansas City Rag
1908 Memphis Rag
1909 Put on Your Old Gray Bonnett
1910 Steamboat Bill
1911 Alexander's Ragtime Band, My Melancholy Baby
1912 Memphis Blues, Look For The Silver Lining
1913 Peg O' My Heart, You Made Me Love You
1914 St. Louis Blues
1915 Jelly Roll Blues, I Ain't Got Nobody
1916 Pretty Baby
1917 Darktown Strutters Ball, Tiger Rag
1918 Ja Da, Oh How I Hate To Get Up In The Morning
1919 Swanee, Baby, Won't You Please Come Home
1920 You Can't Keep a Good Man Down
1921 I'm Just Wild About Harry, April Showers
1922 My Honey's Lovin' Arms, Chicago
1923 Charleston
1924 Tea For Two, The Man I Love
1925 Sweet Georgia Brown, Muskrat amble

Depression Group

The purpose of this group is to help people recognize the symptoms of depression, so they can identify depression in themselves and others. It's useful to provide each member a symptom sheet for later reference. Members also learn how depression causes cognitive distortions and the loss of pleasure in life. Group members should have the opportunity, at designated times, to share their feelings, and hear other members' offered solutions to problems expressed.

Motivation Groups

This group encourages people to share various kinds of information about activities and pleasant social experiences. The purpose is to motivate people to interact socially and establish a richer environment through the discussion of concrete and specific topics such as vacations, gardening, pets, art, hobbies, and nature. Because these groups are a way to recapture pleasure, motivation groups work well in conjunction with depression groups.

Music Therapy

Music therapy helps people in several ways. First, music is a structured, rhythmic event that stimulates the senses, the emotions, and the body, provoking a response from the individual. Second, it provide a means of self-expression, allowing the person to communicate moods, feelings for others, and attitudes about life on a non-verbal level. Third, music facilitates interpersonal relationships and social interactions, such as dancing and singing together. Fourth, music is a powerful way to evoke memory and stimulate thought. Every person has a favorite song, or special memories tied to music.

In the margins are popular songs from past eras.

Medication Groups

Medication groups educate people about the effects and side-effects of medications. This group also learns about good and bad drugs, over-the counter-drugs, and the effects of various herbs, vitamins, and nutrients, as well as about the hazards of abuse, medication compliance, and methods of medication administration (e.g. pills, liquids, gels, inhalents and injections).

Reminiscence Groups

This group provides the opportunity for the exchange of early life experience, such as holiday cele-brations and cooking favorite foods. Such reminis-cences promote interpersonal relationships, increases the sense of belonging, stimulates thought processes, and brings back pleasant memories.

Sensory Training Group

The purpose of this group is to increase function or prevent further deterioration of cognitively impaired people by providing many types of stimuli that arouse the person's senses, promote awareness and elicit meaningful responses.

Orientation Groups

To supplement daily reorientation, participants attend a special class in Reality Orientation lasting approximately 30 minutes and varying in size from two to eight residents. During these classes, participants are given basic information and helped to relearn it by making new associations with words, pictures and objects. Music therapy, combined with orientation, has proven to be especially effective.

Horticulture Groups

Many elderly people require a motivation in order to get out of bed. For many, tending plants provides that

1927 Old Man River, Blue Skies
1928 You Do Something To Me, I'll Get By
1929 Honeysuckle Rose, Am I Blue
1930 I Got Rhythm, Rockin' Chair
1931 All of Me, Lazy River
1932 It Don't Mean A Thing;
1933 Don't Blame Me
 I've Got the World on a String
1934 Stompin' at the Savoy
1935 Porgy And Bess, Blue Moon
1936 I've Got You Under My Skin
1937 I've Got My Love To Keep Me Warm
1938 My Heart Belongs To Daddy
1939 Somewhere Over The Rainbow
1940 Fools Rush In
1941 How About You, I Got It Bad (And That Ain't Good)
1942 White Christmas, That Old Black Magic
1943 As Time Goes By
1944 Have Yourself A merry Little Christmas
1945 Anything You Can Do, Deep Purple
1947 How Are Things in Gloccamora
1948 Buttons And Bows
1949 Scarlet Ribbons
1950 On A Clear Day You Can See Forever
1953 I Love Paris
1954 Misty
1955 Blue Lights
1958 Satin Doll

motivation. People with a plant to care for report more satisfaction in their long term care facilities.

Art Therapy

For many elderly people, art provides an enjoyable, meaningful life experience. This is particularly true once they have had the opportunity to work with in various art media, including painting, drawing, sculpting, pottery and crafts.

Movement Therapy

The goals of this group include release of tension, reduction of anxiety, re-socialization through group interaction and shared movement experiences, improvement of body image, sense of self-worth and self-confidence in one's own body actions, stimulation of verbalization, physical conditioning and exercise.

Recreation Therapy

Recreation provides a way of helping residents direct their attention away from their illnesses toward healthy leisure activity. Recreation motivates and re-awakens in the resident an interest in things that are fun and encourages the healing process.

This program encourages the use of appropriate recreational facilities in the community. Daily recreational therapy sessions may include physical therapy, dance therapy, music therapy, art therapy and a variety of crafts. Crafts include ceramics, wood projects, leather tooling, needle crafting and various other crafts.

Exercise Groups

Constructive physical activity is vital to an individual's well being. An exercise program will delay the body's slowing-down process, contribute to self esteem, and stabilize mood.

Family Support Groups

A family support group is a vital and valuable service offered to the families and friends of the elderly patient. The purpose of the group is to allow open expression of feelings that the family member or friend may be experiencing in their relationship with the patient. The support group also allows the family member or friend the opportunity to problem-solve issues of physical, financial, social, and environmental concerns. In addition, the support group leader teaches participants about the origins and reasons for the problems and difficulties their loved ones are experiencing.

References

1: Ageism

Adams T. The case for breaking through ageism in mental health care. *Nursing Times,* 1996 Mar 20- 26, 92(12):46-7.

Adams T. Working in partnership to end ageism in mental health. *British Journal of Nursing,* 1997 Feb 13-26, 6(3):133.

Coontz, S. *The way we never were* Basic Books, NY., 1992

Fuller D. Challenging ageism through our speech. *Nursing Times,* 1995 May 24-30, 91(21):29-31.

Goulden, Joseph *The Best Years* Athenuem, NY., 1976

[No authors cited] Frequently Asked Questions Age 65 Retirement. Social Security Online. http://www.ssa.gov/history/age65.html

Haight BK; Christ MA; Dias JK. Does nursing education promote ageism? *Journal of Advanced Nursing,* 1994 Aug, 20(2):382-90.

Halek C. Hating your patients. *Nurs Stand.* 1990 Dec 12-8;5(12):46-7.

Laws M. A love hate relationship. *N Z Nurs J.* 1990 Aug;83(7):13-5.

James JW; Haley WE. Age and health bias in practicing clinical psychologists. *Psychology and Aging,* 1995 Dec, 10(4):610-6.

Lash, C. The Culture of Narcissism W.W. Norton, NY., 1978.

McMinn B. Ageism: the challenge for nursing. *Australian Nursing Journal,* 1996 May, 3(10):18- 21.

Ryan A. Focus on ageism [news]. *Elderly Care,* 1997 Feb-Mar, 9(1):40.

Seymour M. Putting an end to ageism. *Canadian Nurse,* 1994 Nov, 90(10):49-50.

Wexler, Nancy (1996) *Momma Can't Remember Anymore* Wein & Wien Thousand Oaks, CA.

2: Leaving Home

Coffman TL. (1981) Relocation and survival of institutionalized aged: A re-examination of the evidence. *The Gerontologist* 21(5):483-500.

Cummings, E. and Henry, W (1961) *Growing Old: The Process of Disengagement* Basic Books, NY.Coffman, S. and Coffman, V. (1986) Aging awareness training for professionals who work with the elderly. *Small Group Behavior,* 95-103.

Havinghurst R. (1961) Successful aging *The Gerontologist* 1:8-13.

3: Families

Grafstrom M; Fratiglioni L; Sandman PO; Winblad B. Health and social consequences for relatives of demented and non demented elderly. A population based study. *Journal of Clinical Epidemiology,* 1992 Aug, 45(8):861 70.

Grimby A. Bereavement among elderly people: grief reactions, post bereavement hallucinations and quality of life. *Acta Psychiatrica Scandinavica,* 1993 Jan, 87(1):72 80.

Howe, G.W. (1994) Neurological trauma and family functioning: toward a social neuropsychology [comment] *Psychiatry* 57(3):275 7 Comment on: *Psychiatry* 1994 Aug;57(3):269 74.

Pillemer K, Finkelhor D. The prevalence of elder abuse: a random sample survey. *Gerontologist* 1988; 28: 51-57

Teusink, J. & Mahler, S. (1984). Helping families cope with. Alzheimer's disease. *Hospital and Community Psychiatry 35,.* 152-156.

4: Memory Problems

Allain H; Raoul P; Lieury A; LeCoz F; Gandon JM; d'Arbigny P. Effect of two doses of ginkgo biloba extract (EGb 761) on the dual coding test in elderly subjects. *Clinical Therapeutics,* 1993 May Jun, 15(3):549 58.

Matteson, William *Stop Memory Loss! How to Fight Forgetfulness over Forty* Matteson Media, Pacific Palisades, CA .,1997.

Erber JT; Szuchman LT. Memory performance in relation to age, verbal ability, and activity. *Experimental Aging Research,* 1996 Jan Mar, 22(1): 59 72.

Sandman, Curt A. Memory rehabilitation in Alzheimer's disease: Preliminary findings. *Clinical Gerontologist,* 1993, v13 (n4):19 33.

5: Confusion

Edmands MS. "Murder!" she said: a case of iatrogenic delirium. *Issues in Mental Health Nursing,* 1995 Mar Apr, 16(2):109 16.

Evans. L. (1987). Sundown syndrome in institutionalized elderly. *Am. Geriat. Soc.,* 35(5), 101.

Haupt.C, Kurz, A Reversibiliry of dementia in hypothyroidism. *Journal of Neurology* 240 :333 335.

Kroeger, L. L. [1991). Critical care nurses' perceptions of the confused elderly patient, *Focus on Critical Care,* 18(5). 395.

Levkofl. 5. E.. Evans. O. A., er al, (1992]. Delirium: The occurrence and persistence of symptoms among elderly hospitalized patients. *Arch. Intern. Med.* 152:21 33.

Ostenveil D, Svndulko K, Cohen SN, et al: Cognitive function in non demented older adults with hypothyroidism. *Journal of the American Geri-atrics Society* 1992 ;40(4): 325 335

Patkar AA; Kunkel EJ. Treating delirium among elderly patients. *Psychiatric Services,* 1997 Jan, 48(1):46 8.

Schor. J. D., Levkoll, S. E.. el al. (1992). Risk factors for delirium In hospitalized elderly. *JAMA.* 267(6), 27.

SunderlJiid, T. (1990). Organic brain disorders. In *The Merck Manual of Geriatrics.*

Touks C, Mental illness in hypothyroid patients. *British Journal of Psychiatry* 1964;110:706 710

War DJ, Pastel ML: Prognosis in myxedematous madness. *British Journal of Psychiatry* 1967; 113:149 151

Warshaw G; Tanzer F. The effectiveness of lumbar puncture in the evaluation of delirium and fever in the hospitalized elderly. *Archives of Family Medicine,* 1993 Mar, 2(3):293 7.

Whybrow PC, Prange J, Treadway CR, Mental changes accompanying thyroid gland dysfunction. *Archives of General Psychiatry* 1969;20:48 63

Yeaw EM; Abbate JH. Identification of confusion among the elderly in an acute care setting. *Clinical Nurse Specialist,* 1993 Jul, 7(4):192 7.

6: Dementia

Alzheimer's Disease: A Scientific Guide for Health Practitioners, NIH Pub 81 2251. Bethesda, MD, National Institute of Health, 1980

Borell L; Sandman PO; Winblad B. Abilities and activities of patients with dementia in day hospitals. *Scandinavian Journal of Caring Sciences,* 1991, 5(1):49 55.

Bucht G; Sandman PO. Nutritional aspects of dementia, especially Alzheimer's disease. *Age and Ageing,* 1990 Jul, 19(4):S32 6.

Burdz,. M, Eaton,. W, Bond, J. (1988) Effect of respite care on dementia and non dementia patients and their caregivers. *Psychol of Aging* 3:38 42.

Carlson DL; Fleming KC; Smith GE; Evans JM. Management of dementia related behavioral disturbances: a nonpharmacologic approach. *Mayo Clinic Proceedings,* 1995 Nov, 70(11): 1108 15.

Clendaniel, BP and Fleishell, A. (1979) An Alzheimer's day care center for nursing home patients. *American Journal of Nursing* 1075:944 945

Fact Sheet: *Senile Dementia and Alzheimer's Disease.* DHEW pub ADM 80 929. Rockville, MD National institute of Mental Health, 1980.

Forsell Y; Jorm AF; Winblad B. Variation in psychiatric and behavioural symptoms at different stages of dementia: data from physicians' examinations and informants' reports. *Dementia,* 1993 Sep Oct, 4(5):282 6.

Funkenstein HH, Hicks R, Dysken MW, et al: Drug treatment of cognitive impairment in Alzheimer's disease and the late life dementias, in *Clinical Aspects of Alzheimer's Disease and Senile Dementia.* Edited by Miller NE, Cohen GD. New York, Raven Press, 1981.

Geiser. R., Hoche. L., King. J. (1988) Respite care for mentally ill patients and their families. *Hospital Community Psychiatry* 39:291 295.

Gugel RN. Behavioral approaches for managing patients with Alzheimer's disease and related dis-orders. *Medical Clinics of North America,* 1994 Jul, 78(4):861 7.

Karzman R (ed): *Biological Aspects of Alzheimer's Disease,* Banbury Report 15. Cold Spring Harbor, NY, Cold Spring Harbor Laboratory, 1983.

Katzman R. Terry RD, Bick K (eds): *Senile Dementia and Related Disorders.* New York, Raven Press, 1978.

Keene JM; Hope T. Hyperphagia in dementia: 1. The use of an objective and reliable method for measuring hyperphagia in people with dementia. *Appetite,* 1997 Apr, 28(2):151 65.

Mace NL, Rabins, PV *The 36 Hour Day.* Baltimore, Johns Hopkins University Press.

Miller NE, Cohen GD (eds): *Clinical Aspects of Alzheimer's Disease and Senile Dementia.* New York, Raven Press, 1981.

Peisah C; Brodaty H. Practical guidelines for the treatment of behavioural complications of dementia. *Medical Journal of Australia,* 1994 Nov 7, 161(9):558 63.

Postoff, R., Collins, A. and Eastwood, M. (1991) *Alzheimer's Disease and Related Disorders.* Toronto: Clarke Institute of Psychiatry.

Reisberg B, Ferris SH, Arnand R, et al: (1983) Effects of naloxone in senile dementia: a double blind trial (ltr). *New England Journal of Medicine* 308:721 722.

Roth M: The psychiatric disorders of later life. Psychiatric Annals 6:57 101, 1976

Sandman PO. Is good care the best treatment for the Alzheimer patient? *Acta Neurologica Scandinavica.* Supplementum, 1990, 129:37 9.

Smith-Jones, SM and Francis, GM (1992) Disruptive, Institutionalized Elderly: Cost Effective Intervention. *Journal of Psychosocial Nursing* 30(10): 17-20.

Thal LJ, Masur DM, Fuld PA, et al. (1983) Memory improvement with oral physostigmine and lecithin in Alzheimer's disease, in *Biological Aspects of Alzheimer's Disease,* Banbury Report 15. Edited by Katzman R. Cold Spring Harbor, NY, Cold Spring Harbor Laboratory.

7: Depression

Alexopoulos GS; Vrontou C; Kakuma T; Meyers BS; Young RC; Klausner E; Clarkin J. Disability in geriatric depression. *American Journal of Psychiatry,* 1996 Jul, 153(7):877 85.

Avorn J, Everitt DE, Weiss S. Increased antidepressant use in patients prescribed beta-blockers. *JAMA.* 1986 Jan 17;255(3):357-60.

Bell IR; Edman JS; Morrow FD; Marby DW; Perrone G; Kayne HL; Greenwald M; Cole JO. Brief communication. Vitamin B1, B2, and B6 augmentation of tricyclic antidepres-

sant treatment in geriatric depression with cognitive dysfunction. *Journal of the American College of Nutrition,* 1992 Apr, 11(2):159 63.

Brodaty H. Think of depression atypical presentations in the elderly. *Australian Family Physician,* 1993 Jul, 22(7):1195 203.

Ciechanowski P, Wagner E, Schmaling K, Schwartz S, Williams B, Diehr P, Kulzer J, Gray S, Collier C, LoGerfo J. Community-integrated home-based depression treatment in older adults: a randomized controlled trial. *JAMA.* 2004 Apr 7;291(13):1569-77.

Conn DK; Goldman Z. Pattern of use of antidepressants in long term care facilities for the elderly. *Journal of Geriatric Psychiatry and Neurology,* 1992 Oct Dec, 5(4):228 32.

Devanand DP; Nobler MS; Singer T; Kiersky JE; Turret N; Roose SP; Sackeim HA. Is dysthymia a different disorder in the elderly? *American Journal of Psychiatry,* 1994 Nov, 151(11):1592 9.

Diagnostic and Statistical Manual of Mental Disorders DSM-IV American Psychiatric Association 2000.

Gaupp R: Depressive states in old age. (Classic Text 42, orig. published 1905). *Historical Psychiatry* 2000; 11:213-225

Krishnan KR, Hays JC, Blazer DG (1997), MRI-defined vascular depression. *Am J Psychiatry* 154(4):497-501.

Krishnan KR, Heyman A, Ritchie JC, Utley CM, Dawson DV, Rogers H. Depression in early-onset Alzheimer's disease: clinical and neuroendocrine correlates. *Biol Psychiatry.* 1988 Dec;24(8):937-40

Krishnan KRR, Hays JC, George LK, et al: Six-month outcomes for MRI-related vascular depression. *Depress Anxiety* 1998; 8:142- 146

Lee MA; Ganzini L. Depression in the elderly: effect on patient attitudes toward life sustaining therapy [see comments]. *Journal of the American Geriatrics Society,* 1992 Oct, 40(10):983 8.

Murphy GM Jr, Hollander SB, Rodrigues HE, Kremer C, Schatzberg AF. Effects of the serotonin transporter gene promoter polymorphism on mirtazapine and paroxetine efficacy and adverse events in geriatric major depression. *Arch Gen Psychiatry.* 2004 Nov;61(11):1163-9.

Post F. *The significance of affective symptoms in old age*. London: Oxford University Press, Institute of Psychiatry, 1962. (Maudsley Monographs No 10.)

Prigerson HG; Frank E; Kasl SV; Reynolds CF 3rd; Anderson B; Zubenko GS; Houck PR; George CJ; Kupfer DJ. Complicated grief and bereavement related depression as distinct disorders: preliminary empirical validation in elderly bereaved spouses. *American Journal of Psychiatry*, 1995 Jan, 152(1):22 30.

Reynolds CF 3rd. Recognition and differentiation of elderly depression in the clinical setting. *Geriatrics*, 1995 Oct, 50 Suppl 1:S6 15.

Rothschild AJ. The diagnosis and treatment of late life depression. *Journal of Clinical Psychiatry*, 1996, 57 Suppl 5:5 11.

8: Suicide

Bron B. [Depression and suicide in the elderly]. *Zeitschrift fur Gerontologie*, 1992 Jan Feb, 25(1): 43 52.

Canetto SS. Gender and suicide in the elderly. *Suicide and Life Threatening Behavior*, 1992 Spring, 22(1):80 97.

Casey DA. Suicide in the elderly. *Journal of the Kentucky Medical Association*, 1990 Jun, 88(6): 301.

Casey DA. Suicide in the elderly: a two year study of data from death certificates [see comments]. *Southern Medical Journal*, 1991 Oct, 84(10): 1185 7.

Conwell Y. Suicide in the elderly [see comments]. *Crisis*, 1992, 13(1):6 8.

De Leo D; Ormskerk SC. Suicide in the elderly: general characteristics. *Crisis*, 1991 Sep, 12(2): 3 17.

Drion H. Suicide in the elderly [letter; comment] [see comments]. *Crisis*, 1992, 13(2):52.

Duffy D. Suicide in later life: how to spot the risk factors. *Nursing Times*, 1997 Mar 12 18, 93(11): 56 7.

Galanos, AN. Suicide in the elderly [letter; comment]. *Southern Medical Journal*, 1992 Mar, 85(3):331.

Heiss HW. [Restriction or fulfillment. Ethical topics on suicide and sexuality of the elderly]. *Wiener Medizinische Wochenschrift*, 1992, 142 (23 24): 1 p. following 538.

Humphry D. Rational suicide among the elderly. *Suicide and Life Threatening Behavior*, 1992 Spring, 22(1):125 9.

Horton Deutsch SL; Clark DC; Farran CJ. Chronic dyspnea and suicide in elderly men. *Hospital and Community Psychiatry*, 1992 Dec, 43(12):1198 203.

Hochbaum GM. Suicide by the elderly [letter; comment]. *American Journal of Public Health*, 1992 Aug, 82(8):1175.

Kua EH; Ko SM. A cross cultural study of suicide among the elderly in Singapore. *British Journal of Psychiatry*, 1992 Apr, 160:558 9.

Kerkhof A; de Leo D. Suicide in the elderly: a frightful awareness. *Crisis*, 1991 Sep, 12(2):81 7.

Lester D; Yang B. Social and economic correlates of the elderly suicide rate. *Suicide and Life Threatening Behavior*, 1992 Spring, 22(1):36 47.

Loebel JP; Loebel JS; Dager SR; Centerwall BS; Reay DT. Anticipation of nursing home placement may be a precipitant of suicide among the elderly. *Journal of the American Geriatrics Society*, 1991 Apr, 39(4):407 8.

Lyness JM; Conwell Y; Nelson JC. Suicide attempts in elderly psychiatric inpatients. *Journal of the American Geriatrics Society*, 1992 Apr, 40(4): 320 4.

McIntosh JL. Epidemiology of suicide in the elderly. *Suicide and Life Threatening Behavior*, 1992 Spring, 22(1):15 35.

Mellick E; Buckwalter KC; Stolley JM. Suicide among elderly white men: development of a profile. *Journal of Psychosocial Nursing and Mental Health Services*, 1992 Feb, 30(2):29 34.

Nieto E; Vieta E; Lazaro L; Gasto C; Cirera E. Serious suicide attempts in the elderly. *Psycho-pathology*, 1992, 25(4):183 8.

Rifai AH; Reynolds CF; Mann JJ. Biology of elderly suicide. *Suicide and Life Threatening Behavior*, 1992 Spring, 22(1):48 61.

Rao AV. Suicide in the elderly: a report from India. *Crisis*, 1991 Sep, 12(2):33 9.

Schmid H; Manjee K; Shah T. On the distinction of suicide ideation versus attempt in elderly psychiatric inpatients. *Gerontologist*, 1994 Jun, 34(3): 332 9.

Skoog I; Aevarsson O; Beskow J; Larsson L; Palsson S; Waern M; Landahl S; Ostling S. Suicidal feelings in a population sample of non-demented 85 year olds. *American Journal of Psychiatry*, 1996 Aug, 153(8):1015 20.

Sverre JM. Trends in suicide mortality among the elderly in Norway, 1966 1986. *Epidemiology*, 1991 Jul, 2(4):252 6.

Tatai K; Tatai K. Suicide in the elderly: a report from Japan. *Crisis*, 1991 Sep, 12(2):40 3.

9: Anxiety

Beck JG; Stanley MA; Zebb BJ. Characteristics of generalized anxiety disorder in older adults: a descriptive study. *Behaviour Research and Therapy*, 1996 Mar, 34(3):225 34.

Bleiker EM; van der Ploeg HM; Mook J; Kleijn WC. Anxiety, anger, and depression in elderly women. Psychological Reports, 1993 Apr, 72(2): 567 74.

Byrne GJ; Raphael B. The psychological symptoms of conjugal bereavement in elderly men over the first 13 months. *International Journal of Geriatric Psychiatry*, 1997 Feb, 12(2):241 51.

Casten RJ; Parmelee PA; Kleban MH; Lawton MP; Katz IR. The relationships among anxiety, depression, and pain in a geriatric institutionalized sample. *Pain*, 1995 May, 61(2):271 6.

Flint AJ. Epidemiology and comorbidity of anxiety disorders in the elderly. American Journal of Psychiatry, 1994 May, 151(5):640 9.

Hocking LB; Koenig HG. Anxiety in medically ill older patients: a review and update. *International Journal of Psychiatry in Medicine*, 1995, 25(3): 221 38.

Lindesay J. Neurotic disorders in the elderly: often missed, poorly treated [editorial]. *British Journal of Hospital Medicine*, 1997 Apr 2 15, 57(7): 304 5.

Markovitz PJ. Treatment of anxiety in the elderly. *Journal of Clinical Psychiatry*, 1993 May, 54 Suppl:64 8.

Marriott P; Smith R. The elderly agoraphobic: a hidden problem. *Australian Family Physician*, 1993 Nov, 22(11):2036 7, 2040 1, 2044 5.

Martin LM; Fleming KC; Evans JM. Recognition and management of anxiety and depression in elderly patients [see comments]. *Mayo Clinic Proceedings*, 1995 Oct, 70(10):999 1006.

Orrell M; Bebbington P. Psychosocial stress and anxiety in senile dementia. *Journal of Affective Disorders*, 1996 Jul 29, 39(3):165 73.

Prigerson HG; Shear MK; Newsom JT; Frank E; Reynolds CF 3rd; Maciejewski PK; Houck PR; Bierhals AJ; Kupfer DJ. Anxiety among widowed elders: is it distinct from depression and grief? *Anxiety*, 1996, 2(1):1 12.

Raj BA; Corvea MH; Dagon EM. The clinical characteristics of panic disorder in the elderly: a retrospective study. *Journal of Clinical Psychiatry*, 1993 Apr, 54(4):150 5.

Rozenzweig A; Prigerson H; Miller MD; Reynolds CF 3rd. Bereavement and late life depression: grief and its complications in the elderly. *Annual Review of Medicine*, 1997, 48:421 8.

Schneider LS. Overview of generalized anxiety disorder in the elderly. *Journal of Clinical Psychiatry*, 1996, 57 Suppl 7:34 45; discussion 52 4.

Sheikh JI; Salzman C. Anxiety in the elderly. Course and treatment. *Psychiatric Clinics of North America*, 1995 Dec, 18(4):871 83.

Simington JA; Laing GP. Effects of therapeutic touch on anxiety in the institutionalized elderly. *Clinical Nursing Research*, 1993 Nov, 2(4): 438 50.

Small GW. Recognizing and treating anxiety in the elderly. *Journal of Clinical Psychiatry*, 1997, 58 Suppl 3:41 7; discussion 48 50.

Smith SL; Sherrill KA; Colenda CC. Assessing and treating anxiety in elderly persons. *Psychiatric Services*, 1995 Jan, 46(1):36 42.

Tucker GJ. Introduction. Part I. Treatment approaches to anxiety, depression, and aggression in the elderly. *Journal of Clinical Psychiatry*, 1994 Feb, 55 Suppl:3 4.

10: Medical Problems

Ancalzi RA; Gemma A; Marra C; Muzzolon R; Capparella O; Carbonin P. Chronic obstructive pulmonary disease. An original model of cognitive decline. *American Review of Respiratory Disease*, 1993 Aug, 148(2):418 24.

Blennow K, Popa C, Rasulzada A, Minthon L, Wallin A, Zetterberg H. [There is a strong evidence that professional boxing results in chronic brain damage. The more head punches during a boxer's career, the bigger is the risk] *Lakartidningen*. 2005 Sep 5-11;102(36):2468-70, 2472-5.[Article in Swedish]

Bonkovsky, H.L.; Kane, R.E.; Jones, D.P.; Galinsky, R.E.; Banner, B. (1994) Acute hepatic and renal toxicity from low doses of acetaminophen in the absence of alcohol abuse or malnutrition: evidence for increased susceptibility to drug toxicity due to cardiopulmonary and renal insufficiency. *Hepatology,* May;19(5):1141 8

Caroselli Karinja, M. (1985) Drug abuse and the elderly. *J Psychosoc Nurs Ment Health Serv,* Jun;23(6):25 30

Chenitz, W.C.; Salisbury, S.; Stone, J.T. (1990) Drug misuse and abuse in the elderly. *Issues Ment Health Nurs* 11(1):1 16

Colledge NR; Barr Hamilton RM; Lewis SJ; Sellar RJ; Wilson JA. Evaluation of investigations to diagnose the cause of dizziness in elderly people: a community based controlled study. *BMJ* (Clinical Research Ed.), 1996 Sep 28, 313(7060): 788 92.

Cosgrove, R.(1988) Understanding drug abuse in the elderly. *Midwife Health Visit Community Nurse,* Jun;24(6):222 3

el Mallakh, R.S. (1989) Migraine headaches and drug abuse [letter] *South Med J,* 82(6):805

Finch, J. (1993) Prescription drug abuse. North Carolina Governor's Institute on Alcohol and Substance Abuse, Durham. *Primary Care,* Mar; 20(1): 231 9

Fooken I. Sexuality in the later years the impact of health and body image in a sample of older women. *Patient Education and Counseling,* 1994 Jul, 23(3):227 33.

Giannini, A.J. (1988) Drug abuse and depression: possible models for geriatric anorexia. *Neurobiol Aging,* Jan Feb;9(1):26 7

Granella, F.; Farina, S.; Malferrari, G.; Manzoni, G.C. (1987) Drug abuse in chronic headache: a clinico epidemiologic study. *Cephalalgia,* Mar;7 (1):15 9

Grimby A; Rosenhall U. Health related quality of life and dizziness in old age [see comments]. *Gerontology,* 1995, 41(5):286 98.

Hasin, D.; Endicott, J, (1985) Alcohol and drug abuse in patients with affective syndromes. *Compr Psychiatry,* May Jun; 26(3): 283 95

Hauser, A.C.; Derfler, K.; Balcke, P. (1991) Progression of renal insufficiency in analgesic neph-ropathy: impact of continuous drug abuse. *J Clin Epidemiol;*44(1):53 6

Jinks, M.J.; Raschko, R.R. (1990) A profile of alcohol and prescription drug abuse in a high risk community based elderly population. *DICP* 24(10): 971 5

Kimball MJ, Williams-Burgess C. Failure to thrive: the silent epidemic of the elderly. *Arch Psychiatr Nurs.* 1995 Apr;9(2):99-105.

Kumar, P.D.; Chandrasekharan, K.G. (1992) 'Cauliflower ear' in an Indian patient with drug abuse [letter] *J Assoc Physicians India* Jul;40(7): 491.

Marcus, M.T. (1993) Alcohol and other drug abuse in elders [published erratum appears in J ET Nurs, 1993 Jul Aug;20(4):168] *J ET Nurs,* May Jun;20(3):106 10

McInnes, E.; Powell, J. (1994) Drug and alcohol referrals: are elderly substance abuse diagnoses and referrals being missed? *British Medical Journal,* Feb 12;308 (6926):444 6

Pennypacker LC; Allen RH; Kelly JP; Matthews LM; Grigsby J; Kaye K; Lindenbaum J; Stabler SP. High prevalence of cobalamin deficiency in elderly outpatients [see comments]. *Journal of the American Geriatrics Society,* 1992 Dec, 40(12): 1197 204.

Rice, D.P.; Kelman, S. (1989) Measuring comorbidity and overlap in the hospitalization cost for alcohol and drug abuse and mental illness. *Inquiry,* Summer;26(2):249 60

Rice, D.P.; Kelman, S.; Miller, L.S. (1991) Economic costs of drug abuse. *NIDA Research Monographs;*113:10 32

Sharma, A.; Newton, W. (1995) Clonidine as a drug of abuse. *J Am Board Fam Pract* Mar Apr; 8(2):136 8

Shelowitz, P.A. (1987) Drug use, misuse, and abuse among the elderly. *Med Law;* 6(3):235 50

Sloane PD; Hartman M; Mitchell CM. Psychological factors associated with chronic dizziness in patients aged 60 and older. *Journal of the American Geriatrics Society,* 1994 Aug, 42(8): 847 2.

Solomon. K.; Manepalli, J.; Ireland,G.A.; Mahon, G.M. (1993) Alcoholism and prescription drug abuse in the elderly: St. Louis University grand rounds [clinical conference] *Journal of the American Geriatrics Society* 41(1):57 69

Sullivan M; Clark MR; Katon WJ; Fischl M; Russo J; Dobie RA; Voorhees R. Psychiatric and otologic diagnoses in patients complaining of dizziness [see comments]. *Archives of Internal Medicine,* 1993 Jun 28, 153(12):1479 84.

Wade, M. (1987) Meeting the challenge of alcohol and drug abuse in the older adult. *Home*

Healthc Nurse, Sep Oct;5(5):19, 22 3

Weiss, K.J.; Greenfield, D.P. (1986) Prescription drug abuse. *Psychiatr Clin North Am,* Sep;9(3): 475 90

11: Pain

Dodrill, C.B. (1997) Myths of neuropsychology. *The Clinical Neuropsychologist.* 11, 1 17.

Eccleston, C. (1994) Chronic pain and attention: A cognitive approach. *British Journal of Clinical Psychology,* 33: 535 47.

Eccleston, C. (1995) Chronic pain and distraction: An experimental investigation into the role of sustained and shifting attention in the *processing of chronic persistent pain. Behavior Research and Therapy.* 33(4): 391 405.

Grigsby, J., Rosenburg, N.L. and Busenbark, D. (1995) Chronic pain is associated with deficits in information processing. *Perceptual and Motor Skills.* 81,403 410.

Jennings, P.J Cancer pain relief (2nd ed.). Geneva:.

Kewman, D.G., Valshampayan, N., Zeid, D. 8 Han, B. (1991) Cognitive impairment in musculo-keletal pain patients. *International Journal of Psychiatry in Medicine.* 21(3): 253 62.

Medina Artiles E, Rodriguez Rodriguez M, Acosta Suarez G. [The care standard of patients at high risk of disuse syndrome] *Rev Cubana Enferm.* 1997 Jan-Jun;13(1):54-9. [Article in Spanish]

McCaffery M, Ferrell BR. Opioid analgesics: nurses' knowledge of doses and psycho gical dependence. *J Nurs Staff Dev.* 1992 Mar-Apr;8(2):77-84.

Schwartz, D.P., Earth, J.T., Dane, J.R., Drenan, S.E., DeGood, D.E. and Rowlingson, J.C. (1987) Cognitive deficits in chronic pain patients with and without a history of head/neck injury: Development of a brief screening battery. *The Clinical Journal of Pain.* 3, 94 101.

12: Hearing Problems

Andersson G; Melin L; Scott B; Lindberg P. An evaluation of a behavioural treatment approach to hearing impairment. *Behaviour Research and Therapy,* 1995 Mar, 33(3):283 92.

Andersson G; Melin L; Scott B; Lindberg P. A two year follow up examination of a behavioural treatment approach to hearing tactics. *British Journal of Audiology,* 1995 Dec, 29(6):347 54.

Andersson G; Green M. Anxiety in elderly hearing impaired persons. *Perceptual and Motor Skills,* 1995 Oct, 81(2):552 4.

13: Vision Problems

Bab, Werner. *The Uses of Psychology in Geriatric Ophthalmology.* Springfield, Ill., Thomas [1964].

Ferris FL 3rd, Tielsch JM. Blindness and visual impairment: a public health issue for the future as well as today. *Arch Ophthalmol.* 2004 Apr;122(4):451-2.

Lightman JM; Rosenbloom AA. Geriatric optometry questionnaire. Journal of the American Optometric Association, 1991 Jun, 62(6):472 4.

Pankow L; Luchins D. An optical intervention for visual hallucinations associated with visual impairment in an elderly patient. *Optometry and Vision Science,* 1997 Mar, 74(3):138 43.

14: Hallucinations

Anderson SW, Rizzo M. Hallucinations following occipital lobe damage: the pathological activation of visual representations. *Journal of Clinical and Experimental Neuropsychology.* 1994;16(5): 651 663.

Arnow, A. J. *Verbal hallucinations: a restitutional symptom.* Bull. Menninger Clin., 1952, 16: 178 183.

Berries GE, Brook P. The Charles Bonnet syndrome and the problem of visual perceptual disorders in the elderly. *Age Aging.* 1982:2: 17 23.

Bick PA, Kinsbourne M. Auditory hallucinations and subvocal speech in schizophrenic patients. *Am J Psychiatry.* 1987 Feb;144(2):222-5.

Buckwalter KC. Phantom of the nursing home. *J Gerontol Nurs.* 1992 Sep;18(9):46-7.

Chen J; Gomez M; Veit S; O' Dowd MA. Visual hallucinations in a blind elderly woman: Charles Bonnet syndrome, an under-recognized clinical condition [letter]. *General Hospital Psychiatry,* 1996 Nov, 18(6):453 5.

Dewi-Rees, W. (1971) The hallucinations of widowhood. *British Medical Journal.* 3:3741.

Eisendrath SJ, Sweeney MA. Toxic neuropsychiatric effects of digoxin at therapeutic serum concentrations. *American Journal of Psychiatry.* 1987; 144(4): 506 507.

Erickson, GD and Gustafson, GJ. Controlling auditory hallucination. *Hospital and Community Psychiatry,* 1968, 19: 327 329.

Fornazzari I, Farcnik K, Smith I, et al. Violent visual hallucinations and aggression in frontal lobe dysfunction: clinical manifestations of deep orbito-frontal foci. *Journal of Neuropsychiatry and Clinical Neuroscience.* 1992;4(1):42 44,

Goffey CE, Cummings, JL, eds. *American Psychiatric Press Textbook of Geriatric Neuropsychiatry.* Washington: American Psychiatric Press; 1994.

Gould LN. Verbal hallucinations as automatic speech; the reactivation of dormant speech habit. *Am J Psychiatry.* 1950 Aug;107(2):110-9.

Grossberg GT; Manepalli J. The older patient with psychotic symptoms. *Psychiatric Services,* 1995 Jan, 46(1):55 9.

Holroyd S, Rabins PV, Finkelstein D, et al. Visual hallucinations in patients with macular degeneration. *American Journal of Psychiatry,* 1992; 149 (12): 1701 1 706.

Lalla D; Primeau F. Complex visual hallucinations in macular degeneration. *Canadian Journal of Psychiatry. Revue Canadienne de Psychiatrie,* 1993 Nov, 38(9):584 6.

Maricle RA, Turner LD, Lehman KD. The Charles Bonnet syndrome: a brief review and case report. *Psychiatric Services.* 1995;46(4): 289 291.

Mikkilineni SS. Gorbien M Rudberg M Case Report: Phantom Boarder Syndrome *Annals of Long-Term Care* 1998;6[12]:401-405.

Snavely SR, Hedges GR. The neurotoxicity of anti-bacterial agents. A*nnals of Internal Medicine.* 1984; 101(1):92 104.

Stewart JT, Yelton JA. Treatment of organic hallucinosis with carbamazepine. *Am J Psychiatry.* 1945;152(1):150. Letter.

Teunisse RJ; Cruysberg JR; Hoefnagels WH; Verbeek AL; Zitman FG. Visual hallucinations in psychologically normal people: Charles Bonnet's syndrome. *Lancet,* 1996 Mar 23, 347(9004): 794 7.

Teunisse RJ; Cruysberg JR; Verbeek A; Zitman FG.The Charles Bonnet syndrome: a large prospective study in The Netherlands. A study of the prevalence of the Charles Bonnet syndrome and associated factors in 500 patients attending the University Department of Ophthalmology at Nijmegen . *British Journal of Psychiatry,* 1995 Feb, 166(2):254 7.

15: Delusions

Arthur, A. Z. (1964) Theories and explanations of delusions: a review. *American Journal of Psychiatry,* 121: 105 115.

Di Bella, GAW. (1977) Educating Staff to Manage Threatening Paranoid Patients. *American Journal of Psychiatry,* 136:3, March, 333 335.

Karkalas, Y. and Nicotra, M. (1969) The capgras syndrome: a rare psychiatric condition. Love hate conflict resolved by directing ambivalent feelings to an imagined double. *R I Med J,* Aug;52(8): 452 4

Meissner, WW. (1986) *Psychotherapy and the Paranoid Process,* Northvale, New Jersey, London: Jason Aronson Inc.

Newhill, C.E. (1990) The Role of Culture in the Development of Paranoid Symptomatology. *American Journal of Orthopsychiatry,* 60(2): 176 185.

Roth, M. (1989) *Delusional (Paranoid) Disorders. In Treatments of Psychiatric Disorders, A Task Force Report of the American Psychiatric Assoiation,* Vol. 2. Washington: American Psychiatric Association.

Sparr, LF, Boehnlein, JK and Cooney, TG (1986) The Medical Management of the Paranoid Patient. *General Hospital Psychiatry,* 8:49 55.

Swanson, DW, Bohert, PJ. and Smith, JA (1970) *The Paranoid.* Boston: Little, Brown and Co.

Walker, JI. and Cavenar, Jr. JO. (1983) Paranoid Symptoms and Conditions. In *Signs and Symptoms in Psychiatry,* edited by JO. Cavenar, Jr. and HK. Brodie. Philadelphia: J.B. Lippincott.

16: Strokes

Donahue, PJ *How to Prevent Stroke,* Rodale Press, Emmaus, Pennsylvania, 1989.

Ebell MH. Predicting short-term risk of stroke after TIA. *Am Fam Physician.* 2006 Sep 15;74(6):1001-2.

Kandzari DE, Granger CB, Simoons ML, White HD, Simes J, Mahaffey KW, Gore J, Rusin MJ. (1990) Stroke rehabilitation: a geropsychological perspective. *Archives of Physical Medicine and Rehabilitation,* Oct, 71(11): 914 22.

Senelick R. and Rossi, P. (1994) *Living With Stroke,* Contemporary Books, Chicago,

Weaver WD, Longstreth WT Jr, Stebbins A, Lee KL, Califf RM, Topol EJ; Global Utilization of Streptokinase and tPA for Occluded Arteries-I Investigators. Risk factors for intracranial hemorrhage and nonhemorrhagic stroke after fibrinolytic therapy (from the GUSTO-i trial).*Am J Cardiol.* 2004 Feb 15;93(4):458-61.

17: Behavior Problems

Busse, Ewald W. and Blazer, Dan G.(1996) *The American Psychiatric Press Textbook of Geriatric Psychiatry* / edited by 2nd ed. Washington, DC : American Psychiatric Press,.

Dawson, PG and Wells, DL (1992) A Content Methodology for Advancing Gerontological Nursing Practice. *Clinical Nurse Specialist,* 6(2):85-88.

Drench ME; Losee RH. Sexuality and sexual capacities of elderly people. *Rehabilitation Nursing,* 1996 May Jun, 21(3):118 23.

Dyck G. (1997) Management of geriatric behavior problems. *Psychiatric Clinics of North America,* Mar, 20(1):165 80.

Lawton MP. Behavioral problems and inter-ventions in Alzheimer's disease: research needs. *International Psychogeriatrics,* 1996, 8 Suppl 1:95 8.

Maletta, G. (1992) Behavioral problems that are not amenable to drug therapy *International Psychogeriatrics,* 4(supplement I):117-130.

Taft, L.B.; Barkin, R.L. (1990) Drug abuse? Use and misuse of psychotropic drugs in Alzheimer's care. *J Gerontol Nurs,* 16(8):4 10.

18: Assessments

Abraham, Ivo (1992) Geriatric Mental Health: Assessing Geriatric Patients, *Journal of Psychosocial Nursing.* 30(9):13-19.

Anderson, Gayle (1992) How to assess the older mind. *RN,* 34-40

Anderson, GP (1992) How to assess the older mind. *RN,* July 34-39.

Bell IR; Amend D; Kaszniak AW; Schwartz GE; Peterson JM; Stini WA; Miller JW; Selhub J. Trait shyness in the elderly: evidence for an association with Parkinson's disease in family members and biochemical correlates. *Journal of Geriatric Psychiatry and Neurology,* 1995

Jan, 8(1):16 22.

Brain, R. W. (1955) Agnosia, apraxia and aphasia, Chapter 83, Vol. 3. In S. AK. Wilson and AN Bruce (eds.), *Neurology.* Baltimore: Williams and Wilkins Co.

Burns, S; Kappenberg R; McKenna A; Wood C (1994) Brain injury: personality, psychopathlogy and neuropsychology. *Brain Injury,* Jul;8(5): 413 27

Crum, R. M., and others. Population-Based Norms for the Mini-Mental State Examination by Age and Educational Level *Journal of the American Medical Association* 18(1993): 2386-2391.

Damasio, A.R. (1992) Neuropsychology, dementia and aging. *Current Opinions in Neurology and Neurosurgery,* Feb;5(1):145 71.

Fidler, G.S. (1984) *Design of Rehabilitation Services in Psychiatric Hospital Settings.* RAMSCO Publishing, Laurel, MD.

Folstein MF, Folstein SE, and McHugh PR. Mini-Mental State: a practical method for grading the cognitive state of patients for the clinician. *J Psychiatr Res.* 1975; 12:196-198

Folslein. M., and Folstein;. S (1990). Mental status examination. in *The Merck Manual Geriatrics.* Merck .

Gurland, B.; Golden, R.; Teresi J. Challop, J. (1984) The SHORT-CARE: An efficient instrument for the assessment of depression, dementia, and disability. *Journal of Gerontology,* 39(2): 166-169.

Koss, E. (1994) Neuropsychology and Alzheimer's disease. *Clin. Geriatric Medicine,* 10(2):299 313.

Marshal F. Folstein, Susan E. Folstein and Paul R. McHugh. The Mini-Mental State A Practical Method for Grading the Cognitive State of Patients for the Clinician. *J. Psychiat. Res.,* 1975, Vol. 12, No. 3, pp. 189-198

Reisberg B, Ferris SH: (1982) Diagnosis and assess-ment of the older patient. *Hospital and Community Psychiatry,* 33:104 110,

19: Interventions

Orange JB; Lubinski RB; Higginbotham DJ. Conversational repair by individuals with dementia of the Alzheimer's type. *Journal of Speech and Hearing Research,* 1996 Aug, 39(4):881 95.

Ryan EB; Hamilton JM; See SK. Patronizing the old: how do younger and older adults respond to baby talk in the nursing home? *International Journal of Aging and Human Development,* 1994, 39(1):21 32.

Thomas LH. A comparison of the verbal interactions of qualified nurses and nursing auxiliaries in primary, team and functional nursing wards. *International Journal of Nursing Studies,* 1994 Jun, 31(3):231 44.

Whitbourne SK; Culgin S; Cassidy E. (1995) Evaluation of infantilizing intonation and content of speech directed at the aged. *International Journal of Aging and Human Development,* 41(2): 109 16.

Wilson BA. Compensating for cognitive deficits following brain injury. *Neuropsychol Rev.* 2000 Dec;10(4):233-43.

20: Specific Behavior Problems

Catastrophic Reaction

Starkstein SE; Fedoroff JP; Price TR; Leiguarda R; Robinson RG. Catastrophic reaction after cerebrovascular lesions: frequency, correlates, and validation of a scale. *Journal of Neuropsychiatry and Clinical Neurosciences,* 1993 Spring, 5(2): 189 94.

Teasell R. Catastrophic reaction after stroke. A case study. *American Journal of Physical Medicine and Rehabilitation,* 1993 Jun, 72(3): 151 3.

Eating Problems

Ackerman BH; Kasbekar N. Disturbances of taste and smell induced by drugs. *Pharmacotherapy,* 1997 May Jun, 17(3):482 96.

Aronow WS. Post prandial hypotension in the elderly. *Journal of the Royal Society of Medicine,* 1995 Sep, 88(9):499 501.

Aronow WS; Ahn C. Postprandial hypotension in 499 elderly persons in a long term health care facility [see comments]. *Journal of the American Geriatrics Society,* 1994 Sep, 42(9):930 2.

Birchall R; Waters KR. What do elderly people do in hospital? J*ournal of Clinical Nursing,* 1996 May, 5(3):171 6.

Bonnel WB. The nursing home group dining room: managing the work of eating. *Journal of Nutrition for the Elderly,* 1993, 13(1):1 10.

Boukaiba N; Flament C; Acher S; Chappuis P; Piau A; Fusselier M; Dardenne M; Lemonnier D. A physiological amount of zinc supplementation: effects on nutritional, lipid, and thymic status in an elderly population. *American Journal of Clinical Nutrition,* 1993 Apr, 57(4):566 72.

Casper RC. Nutrition and its relationship to aging. *Experimental Gerontology,* 1995 May Aug, 30 (3 4):299 314.

Chidester JC; Spangler AA. Fluid intake in the institutionalized elderly. *Journal of the American Dietetic Association,* 1997 Jan, 97(1):23 8; quiz 29 30.

De Castro JM. Age related changes in spontaneous food intake and hunger in humans. *Appetite,* 1993 Dec, 21(3):255 72.

De Castro JM. Age related changes in spontaneous food intake and hunger in humans. *Appetite,* 1993 Dec, 21(3):255 72.

De Jong N; De Graaf C; Van Staveren WA. Effect of sucrose in breakfast items on pleasantness and food intake in the elderly. *Physiology and Behavior,* 1996 Dec, 60(6): 1453 62.

Duffy VB; Backstrand JR; Ferris AM. Olfactory dysfunction and related nutritional risk in free living, elderly women. *Journal of the American Dietetic Association,* 1995 Aug, 95(8): 879 84; quiz 885 6.

Dwyer J. A vital sign: progress and prospects in nutrition screening of older Americans. *Aging,* 1993 Apr, 5(2 Suppl 1):13 21.

Farnsworth TA; Heseltine D. The effect of postprandial hypotension on rehabilitation of the frail elderly with cerebrovascular disease. *Journal of International Medical Research,* 1994 Mar Apr, 22(2):77 84.

Frisoni GB; Franzoni S; Rozzini R; Ferrucci L; Boffelli S; Trabucchi M. Food intake and mort-ality in the frail elderly. *Journals of Gerontology. Series A, Biological Sciences and Medical Sciences,* 1995 Jul, 50(4):M203 10.

Gloth FM 3rd; Tobin JD; Smith CE; Meyer JN. Nutrient intakes in a frail homebound elderly population in the community vs a nursing home population. *Journal of the American Dietetic Association,* 1996 Jun, 96(6):605 7.

Hall P; Driscoll R. Anorexia in the elderly an annotation. *International Journal of Eating Disorders,* 1993 Dec, 14(4):497 9.

Hetherington MM; Burnett L. Ageing and the pursuit of slimness: dietary restraint and weight satisfaction in elderly women. *British Journal of*

Clinical Psychology, 1994 Sep, 33 (Pt 3):391 400.

Holzapfel SK; Ramirez RF; Layton MS; Smith IW; Sagl Massey K; DuBose JZ. Feeder position and food and fluid consumed by nursing home residents. *Journal of Gerontological Nursing,* 1996 Apr, 22(4):6 12.

Jansen RW; Connelly CM; Kelley Gagnon MM; Parker JA; Lipsitz LA. Postprandial hypotension in elderly patients with unexplained syncope. *Archives of Internal Medicine,* 1995 May 8, 155 (9): 945 52.

Jansson L; Norberg A; Sandman PO; Astrom G. When the severely ill elderly patient refuses food. Ethical reasoning among nurses. *International Journal of Nursing Studies,* 1995 Feb, 32(1): 68 78.

Keller HH. Malnutrition in institutionalized elderly: how and why? *Journal of the American Geriatrics Society,* 1993 Nov, 41(11):1212 8.

Lange Alberts ME; Shott S. Nutritional intake. Use of touch and verbal cuing. *Journal of Gerontological Nursing,* 1994 Feb, 20(2):36 40.

Lewis CW; Frongillo EA Jr; Roe DA. Drug nutrient interactions in three long term care facilities. *Journal of the American Dietetic Association,* 1995 Mar, 95(3):309 15.

Lipski PS; Torrance A; Kelly PJ; James OF. A study of nutritional deficits of long stay geriatric patients [see comments]. *Age and Ageing,* 1993 Jul, 22(4):244 55.

McCargar LJ; Hotson BL; Nozza A. Fibre and nutrient intakes of chronic care elderly patients. *Journal of Nutrition for the Elderly,* 1995, 15(1):13 30.

Nikolaus T; Bach M; Siezen S; Volkert D; Oster P; Schlierf G. Assessment of nutritional risk in the elderly. *Annals of Nutrition and Metabolism,* 1995, 39(6):340 5.

Ortega RM; Manas LR; Andres P; Gaspar MJ; Agudo FR; Jimenez A; Pascual T. Functional and psychic deterioration in elderly people may be aggravated by folate deficiency. *Journal of Nutrition,* 1996 Aug, 126(8):1992 9.

Rolls BJ. Appetite and satiety in the elderly. *Nutrition Reviews,* 1994 Aug, 52(8 Pt 2):S9 10.

Rolls BJ. Appetite, hunger, and satiety in the elderly. *Critical Reviews in Food Science and Nutrition,* 1993, 33(1):39 44.

Rolls BJ; Dimeo KA; Shide DJ. Age related impairments in the regulation of food intake.

American Journal of Clinical Nutrition, 1995 Nov, 62(5):923 31.

Rosenbloom CA; Whittington FJ. The effects of bereavement on eating behaviors and nutrient intakes in elderly widowed persons. *Journal of Gerontology,* 1993 Jul, 48(4):S223 9.

Schiffman SS; Warwick ZS. Effect of flavor enhancement of foods for the elderly on nutritional status: food intake, biochemical indices, and anthropometric measures. *Physiology and Behavior,* 1993 Feb, 53(2):395 402.

Sidenvall B; Fjellstrom C; Ek AC. Cultural perspectives of meals expressed by patients in geriatric care. *International Journal of Nursing Studies,* 1996 Apr, 33(2):212 22.

Sidenvall B; Fjellstrom C; Ek AC. The meal situation in geriatric care intentions and experiences. *Journal of Advanced Nursing,* 1994 Oct, 20(4):613 21.

Sone Y. Age associated problems in nutrition. *Applied Human Science,* 1995 Sep, 14(5):201 10.

Steele CM; Greenwood C; Ens I; Robertson C; Seidman Carlson R. Mealtime difficulties in a home for the aged: not just dysphagia. *Dysphagia,* 1997 Winter, 12(1):43 50; discussion 51.

Stitt S; O'Connell C; Grant D. Old, poor and malnourished. *Nutrition and Health,* 1995, 10(2): 135 54.

Stock LZ; Milan MA. Improving dietary practices of elderly individuals: the power of prompting feedback, and social reinforcement. *Journal of Applied Behavior Analysis,* 1993 Fall, 26(3): 379 87.

Tan CD; Hart LL. Caffeine in elderly patients with postprandial hypotension. *Annals of Pharmacotherapy,* 1993 Jun, 27(6):732 3.

Watson R. Measuring feeding difficulty in patients with dementia: perspectives and problems. *Journal of Advanced Nursing,* 1993 Jan, 18(1):25 31.

Watson R. The Mokken scaling procedure (MSP) applied to the measurement of feeding difficulty in elderly people with dementia. *International Journal of Nursing Studies,* 1996 Aug, 33(4): 385 93.

Watson R; Deary IJ. Measuring feeding difficulty in patients with dementia: multivariate analysis of feeding problems, nursing intervention and indicators of feeding difficulty. *Journal of Advanced Nursing,* 1994 Aug, 20(2):283 7.

Zawada ET Jr. Malnutrition in the elderly. Is it simply a matter of not eating enough? *Postgraduate Medicine,* 1996 Jul, 100(1):207 8, 211 4, 220 2 passim.

Sleep Problems

Ancoli Israel S, Kripke D., Mason W (1981) Sleep apnea and nocturnal myoclonus in a senile population. *Sleep,* 4:349 358.

Bixler EO, Kales A, Soldaros CR, et al: Prevalence of sleep disorders in the Los Angeles metropolitan area. *American Journal of Psychiatry,* 136:1257 1262. 1979.

Feinberg I, Koresko RL, Heller N: EEG sleep patterns as a function of normal and pathological aging in man. Journal of Psychiatric Research, 5:107 144, 1967

Feinsilver SH; Hertz G. Sleep in the elderly patient. *Clinics in Chest Medicine,* 1993 Sep, 14(3):405 11.

Institute of Medicine: Sleeping Pills, Insomnia, and Medical Practice. Washington, DC, National Academy of Sciences, 1979 7.

Kales A, Bixler EO, Tan TL, et al (1974) Chronic hypnotic drug use: ineffectiveness, drug withdrawal insomnia, and dependence. JAMA, 227:513-517.

Miles LE. Dement WC: Sleep and aging. *Sleep,* 3:119 220, 1980

Resestein QR: Insomnia and sleep disrurbances in the aged: sleep and insomnia in the elderly. *Journal of Geriatric Psychiatry,* 13:153 171, 1980.

Reynolds C., Spiker D., Hanin I, et al: (1983) EEG sleep, aging, and psychopathology. new data and stare of the art. *Biological Psychiatry,* 18:133 155.

Roffwarg HP, Muzio NJ, Dement WC (1966) Ontogenetic development of the human sleep cycle. *Science,* 152: 619.

Roffwarg HP: (1982) Diagnostic classification of sleep and arousal disorders. *Sleep,* 2:1, 1379 15. Association of Sleep Disorders Centers, US Public Health Service, and Upjohn Co: project Sleep Educational Program. Kalamazoo, MI, Upjohn.

Sloan EP; Flint AJ; Reinish L; Shapiro CM. Circadian rhythms and psychiatric disorders in the elderly. *Journal of Geriatric Psychiatry and Neurology,* 1996 Oct, 9(4):164 70.

Webb W (1974) *The Rhythms of Sleep and Waking,* *in Chronobiology,* Sheving L, Halberg F, Pauly. EDS. Tokyo, Jgaku Shoin

Webb W, Swinburne H (1971) An observational study of sleep in the aged. *Perceptual Motor Skills,* 32:895 838, 1971.

Williams RL, Karacan I. Hursch CJ: flee rroencephalograp h y (EEG) of *Human Sleep: Clinical Applications.* New York, Wiley, 1974

Winger C, Vernikos Daneilis J, Cronin S, et al (1972) Circadian rhythm asynchrony in man during hypokinesis. *Journal of Applied Physiology,* 33: 640 643.

Resisting Care

Carlson DL; Fleming KC; Smith GE; Evans JM. Management of dementia related behavioral disturbances: a nonpharmacologic approach. *Mayo Clinic Proceedings,* 1995 Nov, 70(11):1108 15.

Nelson F. The development of an indirect self-destructive behavior scaled for use with chronically ill medical patients. International *Journal of Social Psychiatry,* 28(1):5-13

Potts HW; Richie MF; Kaas MJ. Resistance to care. *Journal of Gerontological Nursing,* 1996 Nov, 22(11):11 6.

Sloane PD, Hoeffer B, Mitchell CM, McKenzie DA, Barrick AL, Rader J, Stewart BJ, Talerico KA, Rasin JH, Zink RC, Koch GG. Effect of person-centered showering and the towel bath on bathing-associated aggression, agitation, and discomfort in nursing home residents with dementia: a randomized, controlled trial *J Am Geriatr Soc.* 2004 Nov;52(11):1795-804.

Yelling

Bentham PW; Jones S; Hodges JR. A comparison of semantic memory in vascular dementia and dementia of Alzheimer's type. International *Journal of Geriatric Psychiatry,* 1997 May, 12(5):575 80.

Farrell Miller M. Physical aggressive resident behavior during hygienic care. *Journal of Gerontological Nursing,* 1997 May, 23(5):24 39.

Gibbons P; Gannon M; Wrigley M. A study of aggression among referrals to a community based psychiatry of old age service. *International Journal of Geriatric Psychiatry,* 1997 Mar, 12(3):384 8.

Morse JM; Intrieri RC. 'Talk to me' patient communication in a long term care facility. *Journal of Psychosocial Nursing and Mental Health Services,* 1997 May, 35(5):34 9.

Shapiro, Deane H.; Sandman, Curt A.; Grossman, Michael; Grossman, Barbara. Aging and sense of control. *Psychological Reports,* 1995 Oct, v77 (n2):616 618.

Falls

Astrom S; Nilsson M; Norberg A; Sandman PO; Winblad B. Staff burnout in dementia care rela-tions to empathy and attitudes. International *Journal of Nursing Studies,* 1991, 28(1): 65 75.

Beland, I. (1980) Burn-out Syndrome in Nurses, in *Werner-Beland Grief Processes in Long Term Illness.* Reston Publishers, Reston VA.

Blake AJ. Falls in the elderly. *British Journal of Hospital Medicine,* 1992 Feb 19 Mar 3, 47(4): 268 72.

Camicioli R; Howieson D; Lehman S; Kaye J. Talking while walking: the effect of a dual task in aging and Alzheimer's disease. *Neurology,* 1997 Apr, 48(4):955 8.

Corbett C; Pennypacker B. Using a quality improvement team to reduce patient falls. *Journal for Healthcare Quality,* 1992 Sep Oct, 14(5): 38 41, 44 54.

Croft W; Foraker S. Working together to prevent falls. *Rn,* 1992 Nov, 55(11):17 8, 20.

Cumming RG; Miller JP; Kelsey JL; Davis P; Arfken CL; Birge SJ; Peck WA. Medications and multiple falls in elderly people: the St Louis OASIS study. *Age and Ageing,* 1991 Nov, 20(6): 455 61.

Cwikel J. Falls among elderly people living at home: medical and social factors in a national sample [see comments]. *Israel Journal of Medical Sciences,* 1992 Jul, 28(7):446 53.

Cwikel J; Fried AV. The social epidemiology of falls among community dwelling elderly: guidelines for prevention. *Disability and Rehabilitation,* 1992 Jul Sep, 14(3):113 21.

Fleming BE; Wilson DR; Pendergast DR. A portable, easily performed muscle power test and its association with falls by elderly persons [see comments]. *Archives of Physical Medicine* and Rehabilitation, 1991 Oct, 72(11):886

Fried AV; Cwikel J; Ring H; Galinsky D. ELGAM extra laboratory gait assessment method: iden-tification of risk factors for falls among the elderly at home. *International Disability Studies,* 1990 Oct Dec, 12(4):161 4.

Ginter SF; Mion LC. Falls in the nursing home: preventable or inevitable? *Journal of Gerontological Nursing,* 1992 Nov, 18(11):43 8.

Hale WA; Delaney MJ; McGaghie WC. Characteristics and predictors of falls in elderly patients. *Journal of Family Practice,* 1992 May, 34(5):577 81.

Hale WA; Delaney MJ; McGaghie WC. Predicting elderly patients' mobility using fall history and physician assessment. *Family Medicine,* 1990 Sep Oct, 22(5):383 7.

Jech AO. Preventing falls in the elderly. *Geriatric Nursing,* 1992 Jan Feb, 13(1):43 4.

Joshua R. Shua Haim, MD Joel S. Gross, MD Stratford, NJ Lesch-Nyan Syndrome in an Alzheimer's Patient Nursing Home. *Medicine,* June 1997 Vol. 5, No. 7

Kelly WN, Palella TDL. Gout and other disorders of purine metabolism. In: *Harrison's Principles of Internal Medicine.* 199133841.

Lawrence JI; Maher PL. An interdisciplinary falls consult team: a collaborative approach to patient falls. *Journal of Nursing Care Quality,* 1992 Apr, 6(3):21 9.

Loebel JP, Leibovici A. Management of patients with Alzheimer's and related dementias. *Med Clin North Am,* 1994;4:841 859.

Lord SR; Clark RD; Webster IW. Physiological factors associated with falls in an elderly population. *Journal of the American Geriatrics Society,* 1991 Dec, 39(12):1194 200.

Miller PA. Suggestions for improving a falls prevention program [letter; comment]. *Gerontologist,* 1992 Dec, 32(6):859.

Nelson RC; Amin MA. Falls in the elderly. *Emergency Medicine Clinics of North America,* 1990 May, 8(2):309 24.

Perlin E. Preventing falls in the elderly. A practical approach to a common problem. *Postgraduate Medicine,* 1992 Jun, 91(8):237 8, 241, 244.

Petit CD. Falls in the elderly. *Journal South Carolina Medical Association,* 1992 Nov, 88(11): 541 5.

Reinsch S; MacRae P; Lachenbruch PA; Tobis JS. Attempts to prevent falls and injury: a prospective community study [see comments]. *Gerontologist,* 1992 Aug, 32(4):450 6.

Richardson JK; Ching C; Hurvitz EA. The relationship between electromyographically documented peripheral neuropathy and falls. *Journal of the American Geriatrics Society,* 1992 Oct, 40 (10):1008 12.

Ross JE. Iatrogenesis in the elderly. Contributors to falls. *Journal of Gerontological Nursing,* 1991 Sep, 17(9):19 23.

Sherman D. Medication use and falls. Contemporary Longterm Care, 1991 Nov, 14(11): 66, 68.

Shipman KH. Do restraints prevent falls? [letter; comment]. *Annals of Internal Medicine,* 1992 Sep 1, 117(5):442 3.

Sorock GS; Labiner DM. Peripheral neuro-muscular dysfunction and falls in an elderly cohort. *American Journal of Epidemiology,* 1992 Sep 1, 136(5):584 91.

Spellbring AM. Assessing elderly patients at high risk for falls: a reliability study. *Journal of Nursing Care Quality,* 1992 Apr, 6(3):30 5.

Stewart RB; Moore MT; May FE; Marks RG; Hale WE. Nocturia: a risk factor for falls in the elderly. *Journal of the American Geriatrics Society,* 1992 Dec, 40(12):1217 20.

Sumner ED; Simpson WM Jr. Intervention in falls among the elderly. *Journal of Practical Nursing,* 1992 Jun, 42(2):24 34.

Suzuki M; Okamura T; Shimazu Y; Takahashi H; Eguchi K; Kano K; Tsuchiya S. [A study of falls experienced by institutionalized elderly]. Nippon Koshu Eisei Zasshi. *Japanese Journal of Public Health,* 1992 Dec, 39(12):927 40.

Using muscle in the fight against falls [news]. *American Journal of Nursing,* 1992 Sep, 92(9):12.

Vellas B; Baumgartner RN; Wayne SJ; Conceicao J; Lafont C; Albarede JL; Garry PJ. Relationship between malnutrition and falls in the elderly. *Nutrition,* 1992 Mar Apr, 8(2):105 8.

Vlahov D; Myers AH; al Ibrahim MS. Epidemiology of falls among patients in a rehabilitation hospital. *Archives of Physical Medicine and Rehabilitation,* 1990 Jan, 71(1):8 12.

Weller C; Humphrey SJ; Kirollos C; Bowes SG; Charlett A; Dobbs SM; Dobbs RJ. Gait on a shoestring: falls and foot separation in parkinsonism. *Age and Ageing,* 1992 Jul, 21(4):242 4.

Wells. Y. Jorm. A. (1987) Evaluation of a special nursing home unit for dementia sufferers: A randomized controlled comparison with community care. *Aust N Z Journ Psychiatry,*

21:524-531.

White D. Old age is not a reason to fall. *Nursing Standard,* 1991 Nov 13 19, 6(8):20 1.

Wright BA; Aizenstein S; Vogler G; Rowe M; Miller C. Frequent fallers. Leading groups to identify psychological factors. *Journal of Gerontological Nursing,* 1990 Apr, 16(4):15 9.

Agitation

Almeida OP; Howard RJ; Levy R; David AS; Morris RG; Sahakian BJ. Clinical and cognitive diversity of psychotic states arising in late life (late paraphrenia). *Psychological Medicine,* 1995 Jul, 25(4):699 714.

Chou KR; Kaas MJ; Richie MF. (1996) Assaultive behavior in geriatric patients. *Journal of Gerontological Nursing,* Nov, 22(11):30 8.

Cohen Mansfield J. (1995) Assessment of disruptive behavior/agitation in the elderly: function, methods, and difficulties. *Journal of Geriatric Psychiatry and Neurology,* Jan, 8(1):52 60.

Cohen Mansfield J; Werner P; Watson V; Pasis S. (1995) Agitation among elderly persons at adult day care centers: the experiences of relatives and staff members. *International Psychogeriatrics,* Fall, 7(3):447 58.

Cohen Mansfield J; Werner P; Watson V; Pasis S. Agitation among elderly persons at adult day care centers: the experiences of relatives and staff members. *International Psychogeriatrics,* 1995 Fall, 7(3):447 58.

Mintzer JE; Brawman Mintzer O. Agitation as a possible expression of generalized anxiety disorder in demented elderly patients: toward a treatment approach. *Journal of Clinical Psychiatry,* 1996, 57 Suppl 7:55 63; discussion 73 5.

Monfort JC. [Aggressivity in the elderly: when and how to treat?]. *Revue du Praticien,* 1994 Jun 1, 44(11):1426 30.

21: Assault

Atkinson, J.H. (1982). Managing the violent patient in the general hospital. *Post Graduate Medicine:* 71(1), 193 201. 0

Ball, G.G. (1993). Modifying the behavior of the violent patient. *Psychiatric Quarterly,* 64(4), 359 369.

Baltes MM, Wahl HW. The dependency-support script in institutions: generalization to community settings. *Psychol Aging.* 1992 Sep;7(3):409-18.

Barber, I.W., Hundley, P., et al (1988). Clinical and demographic characteristics of 15 patients with repetitively assaultive behavior. *Psychiatric Quarterly,* 59(3),213 224.

Bender, KJ (1998) Addressing Agitation and Aggression in Dementia. *Psychiatric Times,* July.

Bigelow, R. The evolution of cooperation, aggression, and self-control, in the *Nebraska Symposium on Motivation* 1972.

Blair, D.T., and New, S.A. (1991). Assaultive behavior: Know the risk. *Journal of Psychosocial Nursing,* 29(11), 25 29.

Blumenreich, P.E. (1993) Pharmacotherapy of violence. In PE Blumenreich, and S. Lewis (Eds.), *Managing The violent Patient: A Clinician's Guide* (ppA 53 77).New York, NY: Brunner Mazel.

Bridges Parlet, S., Knopman, D., andThompson, T. (1994). A descriptive study of physically aggressive behavior in dementia by direct observation. J*ournal of the American Geriatrics Society,* 42(2), 192 197.

Burgio, L.D., Jones, L.T., Butler, F., and En Rel, B.T. (1988). Behavior problems in an urban nursing home, *Journal of Gerontological Nursing,* 14(1), 31 34.

Carmel, H., and Hunter, M. (1989). Staff injuries from inpatient violence. *Hospital and Community Psychiatry,* 40(1), 41 46.

Chou KR; Kaas MJ; Richie MF. Assaultive behavior in geriatric patients. Journal of Gerontological Nursing, 1996 Nov, 22(11):30 8.

Chou, KR, et al (1996) Assaultive Behaviors in Geriatric Patients. *Journal of Gerontological Nursing,* November. 22(11):30 8.

Cohen Mansfield J. Assessment of disruptive behavior/agitation in the elderly: function, methods, and difficulties. *Journal of Geriatric Psychiatry and Neurology,* 1995 Jan, 8(1):52 60.

Cohen Mansfield, I. (7986). Agitated behaviors in the elderly: Preliminary results in the cognitively deteriorated. *Journal of the American Geriatrics Society*, 34(10), 722 727.

Cohen Mansfield, I., and Billing, N. (1986). Agitated behaviors in the elderly: A conceptual view. *Journal of the American Geriatrics Society,* 34(10), 711 721.

Colenda, C.C., and Hamer, R.M. (1991). Antecedents and interventions for aggressive behavior of patients at a geropsychiatric state

hospital. *Hospital and Community Psychiatry,* 42(3), 287 292.

Distasio, C.A. (1994). Violence in healthcare: Institutional strategies to cope with the phenomenon. *Health Care Supervisor,* 12(4), 1 34.

Dubin W.R. (1981). Evaluating and managing the violent patient. *Annals of Emergency Medicine,* 10(9), 481 484.

Durivage, A. (1989). Assaultive behavior: Before it happens. *Canadian Journal of Psychiatry,* 34(6), 393 397

Engel F, Marsh S. Helping the employee victim of violence in hospitals. *Hosp Community Psychiatry.* 1986 Feb;37(2):159-62.

Flannery RB Jr; Hanson MA; Penk W. Patients' threats. Expanded definition of assault. *General Hospital Psychiatry,* 1995 Nov, 17(6):451 3.

Fornazzari I, Farcnik K, Smith I, et al. Violent visual hallucinations and aggression in frontal lobe dysfunction: clinical manifestations of deep orbito-frontal foci. *J Neuropsychiatry Clin Neurosci.* 1992;4(1):42 44,

Frengley, I.D., and Mion, L.C. (1986). Incidence of physical restraints on acute general medical wards. *Journal of the American Geriatrics Society,* 34, 565 567

Hatti, S., Dubin, W.R., Weiss, K.J.: A study of circumstances surrounding patient assaults on Psychiatrist. *Hospital and Community Psychiatry,* 1982; 33:8.

Lion, J.R., Reid, W.H. (eds.): *Assaults Within Psychiatric Facilities.* New York: Grune and Stratton, 1983; 157 171.

Jacobs, D. (1983). Evaluation and management of the violent patient in emergency settings. *Psychiatric Clinics of North America,* 6(2),259 269.

Jones, M.. (1985). Patient violence. Report of 200 incidents, *Journal of Psychosocial Research Nursing and Health,* 14, 87 95. [I don't have this]

Junginger J. Psychosis and violence: the case for a content analysis of psychotic experience. *Schizophrenia Bulletin,* 1996, 22(1):91 103.

Lanza ML. (1992) Nurses as patient assault victims: an update, synthesis, and recommendations. *Arch Psychiatr Nurs.* Jun;6(3):163-71

Lanza, M.L.: The reaction of nursing staff to physical assault by a patient. *Hospital and Community Psychiatry,* 1983;34:1.

Levy, P., Hartocollis, P. Nursing aids and patient violence. *Am J Psych,* 1976; 133:429 431.

Lion JR et al (1976) A Violence clinic: Three years of Experience. *American Journal of Psychiatry;* 133(4):432-435.

Lion, J.R., Snyder, W., Merrill, G.L.: Under-reporting of assaults in staff in state hospitals. *Hospital and Community Psychiatry,* 1981; 32:497 498.

Maxfield, CM, et al (1996) Training Staff to Prevent Aggressive Behavior. *Journal of Geronto-logical Nursing,* January.

Mehrabian A. *Public Places and Private Spaces* Basic Books 1980.

Miller BL; Darby A; Benson DF; Cummings JL; Miller MH. Aggressive, socially disruptive and antisocial behaviour associated with fronto temporal dementia. *British Journal of Psychiatry,* 1997 Feb, 170:150 4.

Miller RJ; Zadolinnyj K; Hafner RJ Profiles and predictors of assaultiveness for different psychiatric ward populations. Dibden Research Unit, Glenside Hospital, Eastwood, South *Australia. Journal of Psychiatry,* 1993 Sep;150(9): 1368 73

Negley, E.N., and Manley J.T. (1990). Environmental interventions in assaultive behavior. *Journal of Gerontological Nursing,* 16(3), 29 33.

Phillips, P., Nasr, S.J.: Seclusion and restraint and prediction of violence. *American Journal of Psychiatry,* 1983; 140:2

Poster, E.C., and livan, 1.A. (1989). Nurses' attitudes toward physical assaults by patients. *Archives of Psychiatric Nursing,* 3(6), 315 322

Rvan, J.A., and P'osner, E.C. (1989). The assaulted nurse: Short term and long term responses. *Archives of Psychiatric Nursing,* 3(6), 323 331.

Rvden, M.B. (1988). Aggressive behaviors in persons with dementia who live in the community. *Alzheimer Disease and Associated Disorders,* 2(4), 342 355.

Rvden, M.B., Bossenmaier, M., and McLachlan, C. (1991). Aggressive behavior in cognitively impaired nursing home residents.

Snyder W. III: Administrative monitoring of assaultive patients and staff in Lion, assault on

health care professionals. In J. Shepherd (Ed.), *Violence in Health Care* (pp. 1 11). New York, NY: Oxford University Press.

Stokman, C.L.J.: Violence among hospitalized patients. *Hospital and Community Psychiatry,* 1982; 33:986.

Storr A. Human aggression.*Psychiatr Commun.* 1970;12(1):27-30.

Tardiff, K., and Sweillam, A. (1979). The relation of age to assaultive behavior in inpatients. *Hospital and Community Psychiatry,* (10), 709 710.

Treiman D (1986) Epilepsy and Violence: *Medical and Legal Issues Epilepsia,* 27(suppl 2) S77-S104.

Volavka J; Laska E; Baker S; Meisner M; Czobor P; Krivelevich I. History of violent behaviour and schizophrenia in different cultures. Analyses based on the WHO study on Determinants of Outcome of Severe Mental Disorders. *British Journal of Psychiatry,* 1997 Jul, 171:9 14.

Weller P.G., Mungas, D., and Bemick,(1988). Popranolol for the control of disruptive behavior in senile dementia. *Journal of Geriatric Psychiatry and Neurology,* 1(4), 226:

Whittington R; Wykes T. Aversive stimulation by staff and violence by psychiatric patients. *British Journal of Clinical Psychology,* 1996 Feb, 35 (Pt 1):11 20.

Whittington R; Wykes T. Aversive stimulation by staff and violence by psychiatric patients. *British Journal of Clinical Psychology,* 1996 Feb, 35 (Pt 1):11 20.

Wisner, E., and Green M. (1986). Treatment of a demented patient's anger with cognitive behavioral strategies. *Psychological Reports,* 447 450.

Zitrin, A., Hardesty, A.S., Bordock, E., et al: Crime and violence among dementia patients. *American Journal of Psychiatry,* 1976; 133:142 149.

22: Wandering

Algase DL; Kupferschmid B; Beel Bates CA; Beattie ER. Estimates of stability of daily wandering behavior among cognitively impaired long term care residents. *Nursing Research,* 1997 May Jun, 46(3):172 8.

Carlson DL; Fleming KC; Smith GE; Evans JM. Management of dementia related behavioral disturbances: a nonpharmacologic approach.

Mayo Clinic Proceedings, 1995 Nov, 70(11): 1108 15.

Cornbleth T. (1977) Effects of a protected hospital ward area on. wandering and nonwandering geriatric patients. *Journal of. Gerontology* 32, 573–577.

Goldsmith SM; Hoeffer B; Rader J. Problematic wandering behavior in the cognitively impaired elderly. A single subject case study. J*ournal of Psychosocial Nursing and Mental Health Services,* 1995 Feb, 33(2):6 12.

Hussain, R.A., & Brown, D.C., (1987). Uses of two dimensional grid patterns to limit hazardous ambulation in demented patients. *Journal of Gerontology,* 42, 558 560.

McGrowder Lin. R. and Bhart. AA (1988) A wanderer's lounge program for nursing home residents with Alzheimer's disease. *Gerontologist,* 28:607-609

Monsour, N., & Robb, S.S. (1982).Wandering behavior in old age: A psychological study. *Social Work,* 27, 411 416.

Neistein S; Siegal AP. Agitation, wandering, pacing, restlessness, and repetitive mannerisms. *International Psychogeriatrics,* 1996, 8 Suppl 3: 399 402.

Snyder, L., Rupperecht, P., Pyrek, J., & Moss, T. 1978. Wandering. *The Gerontologist,* 18, 272 280.

Stoppe G; Sandholzer H; Staedt J; Winter S; Kiefer J; Ruther E. Sleep disturbances in the demented elderly: treatment in ambulatory care. *Sleep,* 1995 Dec, 18(10):844 8.

Thomas DW. Understanding the wandering patient. A continuity of personality perspective. *Journal of Gerontological Nursing,* 1997 Jan, 23(1):16 24; quiz 54 5.

23: Groups

Bleathman C; Morton I. Validation therapy with the demented elderly. *Nursing Standard. Special Supplement,* 1991 Jul 31(45):20.

Burgio LD; Engel BT; Hawkins A; McCormick K; Scheve A; Jones LT. A staff management system for maintaining improvements in continence with elderly nursing home residents. *Journal of Applied Behavior Analysis,* 1990 Spring, 23(1):111 8.

Burnside I. Reminiscence: an independent nursing intervention for the elderly. *Issues in Mental Health Nursing,* 1990, 11(1):33 48.

Dembicki D; Anderson J. Pet ownership may be a factor in improved health of the elderly. *Journal of Nutrition for the Elderly,* 1996, 15(3):15 31.

Donnelly GF. An assertiveness training program for a group of elders [editorial]. *Holistic Nursing Practice,* 1992 Oct, 7(1):v.

Esposito L. The effects of medication education on adherence to medication regimens in an elderly population. *Journal of Advanced Nursing,* 1995 May, 21(5):935 43.

Fick KM. The influence of an animal on social interactions of nursing home residents in a group setting. *American Journal of Occupational Therapy,* 1993 Jun, 47(6):529 34.

Haight BK; Burnside I. Reminiscence and life review: conducting the processes. *Journal of Gerontological Nursing,* 1992 Feb, 18(2):39 42.

Isohanni M. Coping with institutional life at the old people's therapeutic community. *Psychiatry,* 1990 May, 53(2):148 57.

Lowenthal RI; Marrazzo RA. Milestoning: evoking memories for resocialization through group reminiscence. *Gerontologist,* 1990 Apr, 30(2): 269 72.

Moore BG. Reminiscing therapy: a CNS intervention [see comments]. *Clinical Nurse Specialist,* 1992 Fall, 6(3):170 3.

Radley M; Redston C; Bates F; Pontefract M. Effectiveness of group anxiety management with elderly clients of a community psychogeriatric team. International *Journal of Geriatric Psychiatry,* 1997 Jan, 12(1):79 84.

Rogers J; Hart LA; Boltz RP. The role of pet dogs in casual conversations of elderly adults. *Journal of Social Psychology,* 1993 Jun, 133(3):265 77.

Russell K. Groupwork with the elderly mentally ill. *Nursing,* 1990 May 10 23, 4(10):25 8.

Williams B; Roberts P. Friends in passing: social interaction at an adult day care center. International *Journal of Aging and Human Development,* 1995, 41(1):63 78

Williams Barnard CL; Lindell AR. Therapeutic use of "prizing" and its effect on self concept of elderly clients in nursing homes and group homes. *Issues in Mental Health Nursing,* 1992 Jan Mar, 13(1):1 17.

Yaretzky A; Levinson M; Kimchi OL. Clay as a therapeutic tool in group processing with the elderly. *American Journal of Art Therapy,* 1996 Feb, 34(3):75 82.

Zanetti O; Frisoni GB; De Leo D; Dello Buono M; Bianchetti A; Trabucchi M. Reality orientation therapy in Alzheimer disease: useful or not? A controlled study. *Alzheimer Disease and Associated Disorders,* 1995 Fall, 9(3):132 8.

Zauszniewski JA. Teaching resourcefulness skills to older adults. *Journal of Gerontological Nursing, 1997 Feb, 23(2):14 20.*

Index

About the Author

Dr. Matteson is Licensed Psychologist and accomplished speaker, specializing in mental health and aging, He is the author of three books, *Stop Memory Loss,* a book about preventing dementia, *Caregivers Bible,* a book for professional caregivers of the aged, and (writing as William Cone) *The Abduction Enigma,* a book about how therapist unwittingly induce false memories.

Dr. Matteson is currently a consultant and lecturer in the field of geriatrics. He develops and implements training programs for geropsychiatric hospitals, nursing homes, and board and care facilities throughout the nation.

Because of his expertise he has been featured on many television programs and has been a featured speaker on dozens of radio programs nationwide.

If you are interested in having Dr. Matteson speak at your facility, association, or convention he can be reached at:

SoundMinds
16707 Sunset Boulevard
Pacific Palisades, CA 90272
www.soundminds.net
drmatteson@soundminds.net
888-261-0576

To order additional copies of:

Caregivers Bible @ $40.00

Or

Stop Memory Loss @ $20.00

Shipping/Handling per book: $3.00

Mailing Address

SoundMinds
16707 Sunset Boulevard
Pacific Palisades, CA 90272
drmatteson@soundminds.net
888-261-0576

Order online at
www.soundminds.net